THE REFLEXIVE TEACHER EDUCATOR IN TESO**l**

GW00724600

"This is a highly original contribution to our field. Wise, inspiring and nourishing, it is up there with Earl Stevick's *Memory, Meaning and Method*. Complementing work that takes sociocultural and critical perspectives, it has the ring of truth, and carries with it the shock of recognition. The author's personal voice shines through the narrative. As I read this book I was reminded of why I became a teacher, and why, after 40 years, I remain a teacher."

David Nunan, University of Hong Kong and Anaheim University

"Noble in its purpose, laudable in its substance and engrossing in its style, this extremely valuable book addresses a topic that has seldom been addressed in depth: the reflexive teacher educator. Using a series of absorbing autobiographical episodes drawn from his long and distinguished career as a teacher and teacher educator, Julian Edge maps the different paths that he himself has taken to become a reflexive teacher educator. The profession sorely and surely needs such a book. It not merely fills a gap in the literature, but does so in a highly critical and coordinated fashion. This is one of a kind."

B. Kumaravadivelu, San Jose State University

In this book Julian Edge explores the construct of reflexivity in teacher education, differentiating it from, while locating it in, reflective practice. Written with clarity and style, scholarly yet personal, dealing with reflexivity in an accessible yet non-trivial way, this book – a first in the field, distinctive in terms of *what* the story is and *how* it is told – is a gift to the profession of TESOL teacher education.

Julian Edge is Senior Lecturer in Education (TESOL), University of Manchester, UK.

THE REFLEXIVE TEACHER EDUCATOR IN TESOL

roots and wings

Julian Edge

Routledge
Taylor & Francis Group
NEW YORK AND LONDON

First published 2011
by Routledge
270 Madison Avenue, New York, NY 10016

Simultaneously published in the UK
by Routledge
2 Park Square, Milton Park, Abingdon, Oxon OX14 4RN

Routledge is an imprint of the Taylor & Francis Group, an Informa business

Typeset in Bembo by
Keystroke, Station Road, Codsall, Wolverhampton
Printed and bound in the United States of America on acid-free paper by
Walsworth Publishing Company, Marceline, MO

Library of Congress Cataloging in Publication Data
Edge, Julian, 1948–
    The reflexive teacher educator in TESOL : roots and wings / Julian Edge.
        p. cm.
    Includes bibliographical references and index.
    1. English language—Study and teaching—Foreign speakers. 2. English
    teachers—Training of.
    PE1128.A2E29 2011
    428.2′4—dc22   2010030483

ISBN 13: 978–0–415–88250–7 hbk
ISBN 13: 978–0–415–88251–4 pbk
ISBN 13: 978–0–203–83289–9 ebk

To TESOL teacher educators everywhere –
May it be as good for you as it has been for me.

CONTENTS

Preface   ix
Acknowledgements   xi

1 Of metaphors and myths, voices and vocabularies,
   aims and addressees   1

2 In praise of reflective practice   14

3 In search of reflexivity   26

4 Copying and becoming methodological   49

5 Applying theory and becoming technical   63

6 Theorizing practice and becoming theoretical   79

7 Reflecting and becoming intellectual   98

8 Acting and becoming pragmatic   119

9 Shadows   138

10 So what?   162

References   180
Index   192

PREFACE

We all want to be the hero of our own story, so we all need to take care not to assume that others see things the way we do. At the same time, if you've been doing something for over forty years, you probably hope that you have something to say about it that might be useful to others. In this book, I try not to make that former assumption and still to perform that latter service.

The common ground that I hope to build on is that of reflective practice (Chapter 2). On the basis of that, I introduce the idea of reflexivity (Chapter 3), and extend the book's fundamental invitation, which is for readers to join me in asking two questions:

- What difference does it make to the teacher education that I offer that it is *I* who offer it?
- What difference does offering *this* teacher education make to me as a teacher educator?

This is what I mean by *reflexivity*, and I argue that raising one's awareness of how reflexivity functions lies at the heart of a teacher educator's own continuing development, as well as signposting a road to ongoing development that we can offer our teacher-learners.

In Chapters 4–8, I try to do two things. On the one hand, I draw on auto-biographical data from phases of my life when I came to understand, through experience, dimensions of being a TESOL teacher educator that I regard to be of continuing significance. I have called these phases *becoming methodological* (Chapter 4), *becoming technical* (Chapter 5), *becoming theoretical* (Chapter 6), *becoming intellectual* (Chapter 7), and *becoming pragmatic* (Chapter 8). Allied to these dimensions of being and becoming, I describe and exemplify ways of behaving that I call *copying, applying, theorizing, reflecting* and *acting.* My overall stance is that if I, as a teacher educator, continue to develop along these dimensions and behave in these ways, and if I do so in a fashion that takes my teacher-learners with me, then I might hope to establish a sense of congruence and continuity that will nourish us all. If that were all I do in those chapters, however, the title of this book should probably be 'a' teacher educator in TESOL.

Looking at those central chapters from a different perspective, my purpose is to build a framework for thinking about teacher education and for being a teacher educator that will seem worth evaluating in its own right once the narrative style of its construction has been forgotten. In other words, my intention is to formulate from the experiences of 'a' teacher educator something useful more generally for 'the' teacher educator. Involved here is an argument concerning the relationship between an individual case and what might be generally useful. Let me be clear that I am not trying to work towards *generalizations* as such. Each reader will decide what is useful for her or himself. If enough readers find the framework useful, then I will have succeeded.

(And just among ourselves as language teachers, we know all too well that the correct choice of article is frequently no simple matter. Discussion over the use of 'a' or 'the' in the title of this book has been protracted. The final choice turns on readers understanding it to be a *generic* 'the', rather than a *unique* 'the'. You have to love this stuff.)

Chapter 9 explores occasions when things have gone wrong. I try to learn from how I contributed to shaping those events and how their outcomes reached out to shape me. Chapter 10 draws some interim conclusions and looks again at how the previously identified dimensions and ways of behaving interact and remain meaningful to me, with regard to both personal narrative and professional framework.

All of this telling also includes snatches of an elegiac western movie, a reinterpretation of two Greek myths, a small number of insights drawn from popular song and an increasing level of commitment to the philosophy of American Pragmatism, with specific reference to John Dewey and Richard Rorty.

If this is starting to sound interesting, please consider taking the time to look at Chapter 1, where, as you can see from its title, I go more deeply into such matters as who the book is for and why I wrote it the way I have. I hope to see you there.

ACKNOWLEDGEMENTS

Specifically with regard to the *writing* of the book, my sincere thanks to Naomi Silverman and Routledge reviewers for the ways in which they expressed their enthusiasm for this project right from the beginning. And to Bill Johnston for how he curbed his right at the end. Thanks to Andy Boon, Nur Kurtoglu-Hooton and fellow members of our Research and Writing cooperative at work (Susan Brown, Richard Fay, Gary Motteram, Zeynep Onat-Stelma, Diane Slaouti and Juup Stelma) for comments on chapters along the way. Thanks to Adrian Holliday, Bonny Norton and Mick Randall for joining in, and to 'Kolo' for sharing. The cover drawing, *Icarus Reflects*, is by Clifford Harper, a genius among illustrators, who I thank most specially for taking on the commission, and then for allowing me to name the image and make it mine. All over this book and all through it, my thanks to Mark Clarke for the conversations, linear and cyclical, too many of which had to be electronic, but some of which still taste of beer and jalapeño-stuffed olives. And humble thanks to Ingrid, for unfailing support, great patience, ready insight and countless cups of tea.

Beyond those mentioned above, and others named in the text, there are so many people who have contributed in different ways, and it would be invidious to single out just some of them. What I would like is if we could all get together in our heads and smile over WALSTIB. If you know what it stands for, then you know. If you don't, you could just google it. For a very small sum of money, you could download *Truckin'*, by The Grateful Dead, and enjoy the line and the moment. I would have liked to quote it for you here, but you wouldn't *believe* what those corporate people charge for a few lines of what used to be free.

In all things, and despite all that help, remaining faults are mine alone.

1

OF METAPHORS AND MYTHS, VOICES AND VOCABULARIES, AIMS AND ADDRESSEES

'Just one last job, and then I'm going to quit for good.'

Whenever you hear that line in a movie, you know that something is going to go wrong, badly wrong. Whoever says it is about to take one chance too many, probably for a good reason as far as they are concerned, but we know that there will be some vital factor that they have overlooked, or not taken proper account of. Perhaps things generally have become more complicated than they used to be, or everyone moves a little faster, or the technology doesn't give you the leeway, or maybe it's just good old human error, or a skipped beat of the heart. The mood, anyway, drifts into the elegiac and, as the very word *elegiac* collocates most strongly for me with a certain genre of westerns, I find such titles as *The Wild Bunch* and *The Misfits* rolling through my mind. Like tumbleweed.

They are not bad titles, in fact, to sum up certain perspectives on a working life in TESOL where, just like the teachers interviewed by Johnston (1997), a series of jobs has replaced the concept of a career. *The Wild Bunch* might represent the out-there TEFL years of bright new mornings: sunrise crackling through the giant pillars of Karnak in Upper Egypt; sunrise from the summit of Mt Kinabalu, lighting up a view of the South China Sea washing in on the north coast of Borneo; sunrise over the fallen stone giants of Nemrut Dag in remote eastern Anatolia; sunrise over the Pyramid of the Moon at Teotihuacan, whose ruins were already mysterious to the Aztecs when they discovered them; and dreamily watching another sun come up over the hills of magic, tragic Lebanon, seeing the light creep into the folded valleys around Ba'albek, turning their purple, opaque hollows into endless, rolling slopes of smoky marijuana.

Equally well, *The Misfits* might represent the later, more academic years of trying to establish a niche in university systems where, while some of us who made this journey have been eminently successful, some of us have failed to come to terms, and some of us have done a little of both.

But oh my, what opportunities there have been to articulate ideas and possibilities that had not occurred to any of us until we looked out through the windows that TESOL had opened and found that our initial questions of *What?* had shifted into *How?* before becoming nuanced by *Where?* and *When?*, and that our understandings of *Why?* had been loosened up by *Why not?*, challenged by *Who says?* and deepened by *In whose interests?* Who would have thought that being an English teacher had so much heart and mind and spirit and blood in it?

Rather than jump from the practical to the theoretical when shaping this shift from the schoolroom to the seminar room, some of us discovered the attractions of becoming theoretical in our practice and, striving for the sunlit uplands of such praxis, found ourselves camped out along the marshy borderlands of action research: too theoretical for the practitioners, too practical for the theorists, but at least frequently in interesting company as we constructed our representations around the campfire.

It is perhaps this sense of a working life comprising a series of dislocations and peripheral positions that prompted me to saddle up once more. One more book. One cover to bind them all . . . No, perhaps not. No, I really don't believe in that sort of thing.

Anyway, here we are, however it pans out. A scene is coalescing, for better or worse. The old grey mare has been saddled up for one last job. She's not the fastest anymore, but at least I know she doesn't shy if the action gets noisy. The sun rises one more time. The leather creaks. It begins.

And then, without transition, we are down the road apiece. The saloon is poorly lit. Cards slide rhythmically over the green baize surface. Which scene is this? Is this early or late in the story? Which of those upturned cards is significant here? The Queen of Hearts? The Jack of Diamonds? The Ace of Spades? One needs to know whose symbolism is framing the action. Well, sometimes you do know, sometimes you think you do, and sometimes you haven't a clue. And still you have to act. One is always called upon to make decisions in the face of incomplete information. That doesn't mean, though, that you have to rush in.

'*You learn to draw fast,*' I remember one character saying, '*so as to give yourself time to shoot slow.*'

But then, I remember another one who said, '*The most important thing is to get off the first shot. Just the noise of that will unnerve most people.*'

Yeah, the world's full of folks who know best.

★ ★ ★ ★ ★

OK, before we go any further, two things: One, I've no idea what you're talking about. Two, what makes you think that we need another book on TESOL teacher education?

'Need' is a hard call. I don't know that I'd argue that anyone 'needs' it. If anything, I might say that I 'needed' to write it.

Ah, you mean it's just another 'publish or perish' thing? That's not . . .

No, no, I don't mean that at all. I mean that I have been working in TESOL and teacher education for a long time and writing is one of the things that I have come to see as a part of what I do. But more than that, I have recently come to think that I have a few more things to say that might be useful to colleagues, and I have identified this thematic link, *reflexivity*, that I think can allow me to bring those things together in a way that is coherent. And yes, I want to do that.

It sounds as though this book is much more *about you* than it is *for* anyone else.

I don't see that those two things need to be in opposition. The kind of . . .

Well, let's say this isn't exactly a 'how to' book for people wanting to get involved in teacher education.

Yeah, in simple terms, I'd go along with that. It's not a book of instructions, nor does it try to cover a teacher education syllabus, or anything like that. That's not the kind of contribution I'm trying to make or the kind of impact I would like the book to have. Nor, come to that, is that the only kind of reader interest that needs to be addressed, I think.

OK, so you just talked about 'contribution' and 'impact' and 'addressing' certain readers, and you even used the word, 'need', that you baulked at before. Do you want to say more about those things?

Fair enough. I'll work backwards through your list and I'll try to keep it brief. Yes, I said 'need' in the sense that I think that we need a variety of types of book to keep us motivated and engaged and thinking and developing and healthy. A good 'how to' book is a fine thing, but only 'how to' books would be a thin diet.

As for my addressees, at its broadest I hope to address any fellow TESOL professional with an interest in his or her own continuing development, as well as administrators, researchers and policy-makers who see the professional development of teachers as a focus of their interest or responsibility. But most particularly, as you can tell from my title, I have written this book with those colleagues in mind who work in teacher education.

Well, that's the usual pretty wide net! Did you miss anyone out?

OK, more specifically yet, I want to address those teacher educators who continue to see their endeavours in teacher education as a form of teaching in its own right, in the straightforward sense of helping others to learn, and who remain keen to continue their own self-development through their work.

I write for colleagues who are comfortable with (or at least prepared to entertain) the idea that professional development is a part of personal development: that we do not simply amass bundles of pedagogic functions separate from who we are, but rather that we are whole-people-who-teach and that a continuing exploration of what that means in terms of individual congruence is an appropriate companion to the learning of, for example, how to use new techniques and new technologies. This relation between the personal and the professional is one strand of reflexivity that the book explores.

Is this what you call 'brief'?

Listen up, I'm just getting going. I have written the book for teacher educators who share my perception that, while it is now common to emphasize the need for teachers to pursue their own personal development, to explore and theorize their own experience, as well as to evolve their own style of context-sensitive teaching, there is a serious danger of these topics becoming just that: topics on teacher education courses. I believe that we need lived examples of teacher educators themselves operating in these ways, and that this relationship of compatibility between the ideas that we espouse and what can be seen in our practice represents another element of reflexivity to investigate.

By emphasizing this common interest in exploring and theorizing, it is my intention actively to contribute to a sense of shared purpose and mutually beneficial process between teacher educators and teachers. And if such a sense of common purpose and process is to be established, it falls to teacher educators to take the lead. To put that another way, I want to look at how the experience of teacher-learners working with a reflexive teacher educator is taken forward in their own professional lives. This sense of teacher educator/teacher continuity is another of the meanings of reflexivity that the book takes up.

As I intend to mine my own experience and tell my own stories in the writing of this book, I am writing for readers who are sympathetic to the idea of a narrative truth that does not always boil down to general principles, rules, or instructions. You will need, then, to be prepared to put up with old men's tales, to extend sufficient trust to believe that they are not told without serious purpose, and to challenge yourself with the question, '*What is the significance of this for me?*'

To be quite honest, apart from not being at all brief, this is starting to sound a little overambitious and/or narcissistic.

You may be right. In fact, in a way that completely exposes you as simply a presentational device of mine, you bring me very neatly to my subtitle.

Uh-huh. I'm blown. Do tell.

My mother used to say that parents need to give a child roots and wings. Perhaps your mother used to say the same thing. Or you might have seen the saying on an embroidery sampler in a gift shop. It's not original. But it is powerful. That is probably how clichés get to be clichés. If you can put up with that clichéd reading of the phrase, I think it's fair to say that that is what teacher educators hope to do for the teachers that they work with: help them establish their roots in educational values that are important to them, and help them grow the wings that will enable them to explore their environments and continue discovering new possibilities for themselves in helping others learn. That should not, of course, be confused with the idea of teacher educators taking on some kind of parental role towards teachers. The point that I want to make is that, in order to be effective in helping teachers empower themselves, teacher educators need to be explicitly and overtly engaged in modelling these 'roots and wings' processes.

And you see 'roots and wings' as being connected with being overambitious and narcissistic?

Let's say that I'm prepared to take the risk. But I have to admit to having another agenda in mind here. That phrase, roots and wings, has become evocative, for me, of two well-known Greek myths: the Narcissus myth and the Icarus myth, albeit with unorthodox readings. Indulge me?

Why stop now? I see you have a very battered copy of Graves (that's Robert, not Kathleen) to hand.

Yes, indeed. Well, Icarus was the son of Daedalus, the master craftsman who was imprisoned on the island of Crete by King Minos (because of his designer role in activities involving Queen Pasiphaë and a holy bull that we do not need to go into here). In order to escape, Daedalus created wings from leather, wax and feathers for himself and Icarus. In the telling by Graves (1960:312):

> Having tied on Icarus's pair for him, he said with tears in his eyes. 'My son, be warned! Neither soar too high, lest the sun melt the wax; nor swoop too low, lest the feathers be wetted by the sea.' Then he slipped his arms into his own pair of wings and they flew off. 'Follow me closely,' he cried, 'do not set your own course!'

The effectiveness of this last injunction from parent to child rings down through history. Graves (ibid.:313) continues:

> They had left Naxos, Delos and Paros behind them on the left and were leaving Lebynthos and Calymne behind them on the right, when Icarus

disobeyed his father's instructions and began soaring towards the sun, rejoiced by the lift of his great sweeping wings. Presently, when Daedalus looked over his shoulder, he could no longer see Icarus; but scattered feathers floated on the waves below. The heat of the sun had melted the wax and Icarus had fallen into the sea and drowned.

The story is usually recounted as a cautionary tale about disobedience and, especially, a warning of the punishment that awaits overweening pride. But in Wilson (1998:5), I came across a reference to the myth in terms of its celebrating a defining element of what makes us most excitingly human:

> And so the great astrophysicist Subrahmanyan Chandrasekhar could pay tribute to the spirit of his mentor, Sir Arthur Eddington, by saying: Let us see how high we can fly before the sun melts the wax in our wings.

And then, when reading Levin (1965), whose study of the works of Christopher Marlowe is entitled *The Overreacher*, and the cover of which features a woodcut of Icarus falling, I learned that similar interpretations of the myth go back at least as far as Francis Bacon. Bacon, Levin tells us (ibid.:190), wisely recommends the middle way between extremes:

> But in his parables, De Sapienta Veterum (XXVII), the prosaic Bacon concedes that age goes astray through defect; and whereas defect crawls upon the earth like a serpent, excess makes itself at home in the skies like a bird. The course of Icarus, defying the laws of gravity and common sense, was uncertain and unsafe; yet even Bacon was compelled to admire it, because its youthful swiftness kindled a certain magnanimity.

And in our more recent popular culture, that strand of ambivalence and mournful admiration shines through again in Joni Mitchell's (1977) evocation of Amelia Earhart's pioneering flights, as being as beautiful and foolish as the wings of Icarus ascending. We acknowledge the risk, but sometimes see our best selves in it.

And Narcissus? Is he also a hero?

Well, Narcissus was also a young man, equally wilful in the traditional telling and equally doomed by his pride. In his case, the cause of his undoing was his extreme beauty and his resultant vanity and self-absorption. Women and men, humans and nymphs, all fell in love with him and he spurned them one after the other. One of these broken-hearted suitors, Alpheius, committed suicide and called on the gods to avenge him, a call taken up by Artemis, who in Graves' (1960:287) version, '. . . *made Narcissus fall in love, though denying him love's consummation.*'

While travelling through the woods near Donacon, in Thespia, Narcissus came across a spring of clear water:

and as he cast himself down, exhausted, on the grassy verge to slake his thirst, he fell in love with his reflection. At first, he tried to embrace and kiss the beautiful boy who confronted him, but presently recognized himself, and lay gazing enraptured into the pool, hour after hour. How could he endure both to possess and yet not to possess? Grief was destroying him, yet he rejoiced in his torments; knowing at least that his other self would remain true to him, whatever happened.

Finally, he, too, killed himself and, as his blood soaked into the ground, '. . . *up sprang the white Narcissus flower with its red corollary*' (ibid.:288)

I don't know that anyone has yet tried to argue a case for Narcissus, as has been done in defence of Icarus. Perhaps he does not deserve one. And yet . . .

Both are accused of pride, both died for their faults. Both sought something extraordinary. In both cases, we are offered, as it were, third-party reports; there is no inside story. In neither case is there a word from the central character, from Icarus of how far he saw, from Narcissus of how deeply he looked, or from either of them of what they might have discovered. Icarus had wings and flew higher than he should. Narcissus stayed too long observing himself and put down roots.

I like to think that there is a parallelism between the two, and I see them as emblematic (albeit extreme) of the exploration of the environment that we inhabit and co-create, and of the exploration of ourselves as we engage with that environment. None of us wants to get stuck in the riverside mud, or to burn up over the ocean, but the mutually-shaping interactions between our roots and our wings, our self-knowledge and our environmental knowledge, as we bring them to our awareness and then commit ourselves to future action based on that combined awareness – that constitutes our development, and that constitutes our life. This is the major aspect of reflexivity that I pursue in this book.

Aren't you stretching this just a little too far?

Have you been listening to me at all? It is, of course, true that one can take these things too far, and one can expect to be accused at times of doing just that: of being overambitious, misguided, pretentious or narcissistic. At our best, we might want to reply with Kolb (1984:209):

> If there is a touch of aggressive selfishness in our search for integrity, it can perhaps be understood as a response to the sometimes overwhelming pressures on us to conform, submit and comply, to be the object, rather than the subject of our life history.

Sometimes, however, the accusations will be legitimate. Mistakes are endemic to human experience. Furthermore, while we affirm that we learn from them, we prefer to write about our successes. This book will, however, also look into the dark corners of individual error and failure, my errors and failures, in order to pursue reflexivity into the shadows that we inevitably cast when we walk in the sun.

I believe, as you will have noticed, that this multifaceted concept of reflexivity is one that can help us take the best parts of our professionalism forward in a way that unites teachers and teacher educators. It can also unite our abilities to learn from our experience, from each other's stories, from our intellectual disciplines, from our mistakes, and from our occasional flights of fantasy. That's the kind of impact I would like the book to have.

Altogether then, this book is for people who find the prospect of exploring what a *reflexive* teacher educator might be an interesting and attractive one, either in terms of their own reading, or as a text to read with (other) teachers, or with (other) teacher educators. If this book can play a role in that exploration, then it will have made its contribution. Are things any clearer for you now?

You ask a lot. OK, I'll have to think about it.

I should hope so!

I advise against irony. It seldom works in print. Anyway, I have some sense of your aims and addressees, and you have certainly been free enough with your metaphors and myths. Looking back to the title of this chapter, where do voices and vocabularies fit in?

Hmmm. Good question. You see, I can't tell you everything that I want to say in the same voice. It's like how one learns things in different ways, and knows things in different ways – some things have to be told in different ways. So, you'll hear my voice change now and then, depending on what I'm trying to deal with. Given what we know about communication, I think that that makes sense. I hope that it won't put you off your reading and responding.

And vocabularies?

Well, there's a case in point . . .

★ ★ ★ ★ ★

I have come very late to the philosophy of Richard Rorty and still have a very long way to go if I am to appreciate his thinking in anything like the depth that it deserves. The attraction, however, was immediate when I came across the following line of editorial introduction in Brogan & Risser (2000:45):

> The primary focus of Rorty's work has been to develop this insight: if it does not make a difference to practice, it should not make a difference to philosophy.

For many years, in the field of teacher education, I have been arguing against the validity of the frequently-heard teacher refrain, '*Oh, it's alright in theory, but it doesn't work in practice.*' My argument is not that teachers should try harder to apply the theories that have been worked out for them, not at all. My argument is that if something doesn't work out in practice, then it is most definitely *not* alright in theory. Once one has made allowance for misunderstandings and mistakes, either a theory accounts for the data that it is meant to account for, in this case, teacher experience, or it doesn't. If it doesn't, it's bad theory. Or a theory of something else. The problem with '*Oh it's alright in theory, but . . .*' is that it frequently expresses a generally negative attitude toward theory-as-irrelevance that can then excuse the speaker from further thinking or development.

Rather than dismiss 'theory' in general as irrelevant, what those of us engaged in teaching need to do is to articulate as best we can statements that *do* account for the data of our experience. And if something does not make a difference to our practice, then it does not need a place in these theories of ours.

As I read on, I came across Rorty's stated purpose (ibid.:51), '*to make the best selves for ourselves that we can*', which resonated strongly with what I take to be the underlying tenet of any approach to personal/professional development: my aim is not to approximate as closely as I can some external model of teaching, but to work on my talents and potentials in order to become the best teacher that I, myself, can be, which will necessarily be different in some ways from the best teacher that someone else can be.

An intrinsic part of that self, in Rorty's (ibid.:45) stimulating formulation is a set of words:

> All human beings carry about a set of words which they employ to justify their actions, their beliefs, and their lives. These are the words in which we formulate praise of our friends and contempt for our enemies, our long-term projects, our deepest self-doubts, and our highest hopes. They are the words in which we tell, sometimes prospectively and sometimes retrospectively, the story of our lives. I shall call these words a person's 'final vocabulary.'

'*Final*', I understand not as meaning the last such set of words that one will ever have. Uneasily underpinning this final vocabulary for people who Rorty refers to approvingly (ibid.) as '*ironists*' is an awareness '*of the contingency and frailty of their final vocabularies, and thus of their selves*'. In private, you may agonize over some aspects of it and, as life goes by, (Williams 2003:78): '*Nothing is immune from revision.*'

Even given this sense of '*thoroughgoing fallibilism*' (ibid.: 69), however, the 'vocabulary' is 'final' in the sense that it constructs the current and probably long-term set of concepts and beliefs that are the raw materials with which one thinks. This vocabulary provides the lenses for your perceptions, the bases for your actions. It is key to who you are: key in the sense of central, pivotal, main, and also in the sense of indicative, with each item having the capacity to unlock some other aspect of this interlinked set. It grounds and expresses your habitus (Bourdieu 1977), that blend of genetic and social inheritance and self-construction that you have thus far achieved. Its items cannot be justified except in their own terms. Your final vocabulary is not better or worse than someone else's as measured against an external scale, because there is no external scale. It is what it is. One's final vocabulary does not represent a world that exists separate from it. One uses one's final vocabulary to argue a world into existence.

These thoughts motivated me to spell out here, at the beginning of this book, some of the items that I think of as being a part of my current 'final vocabulary'. I expect these items to be familiar to my readers, but the nuances of how we understand and use them might differ. I am hoping that if I spell those nuances out in advance, you will be forewarned and better able to understand me as we go along, perhaps the better to understand where I go wrong, or how and why you disagree with me.

It may be that I take Rorty's metaphor too literally, or that you are not motivated at this point to read what you might see as a glorified glossary. If that is the case, please skip it. I introduce the terms anyway as we proceed, along with other items that push themselves forward as prominent in my discourse. I have chosen the following, however, because they also structure the book.

Let me begin with five parameters of *doing*:

Copying

I use this term (especially in Chapters 2 and 4) to mean the thoughtful continuation of traditional methods or given models, possibly somehow adapted directly in practice, based on experience of their usefulness, rather than theoretically rethought.

Applying

For reasons that I go into in Chapter 2, it has for some time been thought unhelpful to represent teaching as primarily a matter of applying theories. Nevertheless, there is a sense in which a teacher might have (or obtain) theoretical knowledge that he or she makes use of when teaching. It would be foolish to deny or overlook the potential usefulness of such essentially technical ability simply because of old grudges. For this reason, applying (in the sense of applying theories) receives specific attention in Chapter 5.

Theorizing

To theorize, in the sense I want to use it, is to articulate one's understanding of what is happening and why it is happening. To theorize, bottom-up, *from* one's experience is the counterpart to the technical applying of theory *to* one's experience. I focus on this in Chapter 6.

Reflecting

I mean to invoke the concept of the reflective practitioner, which I look at particularly in Chapter 2. In this sense, reflecting runs all through teacher education. In Chapter 7, I develop a specific usage of the term with regard to broader, intellectual reflection on sociocultural elements affecting the field.

Acting

Sometimes, I want to escape the abstract noun, *action*, and invoke more directly the implied dynamism of the gerund. I mean, therefore, not performance in the dramatic arts, but much more generally, doing things in the social, usually educational, world. I mean deliberate acts as the outcome of thought and possibly planning. As with reflecting, acting runs all through the book. It receives special treatment in Chapter 8.

I continue my 'final vocabulary' statement with five dimensions of *becoming* (and being, and continuing to become). So, when I write about '*becoming methodological*' (Chapter 4), for example, I do not mean that this is something that one becomes and that is an end to it. I mean that this is a dimension of being which one can first access and then along which one can continue to develop. *Becoming* indexes both change and also continuity.

Methodological

I use this term (particularly in Chapter 4) to communicate the recognition of procedural choice and preference that enables teachers to transcend simply repetitive practice, even when those choices remain at the level of untheorized copying or adapting. Development along this parameter also continues when application of theory and theorization of practice are available.

Technical

I use this term (Chapter 5) to invoke the ability to apply ideas and theories, perhaps from educational research, perhaps from informing disciplines such as linguistics, psychology or sociology, perhaps from elsewhere, to the practice of teaching. This can be a part of the overall process of '*becoming theoretical*'.

Theoretical

I use the term *theorizing* (Chapter 6) to invoke the ability to articulate one's own (interim) understanding of what is happening in one's teaching and why it is happening. Such theorization of practice is a counterpart to the ability to apply pre-existent theories in the larger sense of '*becoming theoretical*'.

Intellectual

By the use of this term, especially in Chapter 7, I mean to convey not only the idea of a person who works with ideas and abstractions. I mean also to invoke the kind of thinking and consequent action that relates TESOL to the wider inter-cultural world in which it must operate: a world of politics, racism, religions, globalization and other highly combustible elements.

Pragmatic

I mean to invoke an approach to thought, language and action that sees communication as humanity's way of establishing reality, and usefulness as the goal of exploration. In a changing world, it looks to the future for the justification of its thinking and doing. This is the focus of Chapter 8.

I have chosen these vocabulary items because they are key to my attempt to communicate an overall framework of being and doing in teacher education. I have proposed five dimensions, or ways of *being*: methodological, technical, theoretical, intellectual and pragmatic. I have proposed five parameters, or ways of *doing*: copying, applying, theorizing, reflecting and acting. I do *not* propose that teacher education comprises the careful fitting together of these separate dimensions and parameters.

★ ★ ★ ★ ★

I'm sorry? Then what is the point of it all?

Let me be clear. In my educational culture, we rely a lot on separating things out by analysis and categorization and those processes take us a long way. We do, however, need to remind ourselves that a great deal of our categorization is best understood on an 'as-if' basis. We don't actually divide the world up into its constituent parts, we suggest that it can be useful and/or explanatory to proceed 'as if' the world could be divided up that way. Our purpose remains to understand the whole a little better. Isn't that, for instance, what grammar is all about?

Oh please! Don't lets go there. And yes, I think you may have taken the metaphor of a 'final vocabulary' too literally.

I concede that my voicing of it here might be too heavy, but that is because I feel its weight. It is a powerful concept.

Mmmm. Is there any chance of your giving us a diagram of how these elements fit together?

No. And you're not listening. If you ask me, most diagrams just serve to clarify things for the writer, who already knows what s/he means. I could draw you an arrangement of boxes with arrows indicating that everything is connected to everything else, but what would that clarify?

OK, OK. Another thing that's worrying me is that you haven't yet mentioned *reflexivity* in there.

Oh no. That's going to take me the whole book, with all the vocabulary and voices I can manage. My advice to you is not to believe that any one of them can tell you the whole story.

★   ★   ★   ★   ★

The images in these old movies are not always so clear, and the gambler's hands move so quickly across the table . . . The stranger says that he's looking for reflexivity, that it is worth the search. (How many times have you watched one of these black-and-white 'classics' and found they're not nearly as good as you remember them, or as the film buffs say they are?) Is this just like in *Treasure of the Sierra Madre*? Fool's gold? Where do you stand? Are you just a spectator, or is there a chance that you might become involved? Don't let the gambler's smile fool you. The early cards are always good. The first hit is always free. But once you're in, you're in. No point in asking my advice: I'm in. Just for one more job, though. I'm going to nail this reflexivity thing and then I'm out of here. Just one more job. And this is the one where it all works out fine in the end.

If you're in, pull up a chair.

I'll deal.

2

IN PRAISE OF
REFLECTIVE PRACTICE

This story is going to move around on you, using a lot of flashback and also the occasional imagined future. In this chapter, however, I want to give you my view of the way things are now in TESOL teacher education, before indicating the direction I want to head out in. Naturally, someone wanting to go somewhere else might show you a different panorama. For me, however, the overarching schema in which we work is that of reflective practice so, when our hero comes riding out of those opening titles, this is the background scenery from which s/he emerges.

The state of the art

Since the appearance of Schön's (1983) *The reflective practitioner* and (1987) *Educating the reflective practitioner*, both arising from earlier work in organizational psychology (Argyris & Schön 1974) and translated into TESOL by publications such as Richards & Nunan's (1990) *Second language teacher education* and Wallace's (1991) *Training foreign language teachers: A reflective approach*, the conceptualization of teaching as reflective practice has cast the mould for our vision of what it means to be a teacher. That, at least, is my perception of where TESOL teacher education stands as I write this chapter, in the spring of 2010.

This perception has been consolidated from various perspectives over the years, among them: classroom practice (e.g. Bailey, Curtis & Nunan 2001, Farrell 2007), action research (e.g. Freeman 1998, Burns 1999, Edge 2001b), beliefs and values (e.g. Gebhard & Oprandy 1999, Johnston 2003), individual and collegial development (e.g. Edge 2002a, Palmer & Christison 2007), narrative exploration (e.g. Johnson & Golombek 2002, Casanave & Sosa 2007) and change management (e.g. Clarke 2003, 2007). Canagarajah's (2006b) *TESOL Quarterly* special anniversary issue, emphasized by Johnson's (2006) sociocultural piece on teacher education in that collection, elaborates and reconfirms the currency of the vision.

This seems to me to be a good place for teacher education to find itself, and it is worth recapping why, if only very briefly. Wallace (1991) usefully contrasted a reflective approach with what he called two other models of teacher education, the *craft model* and the *applied science model*. It may nowadays be more accurate to think of all these as elements that will form a part of any teacher education programme, rather than as distinct models, but this does not take away from the strength of the insights that Wallace offers.

A craft approach tends to treat teaching as a group of behaviours that can be modelled by a skilful teacher, and directly copied and learned by a trainee. To the extent that teaching does involve such aspects, the approach can have the advantage of keeping things real, of tying teacher learning into actual situations, and of encouraging close inter-generational continuity and collegiality among teachers. As it stands, however, the apprentice-copying-the-master tradition is limiting in that there is no obvious place for professional innovation or personal growth to enter the system. In a society where the strict replication of given patterns of behaviour is desired, this may be acceptable, but that kind of society is becoming less and less common. Wright (2004:14) gives us a contrasting big picture in dramatic terms:

> From the first chipped stone to the first smelted iron took nearly three million years; from the first iron to the hydrogen bomb took only 3,000.

As physical, cultural, sociological, and psychological dimensions of change have fed into and off each other in ever-accelerating feedback loops, he goes on (ibid.):

> Nowadays we have reached such a pass that the skills and mores we learn in childhood are outdated by the time we're thirty, and few people past fifty can keep up with their culture – whether in idiom, attitudes, taste or technology – even if they try.

The extent to which we can lump together '*skills and mores*', or '*attitudes and technology*', especially in so multicultural a field as TESOL, is a point to which I return (See Chapter 7), but Wright's central point about the ferocious pace of change that humans now need to deal with, along with the need for education to help them do so, remains sound and speaks, therefore, against a reliance only on a craft-based model of teacher education.

The second model that Wallace looks at is what he calls the *applied science model*. The fundamental principle operating here is that teacher-learners should be taught the theoretical bases of pedagogy and of the disciplines informing their specialization and that they should then apply these principles in practice. The strength of this model, and of the tendency that endures in teacher education, is that it respects teachers' intellectual capacity and emphasizes their expertise in their subject areas. The importance of these aspects of a teacher's life has not diminished and they continue to find passionate defenders in TESOL (e.g. Yates & Muchisky 2003), who feel that this importance currently risks being undermined. A weakness of the approach in its stronger forms, however, lies in its central, technocratic concept that teaching essentially involves the application in practice of theoretical understanding developed outside teaching. To deploy Schön's (1992:120) topographical image, researchers are rigorous on the high ground and teachers toil to apply their findings in the swamp below. Disciplinary knowledge and intellectual understanding do have their roles in the make-up of a teacher, but skilful teaching is more than the product of their technical application. Clarke (1994) unpacks for TESOL the problems inevitably caused by a ruling discourse of technical rationality and theory/practice, elaborating the dysfunctional effects that this dichotomy has had across all areas of teacher education. It may be that some readers have their own memories, or even current experiences, of what is involved. Lecturers in educational psychology or second language acquisition, syntax or phonology, complain bitterly about the lack of interest and effort of their students, while the teacher-learners complain equally bitterly about the irrelevance of what they are required to learn. And in between, a great deal of potentially extremely relevant knowledge fails to be constructed and a great deal of motivation fails to be engendered.

Against this background, Wallace introduces Schön's reflective-practice model, in which professional learning arises through the interaction between experience and conscious cognition. We are introduced to the concepts of *reflection-in-action* and *reflection-on-action*. The former arises in situations where the expected flow of a class is interrupted for some reason and the teacher has to rethink, improvise, re-prioritize, or reorient the direction of the lesson. By exploring such incidents, and by encouraging teachers to do so, we have discovered more about the ways in which knowledge, experience and thought interact in decision-making and action. A major technique for such exploration has been stimulated recall (e.g. Gass & Mackey 2002, Borg 2006), in which a teaching session is recorded and then played back while the teacher is invited to comment on critical incidents with regard to what s/he was thinking and/or feeling and what informed his or her decision-making and actions. Schepens et al. (2007) employ this technique in order to investigate the learning processes of student teachers. In so doing, they emphasize a point the importance of which runs throughout this book of mine even when I choose not to repeat it, that is the significance of locally-situated knowledge (ibid.:458):

> Considering professional development separately from the meaningful interaction between student teachers and their learning and work environment would deny the complexity of learning to teach.

Conversely, Meijer et al. (2002) report on the usefulness of the same technique in order to help student teachers learn from the practice of more experienced colleagues because, as they point out (ibid.:406):

simply copying the behaviour of experienced teachers will most probably result in an inappropriate conservatism.

From yet another perspective, in a layered piece of research that used stimulated recall to track developments in the cognitive processes of mentor teachers before and after a period of training in the area, Hennissen et al. (2009:1) report that after training:

> mentor teachers not only seem to emphasize pupil learning and needs when conducting a mentoring dialogue, but simultaneously focus on their own supervisory behaviour.

Here, we have a powerful example of how a heightened awareness of self-in-action can play into the controlled development of one's praxis – a term that I use throughout this book to mean the fusion (in ways that I hope to make clear) of 'theory' and 'practice' as mindful, committed activity (see Edge 1994a, Johnson 2006).

The second concept mentioned above, *reflection-on-action*, refers to the more contemplative type of reflection that takes place beyond the immediate pressures of the teaching moment, when one can think back over what happened and consider what has been learned from it and how this might be used in planning the future – what Loughran (1996) has termed *anticipatory reflection*. The concept of reflection-on-action has helped us understand and implement the cyclical kind of approach to teacher learning that we find also in more formal approaches such as action research, a topic to which I return in Chapter 6. In addition, it has helped us explore another distinction – introduced by Argyris & Schön (1974) – between *espoused theory*, what we say we believe, and *theory-in-practice*, the beliefs that might reasonably be interpreted to be ours by anyone watching us at work. Once more, the exploration of parallels and contrasts found here has proved a very fertile source for teacher learning and therefore made an important contribution to teacher education (e.g. Segal 1998, Lazaraton & Ishihara 2005) as well as to TESOL professionalism more generally (e.g. Walker & Cheng 1996).

All in all, then, reflective practice has provided an approach to the development of professional praxis that allows us to explore the experience of craft learning and intellectual learning in mutually interpenetrative ways (Loughran 1996). It has also provided us with key concepts that have helped shift the understanding of teaching from being seen as a series of behaviours only, to being seen as a complex, multiply-influenced and motivated activity in which awareness and routine both play important roles. It has encouraged us to believe that while routine is important, awareness can help us shape the routines on which we are content to rely and also allow us to develop the innovations that will keep us engaged and alert (Myers & Clark 2002).

Inevitably, caveats and critique have evolved over time. In practical terms, for example, we are sensibly warned that '*the effects of reflection upon practice have yet to be fully realized, for the creation of reflective learning spaces in itself does not necessarily lead to change'* (Clandinin 2008:389). In more philosophical mode, Erlandson & Beach (2008) distinguish two conflicting lines of argumentation that run unacknowledged through Schön's work. At times, the argument appears to involve '*a special reflection-in-action way to think'* (ibid.:419) that, in turn, draws on a Cartesian mind/body duality, with the mind in charge. At other times, this duality is rejected and the body is (ibid.) '*a reciprocal organic-cultural system'* and '*learning to handle practice is not a question of the mind or of thinking but rather of actual experiences of the living reciprocal body'*. A similar tension is pointed out by Fendler (2003), between reflection as formulated by Schön as a form of practitioner intuition, and reflection as envisaged by Dewey (1933), seen as a foundational source in this area, as a way of introducing more rational thinking into a domain too guided by tradition and repetition.

Akbari (2007) raises useful questions about the extent to which reflective practice does, or should, engage with issues of critical practice (in the ideological sense of, for example, Giroux & McLaren 1989, Pennycook 2001) and teacher identity (Norton 2000). I return to these issues in Chapters 7 and 10.

These doubts and concerns, while justified in their own terms, also serve to underline the centrality of the reflective project in contemporary teacher education. In other words, people define their position by reference to it. As I shall soon do, myself.

Furthermore, each critique might be seen to be as much a question of making space for the writer's own interests as one of identifying substantial weakness in its target. It must be true, for instance, that increased awareness does not automatically bring about changes in behaviour. To expect that it should, however, would be to misrepresent the nature of the reflective project, in which increased awareness multiplies the opportunities on which development might be based, leaving commitment to change a question open to the individual. Similarly, while the Dewey/Schön distinction outlined above is certainly of interest, the crucial pragmatic point is that the reflective approach allows for the interaction of craft-based intuition and rational intellect as each becomes a complementary investigative lens for the exploration of their combined potential. To take a final point from the list given above, it may be that many reflective practitioners are not as committed to critical pedagogy as some commentators would wish, but this is not in itself a critique of reflective practice except to the extent that one sees the themes and concerns of critical pedagogy as being constitutive of teaching, which a great many people do not. For those who do, moreover, some form of reflective practice remains the most influential model for carrying such ideas forward into action.

The reflective teacher educator

At this point, I find myself at a pivotal point in my exposition. I celebrate the strength of the reflective approach and I affirm the interest of some of the concerns that have been raised about it. As I have already indicated, I see Wallace's three 'models' more as elements of any sensible teacher education programme. That is to say, teacher-learners should be able to learn, in a craft sense, by copying more experienced teachers (see Chapter 4). They should be able to learn by applying learned concepts in the sense of using them to develop practical procedures for their own particular contexts (see Chapter 5). They should be able to learn by observing the effects of what they have copied and what they have applied, and by articulating their own conclusions. This last step, often called the theorization of practice, is what I see as a key process linking earlier experiential and intellectual learning to future action (Edge 2008a). I return to this theme in Chapter 6. Reflection runs throughout these processes (see Chapter 7) and all are embedded in a context of continuing professional action (see Chapter 8).

Reflection and *action*, thinking and doing, can be seen more generally as describing how it is that any person interacts with his or her environment – a statement of what one does in order to be aware and consciously alive in one's living. From this perspective, *copying*, *applying* and *theorizing* are more specifically what teachers do in order to be consciously alive in terms of their continuing development as teachers.

My discussion so far, therefore, has allowed me to assemble an overall working approach to teacher learning which involves the elements of copying, applying, theorizing and reflecting, all in a context of action. As a way of holding these ideas together, I shall avail myself occasionally of the acronym, CATRA. I see these elements as 'ways of doing' and as parameters for continuing development.

In this approach, a number of legitimate requests arise from the teacher-learner, to which the teacher educator needs to respond. I summarize these in Table 2.1.

These are not to be seen either as watertight categories, or as being in any kind of sequence; they interact in multiple ways, and reflection and action are everywhere.

Reflexive memo 2.1: My telling is balanced on a knife-edge at this point. I have identified elements of teacher learning to be facilitated and legitimate requests that teacher-learners can make, but I can't go there yet, because there is another layer of the story to add, one that refocuses attention on the teacher educator, who is, after all, my

---

TABLE 2.1 Teacher-learner requests

If the teacher-learner is to learn from:	The request to the teacher educator is:
Copying	Show me
Applying	Tell me
Theorizing	Listen to me
Reflecting	Help me think this through
Action	Give me feedback

> primary topic and addressee. I need to move around those elements
> of teacher learning again and see them embodied in the teacher
> educator. That is also how I establish a future link with reflexivity.

If, when talking about being and becoming a teacher, I am prepared to come up
with rather grandiose formulations such as the one above regarding what it is to
be aware and alive and how we enact this experience, then I have always to keep
in mind that the same must apply to the teacher educator. Furthermore, it won't
do just to say these things; if one is to be credible, one has to be seen to be doing
them. This demand is not complicated. It is also explicit in some of the earliest
formulations of reflective practice, which will require, in Argyris & Schön's
(1974:196) terms, teacher educators who:

> are strong enough to invite confrontation of their teaching and to make
> themselves vulnerable to inquiry into the incongruities in their teaching and
> practice; and who, finally, will confront themselves with the conflict of
> values implicit in these incongruities.

Gore (1991:271) is equally forthright:

> We need to ask ourselves questions such as the following: Do we really
> believe in these practices of inquiry-oriented teacher education? Why don't
> we use them regularly in our own teaching? If we argue that we do not have
> time, can we blame teachers for not adopting them as a regular part of their
> teaching? If we argue that teaching is not a priority among the many
> academic tasks before us, can we justify our location in teacher education?

One framework to aid reflection in teacher education that I have found particularly
useful is one that I have copied from work in management training by Boxer
(1985). Its power rises in part from the fact that it provides an analytical lens for
reflecting on reflective practice itself. Like so much of our categorization activity,
it depends on our willingness to suspend our disbelief about how the world can
be divided up into discrete elements and, likewise, to suspend evaluation of the
worth of the activity until we have seen the extent to which it can be useful.

First of all, in order to reflect on experience, whether our own or other
people's, we have to choose a particular incident on which to focus. (Reflection
on 'experience in general' risks avoiding both serious thought and actual events
and becoming little more than a rehearsal of unexplored assumptions or established
prejudice.) When choosing a focus, it is as though we construct a frame around a
certain event and thereby create the picture that we wish to examine and
appreciate. Boxer's first question, therefore, is, '*Who does the framing?*', in the sense
of '*Who decides what we are going to look at?*' Once the picture has been created, we

need some way of appreciating it, of understanding what we can best learn from it. Boxer's second question, then, is, '*Who decides how the picture is to be interpreted?*' For our purposes, we can imagine both decisions being made either by the teacher educator, or by the teacher-learners. With these two questions, Boxer creates a simple four-cell matrix, each quadrant of which can be seen as representing a very different style of using reflection on experience in teacher education. (See Figure 2.1.)

If the framing and the interpretation are both in the hands of the teacher educator, then the style of work is *Instructional*. For example, I might show a recording of a teacher conducting some oral practice and ask teacher-learners to note when s/he uses self-correction techniques, when peer correction, when s/he corrects mistakes herself, and when s/he lets them go uncorrected. I then explain the thinking behind these choices.

If the framing is in the hands of the teacher-learners and the interpretation is in the hands of the teacher educator, then the style of work is *Revelatory*. That is to say, the teacher-learners identify the issue and the teacher educator shows them how to make sense of it. Teacher-learners, for example, might be experiencing difficulties with their own professional reading, in response to which the teacher educator suggests a specific reading strategy. Chapter 5 focuses to a large extent on just such a situation.

If the framing is in the hands of the teacher educator and the interpretation is in the hands of the teacher-learners, then the style of work is *Emancipatory*. That is to say, the teacher educator presents an issue and the teacher-learners need to

Style of work

	By teacher educator	By teacher-learners
By teacher educator	Instructional	Emancipatory
By teacher-learners	Revelatory	Conjectural

Framing the Experience

By teacher educator   By teacher-learners

Interpreting the picture

FIGURE 2.1 Style of work

develop their own way forward. I might, for instance, introduce a series of scenarios in which teachers face dilemmas and ask teacher-learners to decide what they would do next.

Finally, if the framing and the interpretation are in the hands of the teacher-learners, then the style of work is *Conjectural*. That is to say, teacher-learners identify their own issues and make their own sense of them. For example, in order to help them decide how to proceed, teacher-learners are invited to present to a group of peers examples of problems or opportunities that they are facing.

Boxer traces a potential overall development through these styles (Instructional, Revelatory, Emancipatory, Conjectural) as teacher-learners move from dependency to the autonomy that they will need if they are to act as independent professionals and, as one hopes, to continue to develop. At the same time, and this is another ever-present danger in our use of analysis and categorization as a way of exploring and understanding the indivisible, there *is* no fixed linear sequence to these different types of experience. All are useful and appropriate under different circumstances towards different ends. One never escapes the responsibility to give instructions, or the need to demonstrate; nor is it ever too early to encourage speculation.

Nor should one assume that, across these variations, the roles of teacher educator and teacher-learners are fixed. I also maintain my right to ask to be told and shown when that is what I need. And sometimes (very frequently when it concerns computers and software), my teacher-learners are the ones that I ask.

Risks involved

	By teacher educator	By teacher-learners
By teacher educator	Alienation	Fragmentation
By teacher-learners	Impotence	Insignificance

Framing the Experience

By teacher educator   By teacher-learners

Interpreting the picture

FIGURE 2.2 Risks involved

Boxer pursues his analysis with regard to the dangers involved in a situation in which the teacher educator overuses a particular style of working. (See Figure 2.2.) A learner restricted to the instructional paradigm risks *alienation* from the whole process of reflection, asking, '*What has this got to do with me?*', and ends up declaring, '*It's not relevant!*' In overuse of the revelatory paradigm, the risk is one of *impotence*, as the learner has to accept as given other people's ways of making sense. You can bring your own sheep to market, but somebody else shears them. Or choose your own metaphor. With the emancipatory style, the danger is of *fragmentation* as learners may be tied to making sense of other people's pictures, but never their own. They become technically adept analysts, perhaps, but do not gain an overall feeling of self-engendered consistency. The danger when the conjectural paradigm is over-represented, perhaps out of the teacher educator's enthusiasm for teacher-learner autonomy, is that teacher-learners cannot relate their own interpretations to authoritative sources. They may also lose touch with the need to decide and act in real time, so that outcomes drift off into *insignificance*. All of these dangers are threats to the overall concept of the power of reflection and of consequent learning from experience.

One feature of this analysis that I find attractive is the simple elegance with which the basic question, '*Who is in charge?*', is used to demonstrate the powerful connections operating between power, epistemology, identity and social relationships. This alone gives the teacher educator a perspective from which to reflect on his or her role in the development of fellow professionals. More practically, it provides a tool for self-analysis with regard to one's own preferred style of working. If I listen for my own voice as I hear it in my work as a teacher educator, what do I most easily hear that voice saying?

Do it like this.
or
Think about it this way.
or
What do you make of this?
or
What do you want to work on?

Let me not leave that question hanging rhetorically in the text. It deserves an answer. My self-perception is that the second (revelatory) and fourth (conjectural) of these sound more comfortable in my voice, which is why I believe that I am a better teacher educator for experienced teacher-learners than for those entering the profession. Equally, the awareness that this gives me allows me to approach pre-service teacher education in the knowledge that I must take care not to avoid my responsibility to provide instruction and to confront teacher-learners with issues that I believe to be important, even if they do not identify them as such themselves. In Chapter 4, I report on some pre-service teacher education experience of mine which I regard as extremely positive, but in which, in retrospect, I can also probably discern my tendency to favour the revelatory and conjectural over the instructional and emancipatory.

A final strength of Boxer's framework is that it is one that can be shared, where appropriate, with teacher-learners. They can use it to discern better the types of opportunity that are available, as well as to explore their own learning preferences. As an outcome of this reflection, they might also be able to take better advantage of learning opportunities that are not framed and interpreted in their preferred style.

At this point, the elegance of the analysis might also break down. Perhaps my favourite teacher-learner response to this type of discussion over the years is one that I reconstruct here from old notes:

> You know, you made up this scenario for us to discuss and now I want you to tell me what *you* would do. But what I mean is, I want you to tell me so that I'll know what you think. It doesn't mean that I'll take that as 'instruction', it just means I'll know what you think. You can say that's instructional, but it's also emancipatory, because I'll make up my own mind in the end.

I regard this kind of thing as a significant justification of analysis. This individual's understanding was not contained by the analytical framework that he had been offered. He had escaped the *as-if-ness* of the analysis – essentially by introducing the element of perspective – and turned it into his own tool. That is, he was using terminology and concepts learned in the context of analysis to construct an understanding of his experience that exceeded the analytical categorizations with which he had begun. To these old ears, that's what success sounds like.

Allow me to take that last point a little further. During a final feedback session at the end of a methodology module that I had taught on a master's course, one participant said, '*All you have taught me is a lot of new words for talking about what I do anyway.*'

She did not mean this as a compliment. While I paused (certainly a moment for reflection-in-action), another participant said, '*Well, I don't think I've learned any really different ways of teaching, either, but now I understand better why what I do makes sense, and why some things don't work, and I have the words and the concepts to help me talk about it in ways I couldn't before.*' Again, when working with experienced teachers, that sounds to me like a worthwhile achievement in the form of a renewed foundation in the confidence, knowledge and skills required to steer further development. The first speaker shrugged and pulled a face. Truly, we live in a world of multiple realities.

Having praised reflective practice

Reflection and reflective practice have become the watchwords of late twentieth and early twenty-first century professional life and this brief review has risked superficiality. I allow myself this brevity and risk the superficiality for two reasons. First, because my intention here is only to establish common ground with my readers with regard to the contemporary scene in teacher education. I do not believe that I have said anything controversial and, if I have neglected something that you feel is important, I trust you to fill that in for yourself. Second, I take the risk because my next discourse move is not the usual academic one of critique, of showing what needs to be corrected. My aim is not to engage in the usual *displacive* mode of discourse so much as an *augmentative* mode of discourse (Edge 2003a, 2004): I am happy with where we are and I also believe that we can move on positively from here.

Interacting and overlapping with discussions of reflection and reflective practice is the term, *reflexivity*. My aim in this book is to draw out more specific meanings of reflexivity, to identify it among other forms and uses of reflection, to associate it with all the parameters of CATRA that I have sketched above, and to do so by drawing on autobiographical data in a style that might perhaps be described as a type of auto-ethnography (Spry 2001, McIlveen 2008). The aim is to provide stimulation for fellow teacher educators. Believe me, this is not an attempt to join the '*men [who] have sometimes cast their lives into heroic molds in order to project their universal import*' (Tedlock 2003:189), even though the shades of Icarus and Narcissus linger and I have undertaken to defend them, and even though I acknowledge that I also open myself up to the accusations entailed by that defence.

The reflexive invites the autobiographical, and this is what I have to offer after forty-odd years of TESOL. As for its *import*, that evaluation will depend on its readers. The evaluative criteria for the book are, I suggest, the usual ones. You might ask yourself:

- Is it a good read?
- Do I, because of my interaction with this text, know more at the end of it than I did at the beginning?
- Do I feel differently about what I know? Am I in any way excited by what I might go on to learn?
- Do I feel motivated to do something that I might otherwise not have done?

With these self-observing questions at the back of our minds, let us now construct such wings as we can in order to see how close to a useful understanding of reflexivity we can fly.

3

IN SEARCH OF REFLEXIVITY

During our television news broadcasts these days, presenters have taken to saying, '*This report contains scenes that some viewers may find disturbing*.' In like vein, I should warn you that this chapter has its challenges. You could see this as the line in the sand scene. You can quit now and no one will think any the worse of you. But if you're still in, hold your nerve – together, we will find a way through. The gambler has opened a new deck and the stakes are getting higher.

Introduction

In the previous chapter, I highlighted some of the advantages, both conceptual and procedural, that the adoption of reflective practice has introduced into the field of teacher education and development. I also noted my growing interest in the occurrence of the term *reflexivity*, clearly associated with reflective practice, but not well defined in terms of itself, or its role in, or its relationship to, reflective practice. What I want to do in this chapter is to articulate some of the thinking that has emerged as I have worked to understand this concept more intimately. I take this process to be an example of what I have already called the *theorization of practice*: one discerns in one's working environment an opportunity for further intellectual effort that one believes will feed back into and enrich one's praxis. The style and extent of such theorization will be a matter of individual choice at different times, as we shall see through Chapters 6 and 7.

Reflexive memo 3.1: It is so difficult to use the word *intellectual* without fearing that one will put readers off. Even as I write this memo, I wonder about the advisability of the term. But if it has been lost to us because of misuse, or inverted snobbery, or for any other reason, then it needs to be regained, and this can only be done through usage. I remember once referring to myself as '*a working-class* *intellectual'*. During the laughter and mickey-taking that followed, in which I was happy to take part, I realized that I was also actually prepared to defend this self-categorization. I still am. Perhaps I even need to.

Until just before my eighth birthday, my parents, my brother and I lived in a house that had no running hot water and no form of heating except the coal fire in the kitchen. We would bath in a zinc tub in front of that fire on Saturday evenings. The row of terraced houses that we lived in was of the 'two-up, two-down' variety, this expression being a reference to the number of rooms that the houses comprised, with the toilet being located in a small outhouse in a tiny backyard that stopped just far enough away from the railway line for there to be a narrow dirt track to provide access. The houses belonged to Baines' pottery factory, whose huge cylindrical chimney stack dominated the neighbourhood's narrow streets and cobbled alleyways. My parents had managed to get tenancy through negotiations with the rent collector carried out by my maternal grandmother, who also rented across the street from us. She had earlier done the same for her eldest son, so there were now three households of Rowleys and Edges in Granville Street.

When the factory needed the land on which our homes stood, inspectors were called in. The dwellings were declared 'unfit for human habitation' and scheduled for demolition. At least, that is the story I grew up with. Perhaps they really were *'unfit for human habitation'*, according to some bye-laws, but my mother was very put out by the perceived slur on her ability to keep a clean and respectable home.

We were allocated a council house on a public housing project in a part of the city unknown to us. On an exploratory expedition involving a long bus ride and much misdirected walking about, we found the place and discovered that the houses were brand new, in fact, not quite finished. My brother and I could have a bedroom each; there were two indoor toilets, hot running water and a proper, plumbed-in bath. The estate, which comprised only fifty houses, was on the boundary of open fields with a brook, a pond and wooded hills none too far away. We could barely believe our luck. It was not until much later, when I went to university, in fact, that I came to realize the social stigma that was meant to cling to people who grew up *'on council estates'*. But that's OK, I know who my people are. And that's enough of this. For now, anyway.

What is strange is that I started out being defensive about being 'intellectual' and ended up writing so much about being 'working class' . . . More work to do there. See Chapters 7 and 10.

At this point, I want to dig back into my experience in teacher education in order to establish where and how this idea of reflexivity started to become significant for me.

Roots

When, in 1986, members of the International Association of Teachers of English as a Foreign Language (IATEFL) set up a Special Interest Group in Teacher Development, I was an early joiner. I also joined the IATEFL Research SIG at its inception in 1990. The following year, having recently taken up a post at Aston University's Language Studies Unit, I suggested to the director and administrator of the unit, Keith Richards and Alison Birch respectively, that we might host a conference that brought together the overlapping interests of both groups: the desire to develop into the best teacher that one could be, given one's own individual mix of talents and potentials, and the desire to explore and understand better one's professional environment and one's role in it. We called the conference *Teachers Develop Teachers Research* (TDTR) and it became the first of a series held around the world. As we wrote in the publication that followed (Edge & Richards 1993:6):

> we wanted to reclaim the difficult term 'research' to characterize a teacher's personal investigations, and we wanted to establish the personal outcomes of research as a valid point of focus.

> we asked contributors explicitly not to talk about research and development as topics, but to report on their actual experiences.

We had not realized how difficult it would be to bring about either of these aims, or to bring them together. A majority of the initial proposals comprised third-person research by teacher educators, providing reports on the experiences and developmental outcomes of their teacher-learners in ways that were, perhaps, more qualitative and personal than the norm, but which did not feature their own experience and development as a part of the findings of the research. Other proposals featured stories of personal development, but the authors remained reluctant to present this as research.

As we later edited the conference papers, we found ourselves obliged to divide the collection along third-person/first-person lines in ways that we had not intended, but in so doing, we formulated two claims more clearly than we had before (ibid.:122):

> • Firstly, the data of the researcher's personal involvement, whether that be intellectual, emotional, ideological, or experienced on any other frequency, is valid and potentially important.

- Secondly, the exploring teacher must find a voice with which to record and communicate his or her development, whether or not that voice echoes the accents of academic discourse.

In retrospect, although I did not have the terminology at the time, I now see this as my first published attempt (co-written with Keith Richards) to pin down two important dimensions of what I am now calling reflexivity in teacher education.

Reflexive memo 3.2: To my real surprise, I hereby discover that a variant of the desire to insist on being 'working class' and 'intellectual' is there again in the desire to insist on being 'the teacher' and insist on being 'the researcher' *and* to insist that the two are compatible. Not that they have to be, but that they *can* be if that's what you want. It might be, then, that much of my professional development has reflected that autobiographical insistence on the metaphor of expanding one's repertoire, rather than exchanging roles or identities.

My engagement with reflexivity as an integral part of my professional purpose was rooted, then, in the above TESOL-related experiences. In the remainder of this chapter, I pursue the concept of reflexivity further along various other dimensions before returning to establish its relevance, as I now understand it, to teacher education. In those mythological, metaphorical terms for which I have a declared weakness, I shall try to fly a little.

Wings: dimensions of reflexivity

Linguistic

As an English language teacher, the first response I have to the term, *reflexive*, is to think of reflexive verbs and, therefore, in first-person terms, of actions that I do to myself. I act and that action affects me: I warm myself and become more comfortable; I criticize myself and become annoyed or inspired; I fool myself and escape the consequences of my actions, while perhaps storing up problems for the future. In each case there are outcomes, some obvious, some unexpected, some, perhaps, never actually discerned. What I find here is a concept of reflexivity as involving a unitary whole that is at the same time divisible: my self is divisible into an 'I' and a 'me', a subject and an object, a nominative and an accusative. This distinction has a wide-ranging resonance – one which takes us back to Kolb's evocation of the individual wanting to be the subject of his or her life, rather than only an object in it (p.7) – and one to which I shall return repeatedly.

Psychological

One immediate lexical resonance for me is with the Subject/Object shifts that are central to the work of Kegan and his associates (Kegan 1994, Kegan & Lahey 2001) whose topic is (1994:9):

> the evolution of consciousness, the personal unfolding of ways of organizing experience that are not simply replaced as we grow but subsumed into more complex systems of mind.

What stands out in Kegan's (ibid.) *'constructivist-developmental psychology'* is that his concerns centre on *'transformations of consciousness after adolescence'* and he posits particular thresholds that adults need to cross in order to be able to deal successfully with the demands of contemporary life. While this is not the place to go into these thresholds in detail, his point in principle is that (ibid.:134):

> the demands of modern adult life may require a qualitative transformation in the complexity of mind every bit as fundamental as the transformation from magical thinking to concrete thinking required of the school-age child, or the transformation from concrete thinking to abstract thinking required of the adolescent.

One example that he gives (ibid.:87–92) is of a divorced mother deciding how frank to be about her current sex life when asked about it by her ten-year-old daughter. The mother neither wants to lie, nor to burden the daughter with information that she might not be able to interpret appropriately. In Kegan's terms, the mother is called on not to allow herself to be constrained by the one-to-one values of their relationship thus far, in which explicit openness has been fore-grounded as the basis of trust, but to *'stand somewhat outside the relationship,'* to re-evaluate those values and to establish a new relationship with the old relationship itself in the light of what she thinks is best for her daughter. She now sees the mother–daughter pair from an external viewpoint. To make this move does not provide the mother with an automatic answer as to what she should say, but she will now make that decision according to what Kegan calls *'a higher order of consciousness'* in that she is no longer *subject to* the demands of the previous relationship, but can view the relationship and those demands rather as an *object* in a wider frame of reference that she has constructed.

I hope that it is clear from this brief evocation of Kegan's work that, while his use of *subject* and *object* in his subject/object shifts is not exactly in line with the subject/object, nominative/accusative distinction that I called upon previously, there are also elements of similarity. I return to this topic below, but first there is another resonant link to be sounded.

Kegan (1994:8) describes his work as a *'mode of attending to our lives'* that engages a dialectic between the two sides of 'wonder' – wondering *at* and wondering *about*

– without prioritizing either. He suggests (ibid.) that this blend of the aesthetic and the analytical is also '*the lifeblood of wholesome teaching*': too much unfeeling rationality leads us to standardized tests and school league tables, while too much unthinking passion can stoke national, religious and ideological prejudices of the kind that scar our recorded history. While I agree wholeheartedly with this point, and return to it soon, my immediate purpose in taking up Kegan's reference to *wonder* is to note how well it chimes with another such usage, this time in the field of philosophy.

Philosophical

Heidegger, according to Sallis, identifies a sense of wonder as '*the fundamental attunement that – at least for the Greeks – was the origin of philosophy.*

> Wonder, he (Heidegger) characterizes as a stepping back in the face of beings ('Wir treten gleichsam zurück vor dem Seienden') a stepping back that becomes attentive to beings, that they *are* and that they are *so* and not otherwise. Thus to step back is also to be transported to and bound by that before which one has stepped back. Wonder is, hence, the 'dis-position in which and for which the being of beings opens up' (Emerson 1979:190)
>
> *Sallis 2000:38*

It is in this way that the ordinary can become extraordinary for a person who is so dis-posed. I am struck by the parallels between Heidegger's 'stepping back' and Kegan's 'standing outside'. Both achieve a new perspective, but while Kegan emphasizes the objectification of the web of values and relationships one has stepped out of, Heidegger emphasizes the transportation and binding to that before which one has stepped back. I shall want to hold on to both of these metaphors and return to them below.

In the meantime, however, and perhaps rather more prosaically, a further pursuit of reflexivity in the realms of philosophy leads me to logic, where it occurs as a term denoting '*a binary, i.e. two-term, relation which everything has to itself*' (Kirwan 1995:753). This terminology seems very helpful in conceptualizing what I am trying to get a handle on. When one thinks of '*a binary relation which everything has to itself*', one recognizes the presence of a unitary concept as well as a duality, just as one does in the I/me distinction. This opens up the possibility of interaction and mutual shaping between the two elements in binary relation.

Ecological

Ideas of mutual shaping relate also to an overarching schema of ecology, of environment and adaptation, within which I need to introduce two further items of what I have come to think of as my 'final vocabulary'.

Affordance

I learned this concept and term from van Lier (1996), as he interprets the work of Gibson, J. (1979) and Gibson, E. (1991). In my understanding, *affordance* is an interactive, linking concept with the approximate meaning of an *individual learning opportunity*. I call it a linking term because it links a person into his or her context by the means of this opportunity. I might, for example, be watching a game of baseball with a USAmerican friend when the television commentator says something about '*loading the bases*'. I have no idea what this means, so, for me, but not for my friend, this presents an *affordance*: my state of knowledge and the data of my context link up to afford me a learning opportunity. Let me introduce another use of terminology here, one that I learnt from my colleague, Susan Brown. While my baseball-watching companion and I both *perceive* the same situation, I *discern* an affordance. This distinction tips the use of *discern* towards an expression of conscious awareness. This implication suits me as I use *affordance* primarily with regard to teachers' recognition of individual learning opportunities (i.e. discernment of affordances) in their work environments.

Context

I most often use this term in its everyday sense of *surroundings*, or *environment*, whether that be physical, cultural, social, educational, textual, or along some other parameter. Exactly which parameter we are talking about, of course, can already be crucial in identifying what we mean by *context*. If, for example, someone were to ask me for advice on teaching pronunciation, I might ask for some details of their working context. If they were to tell me that they teach in Montevideo, the capital city of Uruguay, a country to the south of South America with a population of approximately 1.25 million, and that the city lies at the mouth of the River Plate, I could not deny that they were giving me information about their working context, but much of this contextual information does not relate very usefully to the matter at hand. So, it is the connection between the context and the contextualized that defines in any particular case what we actually want to mean by the term *context*.

Moreover, we can usefully take this idea of connections further and discover that it is not always easy to draw a line between the context and the contextualized. As we saw in the baseball/affordance example above, my friend and I are in one sense in the same context, and in one sense we are not. I have a learning opportunity, she has a teaching opportunity. (Our roles might be reversed, of course, were we to be watching cricket and the commentator were to point out that the captain of the fielding side had taken out a slip and brought up a short leg.) It is the relationship between the person and the context that defines what the context is for that person. Clarke (2007: Chapter 1) expands powerfully on this ecological theme with direct reference to English language teaching and elaborates on context in the following way (ibid.:32):

This presentation is based on the definition of context developed by the anthropologist Gregory Bateson (1999:289): 'We may regard "context" as a collective term for all those events which tell the organism among what set of alternatives he must make his next choice.' Every day, all of the time, we make decisions based on the alternatives presented by a situation that is in our face at the moment as well as our understanding of larger issues and distant situations.

Nor do we need to stop there. One can follow this theme back to the development of the simplest organism, where the presence of a defining membrane is necessary for the organism to exist identifiably *in* its context, and not simply as part *of* a context, but it is what the organism identifies and responds to in its surroundings that defines what comprises the context *for* that organism, as well as influencing how well that organism survives and what it might become. It is in this sense that Maturana & Varela (1987:25) write of each living organism from the simplest bacterium upwards:

> This circularity . . . this inseparability between a particular way of being and how the world appears to us, tells us that *every act of knowing brings forth a world.*

I find it satisfying to think that the observations we make about teacher development in context are only a particular case of such a general truth: the unitary whole that we need to consider is always organism-in-context. In our particular case (teacher education), we can take the opportunity to see how these two parts of the whole communicate with each other, and it is here that we will discover the mutual shaping of reflexivity.

In qualitative research

My interest in reflexivity as a concept was boosted through my work in qualitative research. The connection with teacher education is a natural one in the sense that reflective practice shades into action research and the role of the teacher or teacher educator as exploring agent is common to both.

A major difficulty when turning to qualitative research for insights into reflexivity, however, is that the term, while ubiquitous, is over- and under-defined to a bewildering degree. At one end of its usage, as noted by Du Preez (2008:510), it merges vaguely into the reflection from which I set out to distinguish it:

> Narrative research is often subsumed under 'reflective practice' or 'reflexive practice' and at times the terms are used interchangeably.

Similarly, D'Cruz et al. (2007:75) write of:

> the richness of critical and constructive practice approaches that may be subsumed or sit together uneasily under what sometimes appears to be one concept, just spelt differently.

In contrast, Finlay (2003a) offers a typology of forms of reflexivity drawn from differing contemporary research traditions. She explains (ibid.:6):

> Five variants of reflexivity are explored: (1) introspection, (2) intersubjective reflection, (3) mutual collaboration, (4) social critique, and (5) ironic deconstruction.

Tellingly, however, she also adds a footnote (ibid.) in which the '*of course*' should bring a smile to the face of any reader who is in this for the long haul:

> Numerous typologies have, of course, been published. Lynch (2000) offers an inventory of 'reflexivities': mechanical, substantive, methodological, meta-theoretical, interpretative and ethnomethodological. Two particular notable, and often referenced, typologies are the ones by Marcus (1994) and Wilkinson (1988). Marcus (1994) identifies four 'styles' of reflexivity: (1) self-critique and personal quest, (2) objective reflexivity as a methodological tool, (3) reflexivity as 'politics of location' and (4) feminist experiential reflexivity as the practice of 'positioning' (of standpoint epistemologies). Wilkinson (1988) offers her feminist distinction between personal (i.e. subjective factors), functional (as related to one's researcher role) and disciplinary (looking at the place and function of the particular research project) reflexivity.

I do not intend to pursue these individual perspectives in detail, but it is important to recognize that we are working in a space the richness of which has been extensively explored.

It is also from qualitative research methodology (most particularly grounded theory, e.g. Charmaz 2003:261–265) that I have taken the general idea of memo writing, a few examples of which I have already introduced without prior comment. In part, they are notes written by me to myself and they establish a relationship between me as the writer of the memos and me as the writer of the main body of the text in which the former is learning from the latter. As they occur in real time, however, what is learned by the former may go on to influence the latter. In addition, I am necessarily working with the idea of a third-party audience in mind, so the memos in their published form are also written for that audience. Furthermore, as writing is a long process of drafting and redrafting, the 'real-time' nature of the relationship between main text and memos is bound to be compromised. Nevertheless, in reflective terms, the memos are an attempt to provide a visible account of reflection-in-action, as distinct from the reflection-on-action of the main text. In reflexive terms, they attempt to bring out elements of the mutually-influencing relationship between the writer and the writing, also in action. While I acknowledge the real possibility that a number of readers will find them annoying, I persevere with them in the hope that a greater number will find them useful.

In the next section of the chapter, I report on my own working version of reflexivity in qualitative research. I then pull together the various dimensions of reflexivity that I have touched on in a statement of their relevance to teacher education. The main part of the book then fills out that statement with examples and discussion.

My working version of reflexivity in qualitative research

To begin with my conclusion, reflexivity in qualitative research is concerned with the ongoing, mutually-shaping interaction between the researcher and the research.

By 'the researcher', I mean the individual carrying out the research. This involves an immediate simplification. There may be more than one researcher, the researcher(s) may see their actual role to be facilitator(s) of participatory research, or as co-participant(s) in researching their own community. I am not going to attempt to deal with these nuances in what follows, which is not to say that I think that what follows has no relevance in such situations. Quite simply, things are complicated enough as they are, and are about to become more so. I intend to attempt to deal with the more straightforward situation of the individual researcher and leave the reader to take on the extra work if s/he feels sufficiently motivated.

By 'the research', I mean everything else that is involved: the cultural, historical, social, ideological setting, the human relationships in that setting, the research paradigm, tradition and literature, the ideology, the formulation of research questions, the gathering and analysis of data, the presentation of findings, the articulation of an argument, the production of texts, the claim of a contribution, the effects, intended and unintended – all of it. In this way, I avoid the various (and extremely useful) subcategorizations above while hoping to stay close to my 'final vocabulary' position (see pp.32–33) that the basic unit of analysis is always organism-in-context. At the same time, I hold on to an earlier clue to the nature of reflexivity (see p.31): the presence of a unitary concept that contains a potential for division and dialogue. In the case under consideration here, the researcher and the research can be seen as the same thing – a unitary concept – but one can also see them as composing an internal reflexive relation.

Furthermore, the mutual shaping of researcher and research is a cycle with no obvious beginning. I become a certain person who asks certain questions, but then I may have become this person because of the questions that I have asked. We are working in an interpretive cycle according to which we understand the world (its events, experiences and texts) on the basis of our current state of knowledge in interaction with currently incoming data. We may assimilate these data into our existing schematic understanding, or the data themselves may trigger a need for large-scale schematic change in order for us to accommodate their significance. An abiding message is that to escape the influence of our own expectations requires dedicated effort. All of this corresponds to a version of what the nineteenth-century German philosopher, Dilthey, called a hermeneutic circle (Rickman 1988:167):

The hermeneutic circle involves the alternation between the detail and big picture, the historical and the systematic, acknowledging no best place to start, and that there is a paradox involved in saying that our knowledge arises from our experience and that our experience is shaped by our knowledge.

Nevertheless, in order to talk about the processes involved, it is inevitably convenient to think in terms of two aspects of this cycle:

- the influence of the researcher on the research;
- the influence of the research on the researcher.

The former is the one more commonly invoked.

The influence of the researcher on the research

For some writers, this is what they mean by reflexivity. There are all sorts of ways in which researchers have an effect on their research, starting from the reasons why the researcher chose this topic area, formulated these research questions, gathered data in this way, chose that form of analysis, referred more to one school of expertise than another, reached this conclusion rather than that, and recommended that course of action rather than the other, even leaving aside such natural desires as to see one's hunches substantiated, one's interventions justified, one's research celebrated, or one's attempts to make the world a better place turn out to be successful.

In order to protect qualitative research from any bias resulting from the above effects, and to defend it from positivist criticisms of a failure of objectivity, a battery of techniques (triangulation, member-checks, audit-trails, peer review, coding validation, etc.) has been developed (e.g. vide Richards 2003). This is as it should be. These techniques do not, however, address the issue of reflexivity; they respond to the results of reflection. It is by reflecting on my research and on my subjectivity (whether approached in terms of gender, class, race, status, etc.) that I can hope to recognize such bias, take steps to make it transparent and thereby seek to correct for it.

Reflexivity, however, is not so much concerned with guarding against such influences as it is with noticing them, accepting them, exploring them and making them a part of the research.

Reflexive research, then, embraces its own subjective nature and sets out to explore in more depth what the effects of its subjectivity have been and will continue to be. As Finlay (2002:531) puts it, '. . . *subjectivity in research is transformed from a problem to an opportunity*'.

The influence of the research on the researcher

This aspect of reflexivity is less referred to, essentially, I imagine, because the end result of a research project is usually seen as being its outcomes in the sense of its contribution to knowledge and/or methodology, or its recommendations, or, in the case of action research, its effect on its context.

The reflexive dimension, however, involves another kind of outcome, that is, change in the researcher. It is unlikely that s/he will have come out the experience the same way s/he went in. Apart from what can be catalogued as having been learned, in a reflective sense, can the researcher also document changes in him/ herself as a person, or changes in awareness about him/herself that are interesting to report? This is what I mean by this second aspect of reflexivity, well expressed here by Sandywell (1996:xiv):

> unlike the closed circle of disinterested reflection, reflexive action changes the form of the self: a reflexive practice never returns the self to the point of origin.

Taken together, these two facets of reflexivity complete a continuing hermeneutic cycle of mutually-shaping change as the researcher constructs the research, works to see how his/her subjectivity influences it, pursues the research goals, and works to see how s/he is (being) influenced, in turn, by these processes and outcomes.

Finlay (2003b:118) makes a slightly different point, in which she reunites the exploration of research question and exploration of self in a way that connects research method again with its philosophical underpinnings. She also achieves this in a way that gave me on reading it an unexpected line back to my mythological framing device:

> as reflexivity continually challenges our practices and understandings, a truth is revealed: 'Since the seer is caught up in what he sees, it is still himself he sees. There is a fundamental narcissism of all vision.' (Merleau-Ponty 1968:138). Hermeneutic revelation of the phenomenon and reflexive uncovering of the self are one.

I have tried to emphasize in this discussion both the unbroken nature of the reflexive cycle and the sometimes strategically useful device of separating out its two aspects. We might note in passing how we have once again identified a unitary phenomenon that we can envisage as two parts communicating with each other, the better to uncover the nature of the whole. In this sense, reflexivity itself opens up to a dialogic conversation-with-self, just as does the reflexive researcher.

Given this strategic usefulness, I shall, when necessary, modify the terms I use in order to distinguish the two aspects of reflexivity referred to, even though the sequential implication entailed is not properly justified. When talking specifically about the effect of the person on the work, I shall use the term, *prospective reflexivity*. When talking specifically about the effect of the work on the person, I shall use the term, *retrospective reflexivity*.

While both these types of reflexivity are available for those who wish to explore them, a warning is called for that applies equally to both. One has, as always, to take care that these issues do not simply become topics to write about or boxes to tick. One does not escape the responsibility of having something interesting to say that actually links the research process to individual disclosure in a mutually-shaping way. As Behar (1996:14) puts it, with regard to what she calls the vulnerability of the researcher writing in this mode:

> Vulnerability doesn't mean that anything personal goes. The exposure of self who is also a spectator has to take us somewhere we couldn't otherwise get to. It has to be essential to the argument, not a decorative flourish, not exposure for its own sake.

Unless, at some point, for example, you see a relevance in my telling you about my childhood home, the telling is superfluous.

With regard to the acid test for prospective reflexivity, the researcher's personal revelations must answer the reader's implicit question, '*So what? What is the actual influence on the research?*' With regard to retrospective reflexivity, the implicit question that the researcher must answer is, '*How come? How do you ground these changes in yourself in the research experience that you report?*'

Reflection and reflexivity revisited

I began this section on qualitative research by pointing out how the terms *reflective* and *reflexive* are sometimes used as if interchangeable. I hope to have established that this should not be the case. Nor, I want to suggest, is it the case that reflexivity is somehow a linear extension of reflection, as though they were on a continuum, as suggested by Finlay (2003b:108).

My suggestion is that there is a twofold relationship between the two concepts. From one perspective, reflection is a broader concept than reflexivity and can contain it. Reflection can address all kinds of issues and some of those issues will be reflexive in nature. In this sense, reflexivity is only consciously accessible via reflection. From another perspective, reflexivity is a more interactively significant concept than reflection. Whereas reflection (whether in-action or on-action) assumes the continuing identity of the person doing the reflecting, reflexivity questions that continuity, foregrounding the change-effect of action-and-reflection on the person concerned, arising from what they have, so to speak, done to themself. In this sense, I recognize a strong affinity with a tradition (e.g. Giddens 1991) which works with a '*conceptualisation of the "self" as reflexive, as a project which is always in a state of becoming*' (Francis & Skelton 2008:311).

This, anyway, is the approach to reflexivity that I have taken, in which the point is not to define reflexivity in terms of its specific components (e.g. the relationship with participants, or with text production, or with methodological decisions), but to appreciate the nature of the mutually-shaping relationship that it involves between an aware organism and all and any elements of its environment.

In all of this, I have already acknowledged the influence of Clarke's (2003, 2007) formulation of the world in the systemic terms of Gregory Bateson (1999), which I see as operating in tune with the broader zeitgeist of Capra (1983, 2001), Prigogine & Stengers (1984), Dawkins (1986), Maturana & Varela (1987), Zohar (1991), Wilson (1998), Rose (2006) and Gopnik (2009) in which the search for understanding in various dimensions of human exploration becomes what is fundamentally a search appropriately described in evolutionary terms for what best *fits*, (with all the reflexive mutuality that that verb entails and purposive activity that the verb implies) and which thereby strives, whether consciously or not, for its own continuation.

I now need to pull the various dimensions of this discussion together in order to argue that a conscious organism's focused awareness on the workings of reflexivity can itself be developmental, and that this abstract statement has specific relevance to the field of teacher education.

Reflexivity in teacher education

Getting one's bearings

The time has come to bring together the brief sightings achieved by flying so high and so quickly over the fields of linguistics, psychology, philosophy, ecology and qualitative research in order to formulate a statement that shows how these glimpses cohere, for me, and are rooted in my work. My purpose, then, is not to define reflexivity in any essentialist way, but to explain what I have come to understand by the term and, better even, how working for this understanding has been developmental for me as a teacher educator. At all stages, I make every effort to keep in mind the aphoristic principle of Rorty (1998:19) that I invoked in the first chapter of this book:

> Pragmatists think that if something makes no difference to practice, it should make no difference to philosophy.

In that introduction (pp.4–7) I also sketched out in discursive style four aspects of teacher education which I find it useful to think of as what I have since called unitary wholes that contain a potential for division and consequent relation:

- the teacher educator and his/her whole-person praxis;
- the teacher educator (viewed in terms of espoused theory *vis-à-vis* theory-in-action);

- the teacher educator (viewed in terms of personal development and professional development);
- the teacher education community (viewed in terms of its distinguishable roles of teacher educator and teacher-learners).

It now seems reasonable to see the first of these as being in some sense qualitatively different from the other three. In logical terms (Sprigge 1995:755–757), we can say that, in the first item, there is an *internal* relation operating, in that the nature of each half of the construct (teacher educator/praxis) is mutually dependent on the nature of the other half and it cannot be otherwise, whether the person concerned is aware of this or not.

The subsequent three constructs demonstrate *external relations*, in the sense that their two halves can be defined independently. That is to say, teacher educators can and do continue to work with espoused theories that they do not, in fact, put into practice. The issue here might be labelled one of *consistency*. They may also possess personal characteristics and values that they do not fully invest in their teaching, as well as develop professional skills that they may not think to take home. The issue here might be called one of *coherence*. Similarly, teacher educators and teacher-learners can and do continue to work in their own ways without achieving the benefits of the mutual collaboration that greater awareness might offer. The issue here can be termed one of *continuity*, not least in the sense that the bringing-in of new generations of teachers to valued ways of working must be high on the priority list of any form of teacher education.

If the above distinctions and definitions are indeed reasonable, one is still left with the question as to what extent they are useful. Their usefulness lies first (for me) in the clarity it gives me regarding the area of work I am trying to cover. Second, it is empowering to see the plausibility (Prabhu 1990) of one's intuitions supported by further theorization. Third, the separation out of congruence from consistency, coherence and continuity becomes suggestive of a goal/means relationship. That is to say, perhaps congruence is best understood in the Yeatsian vision of the inseparability of the dancer and the dance: congruence itself might be difficult to address directly, but stands as a goal.

Issues of consistency, coherence and continuity, however, are directly susceptible to improvement via conscious work on increasing one's awareness in these areas. Perhaps congruence is the unifying epiphenomenon that might arise from such work. Equally, it might be the unitary gestalt that I have attempted to subdivide in a typically analytical search for understanding. Either way, this juxtaposition of goal and means helps to identify a stance and perhaps a direction. To achieve congruence, we work on consistency, coherence and continuity, and thus try to walk a path into being.

The key to action, then, appears to be increased awareness-raising with regard to consistency, coherence and continuity, which might lead to a greater overall *congruence* in the teacher educator's praxis.

Reflexive memo 3.3: Kolb (1984:2) opens his inspirational treatment of experiential learning with the bugle-call:

> We have cast our lot with learning, and learning will pull us through.

I find myself wanting to say that I have nailed my colours to the mast of awareness, in the belief that the increased sense of responsibility that awareness brings will see us through. If this commitment proves to be mistaken, then all that remains will be to learn how to swim in whatever waters our political masters will lead us to founder in.

In formulating this statement of the usefulness of the above definitions and distinctions, I find that I have articulated my way to a new interim realization that fuses the analytical and the poetic elements of the understanding I have been working for and indicates a way ahead. This is what I take Allard et al. (2007:310) to be referring to with their evocative phrase, '*a north star moment*'.

Setting out

As is fortunately so often the case, one does not travel far across the thematic terrain of thought, action, awareness and education without meeting Dewey, who writes (1916:2), '*Life is a self-renewing process through action upon the environment.*' The sense of companionship and guidance is immediately sustaining.

In itself, Dewey's statement invites a wide range of interpretations, from a relatively passive level of consuming sufficient matter and processing it sufficiently well to maintain life functions, to a proactive engagement with our environments in which we seek out those affordances that seem most likely to stimulate our continuing growth. Similarly, when we talk about experience, we might simply mean those situations through which we happen to have passed, or we might mean those interactions to which we have paid close attention and translated into learning opportunities. This distinction is built into such well-known neo-proverbs as, '*We all **have** experience, but we don't all **learn** from it,*' and, '*Some teachers have ten years' experience and some teachers have one year's experience that they've repeated ten times.*'

Dewey (ibid.:139) is careful to give a specific meaning to his use of the term, *experience*, which he distinguishes from '*mere activity*' or '*meaningless transition*'. He characterizes experience as including '*an active and a passive element peculiarly combined*':

> On the active hand, experience is *trying* – a meaning which is made explicit in the connected term, experiment. On the passive, it is *undergoing*. When

we experience something we act upon it, we do something with it; then we suffer or undergo the consequences. We do something to the thing and then it does something to us in return. Such is the peculiar combination. The connection of these two phases of experience measures the fruitfulness or value of the experience.

He continues (ibid.:140):

To 'learn from experience' is to make a backward and forward connection between what we do to things and what we enjoy or suffer from things in consequence. Under such conditions, doing becomes a trying; an experiment with the world to find out what it is like; the undergoing becomes instruction – discovery of the connection of things.

Two conclusions important for education follow. (1) Experience is primarily an active-passive affair; it is not primarily cognitive. But (2) the *measure of the value* of an experience lies in the perception of relationships or continuities to which it leads up. It includes cognition in the degree in which it is cumulative or amounts to something, or has meaning.

My contention is that our contemporary work in a reflective paradigm has properly emphasized what Dewey calls the active and the cognitive – the *trying* and the *meaning-making*, while underemphasizing the passive, the *undergoing*. We have proceeded as though the identity of the acting agent moves on unchanged from one experience to the next, learning more, but not being changed by that learning. To draw again on the terminology of schema theory, it is as though the agent assimilates new learning without undergoing the need to accommodate change in itself. This may, of course, sometimes be the case. The point that I am trying to make is not a dismissive one, but an augmentative one regarding emphasis. Our reports foreground what we have learned, what we have acquired, much more than they feature what changes we have undergone, what we have become. To that extent, they do not represent well the emergent nature of our learning, in the sense that the person entering the next experience is no longer the one who entered the last.

It is at just this stage of the argument that I re-establish contact with the points made in Chapter 2 regarding a distinction between Schön and Dewey, with the former seen as presenting a specifically reflective-practitioner '*way of knowing*', while the latter is concerned more with bringing rational thought into habituated procedures. And now I see the statement that I have been struggling towards . . .

The type of learning from experience that I am seeking to invoke involves, first of all, the ability to be fully engaged in that experience, so that one is both in it and of it, accessing the situatedness of learning in the sense that:

knowledge, which comes coded by and connected to the activity and environment in which it is developed, is spread across its component parts, some of which are in the mind and some in the world much as the final picture in a jigsaw is spread across its component parts.

Brown et al. 1989:36

During such engagement, one is internalizing, in sociocultural terms, the patterns of meaning that social interactions carry (Vygotsky 1978, 1986, Engstrøm 1995, Wells 2007), and possibly experiencing the kind of engagement that Czikszentmihaly (1990) has described as *flow*.

Understandably, in teacher education, we focus a great deal on the cognitive (e.g. Borg 2006), so it is important to keep in mind Dewey's statement above that much of the experience that interests us is not primarily cognitive. What can this actually mean? And how might we evoke it in words, as we must?

'*With difficulty!*' comes the sardonic response, and this is true. But the challenge is there to be responded to, and, '*Through our art*,' is an equally valid response. The affective and even the visceral experiences available to us also need to be expressed if they are to be accounted for. Here is what I consider to be the most effective description of such an experience that I know of. I exemplify here, I should warn, by extreme, not by prototype, and I invite you to amend your current reading style to make space for it.

Dillard (1982:67) has been sitting quietly by a pond for some time. She turns to follow the flight of a bird and then, '*inexplicably, I was looking down at a weasel, who was looking up at me.*'

> Our eyes locked and someone threw away the key . . . Our look was as if two lovers, or deadly enemies, met unexpectedly on an overgrown path when each had been thinking of something else: a clearing blow to the gut. It was also a bright blow to the brain, or a sudden beating of brains, with all the charge and intimate grate of rubbed balloons. It emptied our lungs. It felled the forest, moved the fields and drained the pond: the world dismantled and tumbled into that black hole of eyes. If you and I looked at each other that way, our skulls would split and drop to our shoulders. But we don't. We keep our skulls.

And then Dillard (ibid.:67ff.) goes on to throw in our faces the shadow-side of our ability to 'step back' and observe our experiences as part of our constructivist-developmental psychological growth:

> He disappeared. This was only last week, and already I don't remember what shattered the enchantment. I think I blinked, I think I retrieved my brain from the weasel's brain, and tried to memorize what I was seeing, and the weasel felt the yank of separation, the careening splashdown into real life and the urgent

current of instinct. He vanished under the wild rose. I waited motionless, my mind suddenly full of data and my spirit with pleadings, but he didn't return.

The loss is palpable, but step back we must, for (ibid.:68):

The weasel lives in necessity and we live in choice, hating necessity and dying at the last ignobly in its talons.

The point must be (I say, as I retrace my steps with my head full of data and my spirit with pleadings) to remember at least when we step back, to do so in wonder, as Sallis (above) puts it, *at* the experience of the everyday if we want it to open up to us, and if we want not to lose the feeling of being transported by it and bound to it. Neither in terms of Heidegger nor Kegan is the stepping back to be seen as a separation *from* that with which one has engaged, but as an attempt to establish a potentially richer relationship *to* it than was previously accessible. And thus, reconnecting with teacher education, we can recognize and respect the potential also of situated craft knowledge when we see it embodied, even if it seems superficially to live only '*in necessity*'.

So, yes, we step back and then, as our broader knowledge and values and feelings come into play, we escape the state of being that Kegan (1994) describes as '*subject to*' the rules and constraints of the experience itself and, in Dewey's terms (above), we '*measure its value*'. Both of these statements, however, need further comment.

With regard to Kegan, his framework of increasing layers of complexity and subtlety seems very well suited to capturing the type of reflexivity that we want to deal with. In parallel with the example of the divorced woman talking about her sex life to her daughter, we can imagine a teacher dealing with a disciplinary matter. An unruly student may behave in a disruptive, even dangerous, manner. The teacher witnessing this has to step back from his/her immediate emotional reaction as a person (perhaps one of frustration or anger) and think about his/her role as a teacher. There may be rules to be enforced. However, the teacher may have to step back again from this role as enforcer of rules if s/he sees a bigger picture and recognizes that another reporting of this particular student will lead to suspension from school. Suspension from school will have an effect on the small local community in which both the student and the teacher live. A lack of response may lead to further disruptive behaviour that will penalize other students in the class and could even lead to disciplinary consequences for the teacher if all this comes out. . . . At some point, the teacher must adopt a stance external to the situation as s/he sees it and resolve his/her relationship to the web of value-laden relationships that s/he has thus objectified. S/he must metaphorically frame the picture for which s/he is prepared to take responsibility and in terms of which s/he must formulate a response that s/he can defend as *reasonable* – neither the simple *reaction* of a tired and frustrated individual, nor the depersonalized enforcer of

rational procedures devised far from this particular piece of action. (See Clarke &
Edge 2009 for further discussion of this process.)

Complex as Kegan's 'orders of consciousness' concept can be, here he is at his
clearest (1994:34):

> liberating ourselves from that in which we were embedded, making what
> was subject into object so that we can 'have it' rather than be 'had by it' –
> this is the most powerful way I know to conceptualize the growth of the
> mind.

In the grammatical usage of subject/object that I used when first discussing
reflexive verbs above (p.29), I would say that the capacity we need to develop is
the recursive one of being able to step back from a situation in which we have
been engaged as subject, as 'I', and take up a new subjective position from which
the previous 'I' now appears as 'me'. Each time we step back, there is indeed a
subject/object shift. The shift is brought about as I divide the unitary concept of
myself into its nominative and accusative cases, creating a new subjectivity that
allows me to decide where I want to stand with regard to the web of relationships
that I have made the object of my vision, and into which I shall have to return in
order to be able to act.

And now, at exactly this point, let us remind ourselves of what Dewey says
about how, '*(t)he connection of these two phases of experience measures the fruitfulness or
value of the experience*'. While the cognitive value of the experience might be
measured during the process of stepping back, one can also say that the richer
fruitfulness of the experience can only be measured by what we might call '*stepping
up*' and acting as that once-more emergent 'I' who has undergone some change
and is ready to experience again. To paraphrase Kegan, this is the most powerful
way I know to conceptualize the development of the person. The full engagement,
the stepping back and the stepping up must all be seen as a form of connection,
not separation. If one thinks of the phase of stepping back as the one in which the
cognitive is foregrounded, it must be a cognitive process enriched with the
empathy won through the engagement. If one thinks of the stepping up as the
phase in which full engagement is renewed, the engagement needs to be enriched
with the awareness won through the stepping back. This is how we hope to find
a *reasonable* option among the rational and reactive choices that might ally us too
closely with the forces of order or the forces of chaos (Moorcock 2001).

In the imagery of stepping back and stepping up, we can see also the rhythm
of Dilthey's (Rickman 1988) hermeneutic circles of thought and action, connecting the situated, specifically experienced and the generally, rationally known.
With regard to the processes and procedures of teacher education and development, we can also make out the associated interactive possibilities of applying
theory and theorizing practice that I referred to in Chapter 2 and go on to discuss
in Chapters 5 and 6.

The role of reflexivity in teacher education that I am trying to grasp and communicate involves, at its best, the ability to be aware of the processes that I have been describing above, to articulate that awareness and to pursue the upshot in lived experience. Again: first to live as engaged in my experience as Dillard's weasel, then to 'step back' as a subjective/nominative 'I' in order to learn, in the style of Kegan's *'higher order of consciousness'*, from an objective/ accusative representation of 'me', in context, while maintaining an empathetic contact with that experience, while maintaining a sense of wonder at the everyday and a dual awareness of having *tried* and having *undergone*. Then, with some awareness of what I have learned and who this new 'I' is who has learned, to 'step up' and re-engage weasel-like, because the wholeheartedness of the engagement is as much a part of the cycle as is the functioning of the higher order of consciousness.

I hope to have conveyed an immediacy about this process, a sense of being in-action the whole time, whether stepping back or stepping up. There is a parallel here, already noted, with the way in which Schön writes on reflection as being either in-action or on-action, and that parallel helps me to return to the dissatisfaction that I expressed earlier when dividing reflexivity into prospective and retrospective types. I continue to see a usefulness in that vision, but it needs to be augmented by a sense of reflexivity similar to that I brought out with regard to memo writing, one that is not put on a long-term before-or-after timeline, one that captures the internalizing and externalizing, mutually shaping, interactive relationship between organism and environment, writer and writing, teacher and professional context, moment for moment as it happens. In this choice of the vocabulary of 'internalizing' and 'externalizing', I intend to relate these thoughts again to the Vygotskyan metaphors of learning that Johnson (2006, 2009) has brought to TESOL teacher education as part of what she has termed *'the sociocultural turn'* (see Chapter 6).

As this long, sometimes dense and somewhat disparate chapter draws to a conclusion, therefore, I put aside my long-standing aversion to diagrams and attempt in Figure 3.1 some visual support for the communication of some of the key aspects of reflexivity that I have been working on. In the interaction between the teacher educator and his or her praxis, the question that relates to prospective reflexivity is, *'What difference does it make to the teacher education that I offer that it is* I *who offer it?'* With relation to retrospective reflexivity, the question is, *'What difference does offering this teacher education make to me as a teacher educator?'* And all the time, outside this temporal perspective, a bidirectional shaping is taking place as the teacher educator internalizes the effects of his or her environment and acts to transform that very environment by externalizing his or her own agency.

In all these senses, the discourse of reflexivity augments the *that*-ness of know-ing and the *how*-ness of knowing, the *where*-ness of knowing, the *when*-ness of knowing and the *why*-ness of knowing with the two faces of the *who*-ness of knowing:

it is the unique prerogative of a reflexive being not only to be able to ask after the What and How of beings, but also to ask *Who is it?* and, self-inventively, to ask after the *Who* that is questioning.

Sandywell 1996:290

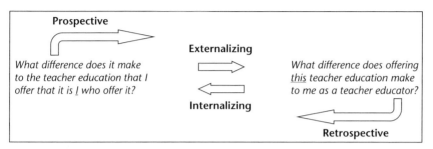

FIGURE 3.1 Reflexivity: two questions and two perspectives (temporal and directional)

The remainder of this book attempts to exercise this prerogative in ways that I know have been useful to myself and which I intend to be useful to the reader. I pursue a twin-track approach to the interrogation of my experience:

1. Drawing on what I see as significant episodes in my experience of teacher education, I make use of the terminology that I have learned in the above discussion, using *prospective reflexivity* to engage with Dewey's *trying* dimension of experience, and *retrospective reflexivity* to engage with his *undergoing*, while knowing all along that this actually indivisible hermeneutic cycle can be broken into only on an 'as-if' basis when one is convinced that such categorization will prove useful in order 'to ask after the who that is questioning'.
2. In parallel with the above historical approach, I take such opportunities as I discern to work with contemporary affordances, with the effects of internalizing and externalizing that occur in the record that I am creating.

In the former case, the questions that are typically operating, in addition to the '*So what?*' and '*How come?*' that we have already noted, are: '*Where was that experience rooted?*' '*What affordances did I discern?*' '*What did I learn when I stepped back?*' '*How did that help me to fly?*' '*Who was I (changed) when I stepped back up?*'

In the latter case, the same questions reoccur in the present tense.

Before I step up to the rest of this book, I want to close this chapter with a statement of one allied principle that one must keep in mind. It is called The Ray Charles Principle, something that I read of several years ago and for which, to my shame, I can no longer trace the source.

An interviewer asked the great man,

> '*What influence do you think it has had on your music that you grew up poor, black and blind?*'

To which he replied,

> '*I don't know – I didn't grow up any other way.*'

In much of what follows, I am the questioner and the informant, and 'I' didn't grow up any different than 'me'. In addition to the identity features already mentioned, others that will come into play include the fact that I grew up a monolingual speaker of British English; I married into another language in which I can now live with great pleasure and I have a learned survival ability in a small number of other languages; I have lived in a number of different countries and cultures, and now live in the one I was born in; while convinced by the socio-psychological importance of myth (vide Campbell 1973), I have no beliefs in the realm of the supernatural.

I will miss some perspectives and wrongly presuppose others, but I will do my best to explore. There will be surprises. As Forbes (2008:453) says, it is a problematic business:

> In continuously subverting my previous positions and identities, less essentialist and more energizing, albeit more uncertain and fragmented, selves emerge – a personally risky experience.

But one is always called upon to act in the absence of sufficient knowledge of what the outcomes might be, and there comes a point at which you either take the leap or you don't.

It is important to count the cards. It is important to know the odds. But the numbers and the odds don't make up the whole game. Not even the most interesting part of it.

So, here we go. The next five chapters will survey the teacher education experience that I have tried and undergone, through activity that I characterize as Copying and becoming methodological in a craft sense (Chapter 4), Applying theory and becoming technical in an applied science sense (Chapter 5), Theorizing practice and becoming theoretical through a mode of exploration and articulation (Chapter 6), Reflecting and locating the above activities in a broader intellectual context (Chapter 7), and dealing with all of the above in Action, in a way that I shall want to refer to as pragmatic (Chapter 8).

As I deal with my own discoveries, I rely on my readers to work on theirs.

4
COPYING AND BECOMING METHODOLOGICAL

Introduction

When writing earlier (p.15) about what Wallace (1991) called a craft model of teacher education, I pointed out the usual critique of such an approach, namely that it can overemphasize a reliance on the reproduction of what already exists, and so constrain creativity. At the same time, I suggested that elements of the craft tradition, of copying what already exists, and of modelling what is to be copied (Loughran 1996) should still have a role to play in our work as teacher educators.

One reason for this arises for me from an overall attitude to craft itself. The ancient tradition of *apprentice, journeyman, master* (leaving aside, on this occasion, the unfortunately in-built sexism of its historically-bound terminology) has honoured and nourished, time out of mind, those ways of knowing that Aristotle named as *techne, phronesis* and *nous* (Irwin 1999) – experientially-based knowing how to make things and how to behave, along with an intuitive grasp of what is going on. These qualities do not preclude intellectual capacity or creative facility. Indeed, the development of these latter two in the absence of the former three might be seen as risking the rise of a culture over-committed to novelty and cleverness and in apparent flight from the kind of overall wisdom (*sophia*) that we might expect to need, whether we think of these issues with regard to TESOL, or to education in general, or indeed to the overall culture in which we live.

Reflexive memo 4.1: I always struggle at moments such as this with the idea that I may simply be presenting the typical symptoms of grumpy old man syndrome. I invite a thought experiment: imagine yourself reading an article about some aspect of TESOL methodology. You encounter a sentence beginning, '*The traditional way of doing this* *is X.'* What comes next? Is X about to be praised as a way of upholding good practice? I suspect not. *'Traditional'*, in this environment, signals that-which-must-be-changed. This may not, however, be how tradition is viewed by all readers. Nor was it the way in which I used the word, *tradition*, in the previous paragraph. This issue deserves further thought. I return to it in Chapters 5 and 8.

More immediate to our current topic is the well-recorded observation, originating with Lortie (1975), that teachers-to-be spend a long *'apprenticeship of observation'* in the practice of teaching, in the sense that they spend many years in school being taught and thereby subconsciously assimilating and constructing a model of what it means to be a teacher. We also know that the influence of this apprenticeship is likely to be stronger than whatever they are taught on their teacher education programmes, especially if they return to teach in the same environment in which they themselves were taught (Johnson 1994, Tsui 2003). Now, to the extent that this process represents some kind of unconscious drift into repetitiveness, it is easy to agree that it is unwelcome. This is not to say, however, that there are not positive aspects of what has gone before that are worth taking on, where the wisdom of teaching is expressed in action that needs to be local, because action has to be specific and cannot allow itself the simplifying privilege of generalization. Copying can make good, rooted sense, as can adapting to changing circumstances without the necessary intervention of theoretical abstraction to drive such change, as can the expression of emergent sensibilities. Awareness is what counts, awareness of just what it is that one is doing, trying, undergoing.

Nor should one allow one's understandable professional focus to narrow one's awareness of the broad theme that one has engaged here. Taking a tradition forward is not an issue restricted to teaching. One sees such possibilities in various cultural traditions, the carvings and designs of Canada's northwest coast nations (McNair et al. 1984) being one that I am lucky enough to be slightly familiar with, thanks, of course, to English language teaching.

Reflexive memo 4.2: This last, apparently throwaway comment in fact indexes an important truth already hinted at in Chapter 1: a life in TESOL has been deepened in ways that are scarcely thinkable without it. The actual experience that has just flooded out of my memory banks has been described with typical emotional vividness by Winterson (1996:3):

I was in Amsterdam one snowy Christmas when the weather had turned the canals into oblongs of ice. I was wandering happy, alone, playing the flâneur, when I passed a little gallery

> and in the moment of passing saw a painting that had more
> power to stop me than I had power to walk on.

> Except that I was in Vancouver, and it was a lithographic reproduction
> of a design for a drumskin by the Nuu-Chah-Nulth artist, Joe David,
> entitled '*Octopus and Jellyfish*'. I had never seen anything like it, or like
> the objects surrounding it, in my life. I learned later that while David
> is a new master *of* the tradition, neither octopus nor jellyfish had ever
> previously been represented *by* the tradition, and yet this piece was
> seen as being unquestionably *in* the tradition. What was I doing in
> Vancouver? A TESOL Convention. Why else would I have been
> there?

It is in this sense of trying to master a craft and looking to learn from what has
been done and what is being done, to copy from others but to understand why,
to respect where one has come from without being limited by it, and to carry over
ideas and practices from one domain to another, that I mean *Copy* to be understood
when I suggest that it is an important part of our teacher education praxis. It is
true that I have just blurred a distinction between craft and art, but let it stand. It
is a distinction worth the blurring and, anyway, understood differently in different
times and places (e.g. Tully 1992). We cannot all become great artists, but there
is an art to what we do. We can, moreover, each work on our craft and decide,
both individually and with our colleagues, which elements of it we wish to preserve and to renew.

Let us get down to earth.

Roots

MaryAnn Christison (Palmer & Christison 2007:4) writes:

> I think I had always wanted to be a teacher. As a young child I used to line
> up all of my dolls and stuffed animals in a row and pretend they were my
> students.

This is in stark contrast to my own early attitude towards becoming a teacher.
When I graduated from university in 1969 with my degree in Modern Arabic
Studies (that's another story, see Edge 2010), I applied to the United Nations
Association for voluntary work. With little thought that I was not well qualified
actually to do anything useful anywhere, I responded to the question regarding
the kind of work that I would be prepared to take on with: '*Anything except
teaching.*' I was promptly offered a post teaching English at Amman Teacher
Training College, Jordan. Apart from one of those *Wild Bunch* memories that I

referred to in Chapter 1, what tied me in to the work itself was a growing fascination with how one could help other people to learn one's own language.

Reflexive memo 4.3: That expression *'to learn one's own language'* flowed from my fingers directly out of that time as I recall it. I would no longer maintain that ESOL students are trying to learn 'my' language, but that was how it felt then. My own mediocre record as a language learner and a grumbling dissatisfaction with how I had been taught were also a part of my motivation to understand the learning/ teaching processes involved. It seemed a worthwhile undertaking, neither more nor less.

By 1981, I was working in Turkey with, viewed chronologically, a teaching diploma, a year's teaching experience in each of Britain and Germany, four years in Egypt, an MA, two more years in Singapore and half a year in Beirut behind me. The job in Istanbul was in pre-service teacher education, working on a four-year undergraduate programme not too dissimilar from the one that I had taught on at the University of Alexandria. Out of this three-year experience in Turkey came a series of tryings and undergoings that can help me illustrate what I mean by copying, and what I mean by *becoming methodological*, for the students that I was teaching, for some of my colleagues and for myself.

The overall arrangement of the four-year course that I came into was one in which the students spent their first two years on language improvement and the last two years on professionally-related topics such as linguistics, psychology of learning, methodology and, in their final year, teaching practice. Junior colleagues tended to teach the earlier years and more senior ones the later. In retrospect, I would say that the curriculum changes that we made were a direct attempt to shift the whole participant experience from a discourse of 'student' to one of 'teacher-learner', and to have everyone profit directly from our teacher-learners' apprenticeship of observation, although the terminology was not known to us at the time.

We had an annual intake of eighteen- and nineteen-year-old women and men, predominantly the former, some of whom were responding to the kind of motivation that Christison describes above, and some of whom were there because their school-leaving grades meant that they couldn't study what they wanted to, leaving Education as the best Faculty that they could get into with the grades that they had. Once there, the attraction of our course was that this was their best chance to improve their English and thus open up the possibility of some kind of tourist-related or other commercial employment. This scenario mapped very well onto the one that I had known in Egypt and I do not believe that it is restricted to those two countries.

Whatever the reasons for their being there, or their thoughts about their future careers, it seemed fair to note that these young people were stepping into a whole new period of their lives and that they were up for something new. A programme that cast them for the next two years back into the roles that they had just left, of semi-remedial language learners, did not capture the potential of this moment. The changes that we made to the programme were aimed at helping them do just that. I now see that they could all well be themed under the heading of *becoming methodological*, while also indexing issues of imagined identity (Pavlenko 2003).

First of all, we brought out into the open with the new entrants our shared awareness of their mixed reasons for being with us, and, in turn, made clear our motivation in working with them: namely, to ensure that those of them that did go on to become teachers of English would have had every opportunity to become the best language teachers that they could. From now on, we would treat them all as teachers-to-be. We assured those who felt that they had no intention of going into teaching that their best chance of benefiting in terms of improving their English was nevertheless to go along with our approach, partly because teachers have to learn the language really well, and partly because fitting in with where we were putting our efforts was just plain common sense if they wanted to obtain maximum benefit from those efforts. I have no explicit data from that time and can only report anecdotally that in terms of energy level, commitment and engagement from that year's students and the next, I believe that we had them with that particular hello. They were being spoken to as motivated agents, as the subjects of their own lives, and I believe that this made a difference.

Reflexive memo 4.4: As I wrote the last few sentences, a sense of internal contradiction grew. How can I be claiming a respect for tradition and simultaneously praising fundamental change? Well, because these are the borders where judgments must be made. That is how organism and context interact. Hence the octopus and the jellyfish. Hence, too, my respect for my own traditions:

> I myself always *reason*, and . . . I thus *induce the scholar to reason*: that I am not content with his *memory*, but force him to give me the use of his *mind*.
>
> William Cobbett, *Political Register*,
> 6 December 1817, col. 1094

We began to mix an explicit awareness of methodology into the teacher-learners' language improvement classes in various ways. First, we invited them to bring their English textbooks from secondary school into class and we talked about how they had been taught. In this situation, the textbook was standard, but what came out in discussion were differences in how their teachers had used the materials, where the emphasis had been put, which bits had been missed out and, crucially, which parts of the lessons and which types of material they had themselves most enjoyed and found useful. These discussions, carried out mostly in English and allowing for occasional mutual help via translation from the Turkish, opened up the students' thinking with regard to differences in learning and teaching preferences and in the use of different learning and teaching strategies, while also starting to build the professional metalanguage of teachers and teaching. Perhaps most fundamentally, the idea was grounded that these issues were open for discussion. And once that idea was in play, we could then help them distinguish what we meant by *discussion* (involving the need to learn and to listen and to reason and to accept difference) from both the repetition of unquestioned dogma and the unjustified assertion of individual opinion. In plain educational terms, I take this kind of work to be commonly required with most first-year undergraduates under most circumstances, anywhere.

Second, we invited comparisons between the textbooks that they had used at school and the books and other materials that we were using with them at the university. We began to talk about the language-learning assumptions that must lie behind these differences and, again, we talked about preferences and reasons from the perspectives of learners and teachers. An important point here was the need to demonstrate respect for the teachers through whose hands they had passed, while maintaining the right to differ about ways of teaching. Both I, as a foreigner, and my Turkish colleagues, worked to hold that line of respectful difference and to make it an issue.

Third, we introduced a one-hour 'methods review' class at the end of the week in which we looked back at what we had done over the course of the week, not with regard to the English they had learned, but with regard to how we had taught the classes. Why hadn't we done this exercise? Why did we spend so long on that one? Why? Why not? How else? These questions were restricted to the classes that had been taught by the teachers running the methods review class. We did not entertain questions about the teaching of other colleagues because, as we explained, our answers would have been guesswork. Nevertheless, it does not take too long to see that the way in which we were moving the relationship between ourselves as university 'professors' and the undergraduate student body was not necessarily comfortable for all members of staff.

All I can say is that this is something to be negotiated in each situation. These ideas were clarified among staff members first and those interested in being involved were, so to speak, given permission to go ahead by those who did not want to take part. The students, or teacher-learners, behaved impeccably with regard to seeing and observing the implicit borders that it would be inappropriate to cross. This remained true when one or two of us extended the principle of the 'methods review' class to every class. That is, our teacher-learners were told that it would be not only acceptable, but actively welcome, if they were to raise their hands at any point during a language improvement class to ask, '*Why are we doing this now?*' We, as teachers, would expect to be able to give them an answer.

They did not, in fact, avail themselves of this opportunity as often as we had expected, and never in a way that was meant to be disruptive. As with the other *becoming methodological* activities in which we engaged our teacher-learners, the effects were felt at various levels. In curriculum terms, issues of teaching methodology were being introduced as they arose in action. While piecemeal in terms of theoretical coherence, these issues drew a different kind of coherence from the authenticity of their emergence – a syntagmatic coherence, perhaps, rather than a paradigmatic one. At the same time, the teacher-learners were laying down an experiential-conceptual basis for the more theoretical treatment of methodology that awaited them later in their university career. They were also building a vocabulary with which to talk about their teaching and learning, while becoming accustomed to treating teaching and learning as something to be talked about. In this regard, the point was made again (and again) that there was room for individual difference in teaching, just as long as that difference was the outcome of aware, informed and thoughtful action, or of trying and undergoing, as I might now put it.

Reflexive memo 4.5: I have pondered long and hard about whether or not to call this chapter, *Becoming Pedagogical*. 'Pedagogy' and its derived terms are not widely used in my educational culture, but certainly the connection between the teacher as the mindful embodiment of pedagogic praxis, rather than the operator of a methodological delivery system (the goal and vision of most governmental policy-making) is what we were seeking, and is well caught by Gray's (2001:32) observation that it is a, '*sense of individuality that distinguishes pedagogy from methodology*'. Gray goes on (ibid.) to quote Brown (2000:188):

> Methodology tends to stay on the page, while pedagogy implies a sense of energy; it tells us how the teacher interacts with the methodology to engage pupils in their learning.

Having created, over the course of the first year's study, a context in which it became normal for teacher-learners to compare the materials and methods of their school experience with what was happening in their current language improvement classes, and then to discuss the thinking behind what was happening in those classes, the next step was to involve the teacher-learners in a little teaching. We did this by dividing the class into small groups of three or four (class size was around thirty) and having them look ahead to upcoming units of work. Each group would be assigned a short activity for which they would be responsible when the class got there. The activities chosen were ones where the teacher-learners could inform themselves about what language would be correct and appropriate, and ones with a relatively clear procedure to follow. When the class reached such a point, one or two members of the group would take over the teaching of their classmates for the duration of that activity. This was, then, a kind of peer micro-teaching, but in a situation where what was to be taught was indeed a part of the class's planned curriculum. Direct comment and feedback was kept to a minimum and expressed almost entirely in terms of praise. The main purpose of the process was to have the teacher-learners experience for themselves what it was like to be that person at the front of the class – to try and to undergo. It was stressful, but became less so. Also, it became possible to refer to positive elements of what happened in these micro-teaching sessions during the end-of-week methodology discussion classes mentioned above.

I have described the above period of work from an applied linguistics/language-awareness perspective in Edge (1988a) and anyone interested in pursuing that track could follow it up there and in a direct line through Wright & Bolitho (1993), Hales (1997), Johnston (2000), Andrews (2003) and Svalberg (2007). The point that I want to foreground here, however, is the transformative personal effect that such experience had on the teacher-learners. By the end of their first year, their status had changed in their own minds from being remedial language learners to being apprentice teachers. By the end of the second year, they were accustomed to talking to their teachers about the teaching taking place and they were accustomed to standing up in front of their peers and trying their hand. They were, in this, essentially trying to copy what they understood to be the best of what their apprenticeship of observation, enhanced by discussion, had shown them. This chosen copying was only a first step to becoming a teacher, but it was such a step. It was a type of peripheral participation (Lave & Wenger 1991) in a new world of discourse and identity. As teacher-learners, they had begun to become methodological. They were, consequently, ready to study methodology and to go on teaching practice in a way that exceeded by far the state of preparation of those students ahead of them in the system, who had studied two years of remedial English, followed by lectures on methodology given by lecturers now too senior to do any language teaching.

The process of becoming methodological that I have described so far has focused to a large extent on the teacher-learners more commonly referred to as our students. A great deal of methodological learning was also going on, of course, among ourselves on the teaching staff, most especially as we copied and borrowed ideas and procedures from various places and worked to make them appropriate in our particular context. As we worked to help our teacher-learners establish their roots, we were simultaneously spreading our wings.

Wings

One example of this concerns translation, not an area in which I had any expertise, particularly not with Turkish, a language in which I achieved only a survival level of competence. At the time, however, there were grumblings from the students about how boring translation classes were, and the junior members of staff responsible for them were feeling the pressure. What we 'copied over' in this instance was a set of procedures, taken from regular ESOL classes, that featured pairwork and groupwork on a divided-information task involving a need to communicate, followed by an opportunity to focus on linguistic form. Cast in the mould of a translation class, it went like this:

1. We selected two short texts of appropriate content and language difficulty that were also as self-contained as possible. For final-year students in our TESOL programme, for example, this text from Stevick (1982:21) was one that we used:

   > There are a few questions that have occupied language teachers for centuries and probably always will. Of these, perhaps the most basic is, 'How does a person come to control a language anyway?' We all achieved this feat with our first language and many of us have gained some ability in other languages by learning them in school. The term 'acquisition' is sometimes used for the former, and 'learning' for what goes on in the classroom. There has been considerable discussion about whether these two processes are essentially the same, or essentially different. Until very recently, however, people have generally assumed that one followed the other with perhaps a few years' overlap. The ability to 'acquire' supposedly died out at about the age of puberty, while 'learning' became possible only in the early school years as the necessary 'readinesses' developed.

2. We divided the class in half. One half got one text to translate, the other half got another. We set an appropriate time limit for the students, working in pairs, to produce a legible translation into Turkish. The teacher would circulate and help with issues of comprehension, but leave translation to the students.

3. We collected the original texts and had pairs of students exchange their translations so that each pair got the translation of the text that they had *not* read in English. We then set an appropriate time limit for the students to produce an English translation of the text in front of them. Again, the teacher circulated and answered questions about vocabulary and structure, but not directly about the translation.

4. We put those pairs together who had back-translated each other's translations and gave out the original texts. At this point, the big challenge that we set our students, or teacher-learners, as I should say, was *not* to concentrate on correcting anything, but to concentrate on learning something. We asked them first of all to compare the original text with its retranslation into English and to discuss such questions as:

   a. Have meanings been changed, or lost, or become unclear?
   b. Which words have changed? How important is this?

    c. Have sentence structures changed? How important is this?

    d. How are sentences linked together? Has this changed? How important is this?

5. Where important changes were found, the group would go back to the Turkish text and try to find out where, when, how and why this had happened.
6. In a whole-class feedback stage, each group would be asked to comment on the most interesting translation question that they had encountered, to offer alternative versions, and to state what they had learned.

My Turkish colleagues, with their bilingual competence, adjusted and adapted the procedure as they saw fit. What pleased me was the way in which my under-graduate teacher-learners were happy to take responsibility for negotiating the Turkish among themselves when I was in charge of the class. Some items of feedback that I noted at the time were:

- We usually use a safe range of language; this encourages us to widen our range and that will make us better translators.
- It's interesting to be able to make an immediate comparison; it also makes us see our mistakes more clearly.
- It's very interesting to see how somebody else interprets your translation.
- Before, I used to think my mistakes weren't important, but now I can see how everything goes wrong.

Other benefits, particularly relevant to teacher-learners, were the building of a metalanguage to enable participants to talk about English, along with an increasing awareness of the importance of choice in language use and, therefore, of rules as things to use rather than only follow, in addition to a need to explain one's choices.

There is another reason why this particular procedure has stuck in my mind. The line from the Stevick text above, '*The ability to "acquire" supposedly died out at about the age of puberty*', was retranslated as, '*The ability of acquisition disappears in adultery.*' At the time, this caused some furious scrabbling backwards and forwards in bilingual dictionaries (and therefore itself a fine learning moment), a quantum of embarrassment in a mixed-gender class of young adults, and finally a great deal of laughter. It also gave me (Edge 1986a) a memorable title.

While the translation class exemplified a copying-over of procedures from one domain of teaching into an adjacent one, another procedure that we developed in Turkey proved itself copiable across very different environments. On this occasion, I was involved in in-service courses for secondary-school teachers and we were employing rounds of peer-microteaching for half of each day. While it has long been established (e.g. McIntyre et al. 1977) that teacher-learners under such circumstances value the comments of their peers very highly, most of the course participants had no experience of peer-microteaching, or of having their teach-ing commented on by anyone, much less by their colleagues. Participants felt threatened by the idea of being criticized and, by the same token, unwilling to express critique of others. The procedure we devised went as follows:

1. A teacher-learner carries out a peer-microteaching task.
2. The participants form small groups to discuss what happened.
3. The teacher circulates and listens to what is being said, to the extent that s/he wishes to.
4. The class reassembles and we repeat the above steps.
5. After three or four rounds, we pause and each microteacher is asked to give feedback on their own performance, including reference to peer comment if they so wish.
6. Colleagues and the teacher educator add their own comments at this point.

We emphasized throughout that comments from peers and the teacher educator should be aimed at the teaching point in question, not at individual performance. The difference between saying, '*I think it's a good idea to give learners a chance to correct their own mistakes,*' and '*She should have given us a chance to correct our own mistakes,*' is quite significant in terms of the relationships involved and, therefore, with regard to what is at all *sayable* and *learnable from*.

In the above procedure, teacher-learners had the opportunity to exchange critical ideas among themselves without the direct presence of the individual microteacher of the moment, while microteachers had the chance to gather themselves and to reflect on their experience while hearing some comments from their peers, before then having the opportunity to say what they wanted to about what had happened. Saving the general discussion for a little later also helped establish the focus on the teaching topic rather than on personal performance. As ever, a part of the procedure was discussing with the teacher-learners the purpose of the procedure, thus bringing into play the underlying principle already invoked above: awareness is what counts.

The particular point that I want to make here about copying-over, however, is that twenty-five years later, I heard from someone whose work I had long admired but had only recently met, Alan Waters (personal communication, July 2009), how useful the 1984 article detailing this procedure had been to him:

> it was in the context of wondering how to handle the (public) post-practice teaching observation and feedback in the MA in ESP that I was involved in setting up in Thailand just at the time when your article came out. Basically, it seemed to fit the bill perfectly, so we adopted it more-or-less wholesale, and it seemed to do very much what we hoped, especially as we had, on the one hand, some very face-protective participants (we were in a very face-protective culture, after all!), but some others who were willing to be more 'barbed' in their comments. Perhaps I might add though that we had relatively large amounts of time to carry out the full process you described,

whereas in some other situations where I have subsequently worked, unfortunately this hasn't been the case (though have still found it possible and useful to 'salvage' elements of the procedure).

Copying, therefore, is not an activity restricted to beginners. The more skilled and experienced one is, the more able one is to recognize just what can be copied, even across contexts as apparently different as Turkey and Thailand, as well as being able to know what to cut, extend or adapt. Or, to put that another way, the more skilled and experienced one is, the more able one is to recognize which sets of possibilities and choices actually comprise the context in which one is operating, and the more able one is to make telling comparisons among the patterns that one recognizes (Goldberg 2005).

Reflexivity

The work reported here, the *trying*, was a formative part of my own *becoming methodological* experience. I saw how procedural ideas could operate coherently in different domains and successfully be copied over from one to another so long as one remained alert to the ways in which the commonalities and the specificities matched up, and as long as one worked with awareness and respect all round. I felt that I was positively and productively involved in a craft tradition, both developing my own art/craft potential and helping induct others.

Reflexive memo 4.6: As I write 'awareness' and 'respect', I find that I am happy with the collocation. I feel a congruent bringing together of the cognitive and the affective, of the prospective and the retrospective, the teacher and the researcher-to-be and, in very personal terms, of the working class and the intellectual.

As readers may have noticed, the work also formed the content of a series of articles in *ELT Journal* (Edge 1984, 1985, 1986a, 1988a). Looked at from the perspective of *undergoing*, then, this experience of becoming methodological also changed me in the sense that I became a writer. That is to say, to be more careful, that this period, through the affordances that it provided, clearly in interaction with some emergent desire on my part to articulate what I had experienced, led me into a period of trying and undergoing during which writing about what I did became a part of what I do.

I know that I now consistently say to MA participants that in doing this degree, they take on a responsibility for their generation to forge the links between what is happening in the field and what is happening in the journals. They are the ones properly located to do that. It will be good for them and good for the profession. I don't think that I harm anyone with this assertion, but I do now note that I am suggesting that they do what I did, and anyone with an interest in reflexivity must regard this fact as potentially significant. In the context of this chapter, the suggestion represents a level of copying that I had not been aware of when I began the chapter. I would want to step away from the idea that any individual modelling was intended. I would, however, want to stand by the suggestion that 'making writing about what you do a part of what you do' is now a legitimate part of our craft. Of course, it's not for *everyone*, and I must be more careful to make that clear. At the same time, it is available to *anyone*, and that also has to be made clear. I do not know of a journal or magazine editor who complains about having too many submissions from thoughtful teachers writing about what they do.

Another kind of modelling was deliberate, however. My colleagues and I did want to model the kind of teacher who was open to question and whose sense of authority depended on their ability to respond to such questions, rather than on an insistence on a status differential. We did want to model the kind of teacher in whose presence it was easy to see a connection between the ideas that they spoke and taught and the way in which they behaved. And in modelling, we did hope to be copied. In other words, issues of what I have called consistency and continuity were certainly on our minds.

It takes either several years of situated experience, or a rigorous data-gathering process, or both, in order to make claims of success in such ventures. In this instance, I can provide neither and have only memories and anecdotes with which I hope to have exemplified the initial element of my CATRA acronym, some various roles of copying in teacher education, along with some reflexive considerations of copying in action.

This current writing experience has also afforded me the opportunity to step back even from the remembering/writing relationship itself, and to take up a learning relationship with that relationship. I see how my teacher education was prospectively shaped by a combination of awareness and respect that attempted to encompass both my own heritage and that of my working environment. I am forced to acknowledge that the main driver of my work was my own inheritance. My respect for the traditions of my environment was more instrumentally oriented, in the sense of affording me a respectful means of achieving my goals, rather than demonstrating a truly open mind about the need for change, or the direction in which that change should move.

Of course, I am aware now, in ways that I was not then, of the cultural-political significance of the endeavour in which I was engaged. I have no argument with Pennycook's (1989) exposition of the '*interested*' nature of methodology, or with his (1994:152) statement that, '*the promotion of particular teaching approaches is closely linked to . . . the promotion of particular forms of culture*'.

However, I cannot deal with everything at once, and I have made a decision to address the various impacts of critical thinking at a later stage of this telling (see Chapter 7). For now, I shall restrict myself to two comments. First, becoming methodological is a process saturated with ideological content and this fact is not changed by anyone's refusal to acknowledge it. Second, as I look back at, and look inward with regard to, the period I have described, in all honesty and humility, I cannot bring myself to think that the work my colleagues, our teacher-learners and I did together was out of place or harmful. The roots were taking and we all were flying high.

Over the next two chapters, I bring into the equation some considerations of theory, its application, its derivation, and the reflexive consequences of both in the life of a teacher educator.

5

APPLYING THEORY AND BECOMING TECHNICAL

Introduction

In the previous chapter, I wrote about some of the methodological strategies that I developed while working as a university-based, pre-service teacher educator in Turkey. I related these strategies to the idea of a craft-based type of professional education, in the sense that teacher-learners were encouraged to copy and adapt procedures from their previous and current experience. In addition, ideas and attitudes were modelled in order to be passed on. I also took procedures from one area of my work and copied them, in somewhat adapted form, to another.

All of this is meant to be of a piece with the 'copy' element of teacher education praxis that I introduced in Chapter 2 as part of the CATRA acronym. Such copying, as an element of praxis, is common to teaching and to teacher education. Establishing this commonality is an important part of building consistency and continuity as I have defined them (pp.39–40).

In this chapter, I track another kind of professional development that took place for me as teacher educator and which consequently made parallel demands on the teacher-learners I was working with. This style of work exemplifies what Wallace (1991; see Chapter 2 above) defined as an applied science approach, encouraging technical rationality, and which I described as involving the application of theories, the first A in my CATRA acronym. I see such theory-application as one aspect of the larger concept of *becoming theoretical* that is filled out in the next chapter.

Reflexive memo 5.1: Please note the way in which the adverb, *consequently*, in the first sentence of the previous paragraph stole in unbidden as a signal of the effects of prospective reflexivity. That is to say, what was developmental for me shaped my demands on my teacher-learners. This is the shadow-side of consistency and continuity, the distinct possibility that my affordances are their constraints.

Roots

My undergraduate students in Istanbul (and earlier in Alexandria) made good progress in terms of their spoken ability and confidence in themselves as potential teachers. What I also wanted them to have was an ability to profit from the literature of our field. By this I do not mean an ability to consult heavyweight texts or journals that report on cutting-edge research, or dispute over theories of second-language acquisition. That would have been an unrealistic and demotivating demand on the great majority of the young people that I was working with. I wanted them to be able to read what I called 'methodology texts': short magazine articles from publications such as *Modern English Teacher, English Teaching Professional, Forum,* or perhaps *TESOL Journal* and *ELT Journal,* that dealt specifically with classroom teaching. I wanted them to be able to recognize a teaching procedure and evaluate it for their own use. This proved difficult, more difficult than seemed reasonable at the time. In what follows, I present my own brief interpretation of what happened and what it meant. Anyone wanting to check the detail or challenge the evidence could go back to Edge (1985, 1986b, 1989).

In 1983, in response to hearing me talk about my students' difficulties in reading methodology texts, a fellow conference participant suggested that I read Michael Hoey, a linguist at Birmingham University, England. When I did, I was struck by three major points: first, one of linguistic detail; second, one of broad cultural significance; third, by the fact that these first two points were intimately related and fundamental to my purpose.

First, then, the linguistic detail: an extraordinary amount of English text is organized by what Hoey (1983) describes as a Problem/Solution pattern, semantically organized as Situation-Problem-Response-Evaluation. Not only does this pattern have formal schematic reality for us as writers and readers, the pattern is also clearly signposted in our texts by lexical and grammatical signals. An analytical glance back at the previous two paragraphs, for example, will identify the pattern emerging in terms of:

SITUATION: Place and time signalled by prepositional phrases, *in Istanbul, earlier in Alexandria,* and *in 1983.*

PROBLEM: *Students . . . to be able to recognize a teaching procedure and evaluate it for their own use* – initially signalled as goal by *I wanted* and then identified as problem by, *difficult, more difficult than seemed reasonable, difficulties in reading.*

RESPONSE: Read Michael Hoey, signalled lexically by *in response to* and discoursally by cohesive tie between *read Michael Hoey* and *I did.*

EVALUATION: Still in progress, but begun by, *I was struck by three major points,* which not only suggests that a positive evaluation of the response will emerge (thus turning it into an at least partial solution to the problem), but which also organizes our expectations for how the next part of the text will proceed.

Some things are blindingly obvious, but only when they have been pointed out. I recognized immediately that I was being shown the typical semantic organization of a methodology text in teachers' magazines. To simplify somewhat:

SITUATION: This is where I work and who my students are.
PROBLEM: This is a difficulty that I have had when teaching them.
RESPONSE: This is what I do about it.
EVALUATION: These are the results I now get, which suggest that the problem is solved.

Second, and with regard to cultural significance, the obviousness of this textual organization had to be considered in relation to the following, broader proposition of Hoey's (ibid.:178):

> If the claim is correct that there are an infinite number of discourse pattern possibilities, then the prevalence of any recurring patterns must be explained. This can be done if they are seen as culturally approved patterns which reflect (and perhaps to some degree influence) the Western world's concern with problem-solving and classification.

Reflexive memo 5.2: I have returned to this quotation many times over the intervening twenty-seven years, but only precisely now have I seen quite so explicitly the central reference to reflexivity ('*reflect and influence*') that is built into it. This is another example of a feature of a context becoming an affordance (only) when the person in that context discerns it.

This reflexive relationship, between the textual organization and signalling on the one hand and the cultural approval and concern on the other, simply did not obtain for my teacher-learners. Their experience of reading English had been confined to passages designed to practice their grammar, or to introduce sets of vocabulary, or to test their reading comprehension by requiring them to answer different types of question, frequently multiple-choice. More generally speaking, their experience of reading in an educational setting was of being required to reproduce the content of what had been set for them to read, with memorization the surest path. This was for me very much a moment of stepping back in *wonder at* the significance of what I had been shown. And then I started to *wonder about* it and where it would lead.

As a first step, I discovered that if I treated a methodology text as a reading comprehension passage, then my students could score reasonable marks if tested in the (to them) usual way. Nevertheless, when I then asked them, '*So, what do you think about the writer's suggestion?*' my question remained opaque to many. What was missing, with regard to making sense of the text by linking textual organization and signalling to cultural approval and concern, was an understanding of the pragmatic significance of the semantic pattern that Hoey's formulation of what he called *relational analysis* had made clear. In my application of his work, the archetypal pattern of pragmatic significance in methodology texts functions in this way:

SITUATION: I am telling you about where I work so that you will recognize me as a genuine teacher and so that you can compare where I work to where you work. This should help you see how useful my ideas might be for you.

PROBLEM: I am telling you this because I think that you will recognize this issue as something that might be troublesome for you, too.

RESPONSE: These are my suggestions for what you might do.

EVALUATION: This is the evidence I have to help convince you that my suggestions are good ones.

Even if/when they could understand this in conceptual terms, my students still faced three particular challenges. First, at a linguistic level, they had to realize that the author's Response/Suggestion might come in a number of different grammatical realizations, featuring different tenses, voices and modalities, and represented in first, second, or third person. For example, a writer's suggestion regarding the assigning of specific student roles during group work might appear as:

IMPERATIVE: Assign a different role to each student.

PAST SIMPLE: I assigned a different role to each student.

PRESENT SIMPLE: The teacher assigns a different role to each student.

MODAL: You should assign a different role to each student.

HABITUAL 'WOULD':   I would assign a different role to each student.

PASSIVE: Each student is/was/should be assigned a different role.

The reader has not only to understand all of the above in propositional terms, they also all need to be interpreted in illocutionary terms as suggestions for action, and all for the same action. This represented a fundamental shift of attitude for the readers I was working with: it was no longer important to remember what the writer actually *said*, nor was it enough to remember what writers said that *they* had *done*. What was important was to understand what the writer *suggested* that *you* do. This is a radically different form of reading.

Furthermore, understanding the text, even in the novel way outlined above, as suggested action, rather than only information, was still not sufficient. The second challenge that my teacher-learners faced was that they were being called on to evaluate the suggested action. In other words, the text was no longer an undisputed source of content to be learned, or even instruction to be followed, it was a source of opinion and argument, formed in one situation, about which the reader had to make a judgment from the perspective of his or her own situation. Nor, if one continued down this road, were simple same/different comparisons, or yes/no decisions, acceptable as satisfactory reader responses, because there might well be useful tips to be found in procedures devised in situations very different from the reader's, even when a common problem was not recognized, or when the teaching procedure as a whole would not be appropriate.

The third challenge, implicit in the previous two, was that such evaluation needed to be carried out not only in conceptual terms, but with regard to practical teaching in the teacher-learner's particular situation. In the terms of Chapter 4, the thoughtful copying-over of pedagogic ideas had to begin with the processing of these suggestions in text, and then continue with the discernment of the affordances that they offered in context. With regard to interaction between the elements of my CATRA acronym, the application of (discourse-analytic) theory was meant to be opening up new possibilities for my teacher-learners' thoughtful copying in terms of their methodology.

The effects of all this on my teacher education praxis were significant at several levels.

With regard to practical methodology, Hoey's model of relational analysis provided the basis for a reading worksheet that teacher-learners used to take notes on the articles that they read. In its somewhat developed form, it looked like Figure 5.1.

Full title and reference:

Situation
Setting   details of context, students, level, purpose, etc.
State of the art   current opinions/practice in this area of TESOL

Focus
Problem   a particular difficulty that needs to be addressed
Purpose   the students', teacher's, or writer's specific goal

Response
Principle   the arguments underlying the writer's suggestions
Practice   the teaching procedures suggested

Evaluation
Evidence   positive outcomes actually reported by the writer
Criteria   ways to judge if the suggestions are working

Reader Comments

FIGURE 5.1 A reading worksheet

Reflexive memo 5.3: I still feel a thrill as I type out this framework. It marked a significant turning-point in my development from being methodologically capable to being theoretically informed in my praxis.

In text-analytical terms, I introduced the terminological shift from problem to focus as the second major semantic building block because it seemed an appropriate way to distinguish between problem as a category of discourse analysis, and a real-world problem in the sense of difficulty. As far as difficulties are concerned, and especially in intercultural terms, readers have to learn to recognize how writers from a different culture signal the focus that they are identifying. This is where my earlier comment (see pp.49–50) on the use of the term *traditional* fits in. In our field, one can assume that its use is pejorative and intended (not necessarily consciously) to signal the problem that needs to be addressed.

A point of at least equal significance, however, is that teachers should escape the assumption that either education itself, or professional development, is best seen as problem-focused. If we want a single term, I would say that both should be seen as aspiration-focused. Over the intervening years, this point has been made in formal terms by the emergence of appreciative pedagogy (e.g. Yballe & O'Connor 2000: 477), which emphasizes: '*the profound connection between positive vision and positive action*'. More generally, teacher-learners need to be encouraged to examine their strengths, explore their successes and pursue their interests. An affordance can be found in something positive or negative, or not cast in terms of that dichotomy at all. The point is to identify your focus and work on it.

What students came to see when using this note-taking aid was that, while the text they were reading was not necessarily explicitly organized in the above sequence, and while not all texts supplied all the information indicated, the archetypal pattern still functioned as a background schema. Moreover, they started to respond to it. It helped them read and it helped them remember, with regard both to an article's semantic content, as well as to what the writer was suggesting.

With reference to this latter pragmatic significance, we focused particularly on the response section, looking for procedural ideas and transforming them, no matter what their original grammatical form, into explicit lists of imperatives so that the suggestions became very clear. We then searched the text for the principles that underpinned those procedural suggestions, asking ourselves whether the procedures seemed suitable and the principles convincing.

At a conceptual level, other changes were afoot. I have already mentioned the necessary shift in the reader's relationship to the text, which was no longer something to be understood, learned and repeated, but which had to be transformed into action and evaluated as such.

Reflexive memo 5.4: Here the earlier quotation from Cobbett (see p.53) is again relevant, as is the observation that I was deliberately introducing my own tradition of educational thought, and that, in this case, of course, *tradition* is not intended to signal a problem: it is *my* tradition, after all. I note also my enjoyment of the *revelatory* nature of this work (see p.21).

This shift, in turn, challenged the fundamental relationship between reader and writer. It was no longer the case that the writer was the higher central authority, leaving the peripheral reader to interpret the message being sent; the writer was also a local, but simply from somewhere else. The reader thus became the local authority right here, whose responsibility it was to exploit the resources available in texts as s/he saw fit. I came to describe these two approaches to reading as an *interpretive* approach and an *exploitative* approach respectively. The distinction has served me well. Once the distinction is clear to teacher-learners it also helps drive home another point that teachers frequently make to their language learners, that different styles of reading and different strategies are appropriate for different purposes. Here we have the same principle made meaningful in a more sophisticated way for teachers themselves.

Yet another consequence of the application of this discourse-analytical approach to our professional situation was that issues of individual difference again came to the fore. The evaluation of a teaching procedure, students came to see, was not only a matter of comparing and contrasting situations, focuses and responses in an objective way. What also counted was teacher preference. Different teacher-learners were attracted by different types of procedure, and convinced by different arguments, just as they had found themselves motivated by different activities as learners (see Chapter 4). In this way, another corner-stone of a 'no best method' attitude was laid, also a basis for a developmental approach to continuing to become a teacher, by continuing to try and to undergo.

The effects that I recount here were exciting and energizing in class. Through their achievement of a new level of technical rationality, young adults found ways to interact with their educational resources, with their career prospects and with each other that were new and motivating. I leave this scenario for the time being and return to re-view it later in the chapter under the lens of reflexivity.

Wings

Hoey's work on relational analysis, and most particularly his clarifying of the mutually-shaping relationship between culturally-preferred patterns of discourse organization and the signalling that assists the recognition of such patterns, was transformative in my professional life (forming the basis of my doctoral research) and remains important today. In this section of the chapter, I outline three ways in which this engagement with an application of linguistic theory gave me the feathers and the wax I needed to construct wings for different kinds of flight: engaging with theory, extending the application, and making larger-scale connections.

Engaging with theory

As I have said, working with Hoey's ideas on discourse organization led me to formulate the concepts of *interpretive* and *exploitative* reading (Edge 1986b) in the context of developing a professional reading strategy for teacher-learners.

Thinking further along the lines of what I had called exploitative reading led me to engage with language description at a level of abstraction that I had not expected, and which I continue to find stimulating. I had learned when doing my MA in the late 1970s about Speech Act Theory as it had arisen from the work of Austin (1962) and Searle (1969) and entered TESOL most significantly in the shape of an emphasis on teaching what we called language *functions* (e.g. Wilkins 1976), our working synonym for speech acts. Austin's great insight was that when we *say* things, we also *do* things by that saying. Under most circumstances, the utterance, '*I could carry your bag*,' will neither be meant nor understood as a statement to be judged in terms of its truth regarding the speaker's physical strength or hypothetical ability, but as the making of an offer which requires either to be accepted or declined. Offering, accepting and declining are all speech acts. Taking the terminology of the theory a little further, utterances have a *locutionary* content (the semantic meaning of the utterance), an *illocutionary* force (the intended function of the act) and a *perlocutionary* effect (the consequence of the utterance as it is received, whether the intended one or not). Discussion of these and related concepts of semantic and pragmatic meaning have continued over the intervening years, with Medina (2005:28) summing up the contemporary situation in this way:

> It has become increasingly clear that a theory of meaning must provide an account of the semantic significance of the illocutionary aspects of language, and yet no fully satisfactory account has been developed either within Speech Act Theory or outside it . . . Moreover, a theory of meaning must not only take into account the illocutionary force of utterances, but must also pay attention to their perlocutionary effects.

What struck me then, and continues to intrigue me now, is that the approach to an understanding of perlocutionary effect has remained doggedly attached to its relationship to the illocutionary intent of the message-sender. In the terms of my two models of reading, it deals always (and perhaps only) with interpretive reading, where the responsibility of the reader is accurately to understand the message sent by the writer. But what of the exploitative reader, one who is, for example, out to take out of methodology texts any ideas and/or procedures that might be useful to his or her praxis?

Let us imagine a scenario in which I have an extra afternoon class to teach because a colleague is sick. With little notice or time to prepare, I skim through a professional magazine in the staffroom. In some haste, I see a series of teaching steps (clearly signalled in the text by numbering 1, 2, 3, and the use of imperative verbs) that sound reasonable as the basis for an activity. I go into class and, on the basis of this procedure, enjoy what seems to be a successful lesson.

Now, it is possible (without putting a percentage on likelihood) that the writer of the article that I hastily skimmed had provided this procedure as something s/he regarded as a well-known (traditional, perhaps) approach that needed to be criticized and changed; that is, the writer saw this procedure as the problem, rather than the response. Are we to account for my successful class as the unintended perlocutionary effect of a misunderstanding? We can do, but the complications of this seem to me to be lessened considerably if we move away entirely from the writer-to-reader message-sending schema that still dominates our thinking.

If, instead, we model our explanation on the meaning-creation of the exploitative reader, acting with purpose towards his or her own ends, then what counts is the semantic and pragmatic meaning that the reader, in interaction with the text, creates from it. To capture this idea, I allowed myself the luxury of inventing the term, *ablocutionary value*, defined (Edge 1989:415) as: '. . . *the semantic and pragmatic value assigned by the individual reader*'.

From this perspective, it can be interesting, but only secondary, to pursue the question of the match between the writer's illocutionary intent and the reader's ablocutionary value. Where there is a partial mismatch, the situated justification of the reader's ablocutionary value is of at least as much interest as a message-sending-oriented investigation of misunderstanding. Where the reader/writer relationship is one of actual disagreement, of course, the concept of ablocutionary value takes on even more weight, because it is the reader's situated, exploitative evaluation of worth that is paramount.

I am not oblivious to the fact that, since the 1989 publication of my article on ablocutionary value, the take-up of the concept has been minimal, although Reeves (1994:59) took the point precisely:

> a reader-oriented conception of communication such as this one has the effect of promoting the status of the reader, relative to text and writer.

The case remains, anyway, an exemplification of what I mean by the way in which a reflexive relationship can grow up between a theory applied and the application returning to inform theory. Nor, I must admit, do I actually accept the verdict of my peers on this concept. My feeling stubbornly remains that if I had stayed in the domain of discourse analysis and shifted more enthusiastically into the philosophy of language, I might have made a little space for my foundling among the difficulties of Derrida's (1982) différance, deconstruction and de-authorization of the text, but I took another job and I had to let it go. Non, je ne regrette rien.

Pulling back, then, from the doomed flight of ablocutionary value, I have decided to allow myself to mention the satisfaction that I felt when seeing the interpretive/exploitative analysis used by Hoey (2001:13ff.), as this provides a more achieved example of the type of reflexivity that I am trying to invoke here: the application of linguistic theory leads to the formulation of concepts in pedagogic practice which, in turn, prove useful to the subsequent work of the original theorizer. To put it reflexively, the unitary whole of working with language divides into the descriptive and the educational and these two parts communicate with each other in mutually shaping ways.

While this section has looked at what we might call theory-application reflexivity, the next section provides an account of another type of reflexive mutual shaping in the technical rationality matrix.

Extending the application

As well as having direct and powerful application in support of teacher-learners' reading, Hoey's theories of discourse organization have proved enormously useful with regard to their writing (Wharton 1999, 2008, Edge & Wharton 2001).

One can see this either as another case of theory-application, or as an example of how one application can be taken as a model and copied over into another area of activity. The actuality is almost certainly a mixture of both, but this momentary stepping back to achieve a perspective on what is happening serves also as a reminder that both the Copying and the Applying elements of the CATRA acronym are in play, just as the previous section highlighted the R of Reflection and the T of Theorizing.

The rubric for the assignment that my current MA students have to write in the context of the methodology module runs as in Figure 5.2.

No one has trouble thinking that they understand these instructions, but we spend a serious amount of class time looking at articles that demonstrate this pattern, as well as talking through the ideas and projects that students want to write about, before this shape is actually achieved in textual form. Once it has been, an important step towards what Lave & Wenger (1991) call '*legitimate peripheral participation*' in what I think of as an authentic TESOL world of discourse has been taken: the importance of context is emphasized, as is the need to develop a clear purposive focus for one's writing, as is the need to express oneself in terms both of ideas and actions, and the need to be accountable for one's efforts and their effects.

The power of what is being understood and achieved here continues to be significant for teacher-learners with whom I work. MA participants regularly refer to its usefulness in their reading, writing and teaching.

Reflexive memo 5.5: I am not looking to avoid the cultural-political shadow-side of what I have written so far about applying theory. Everything that I wrote in Chapter 4 about the 'interested' nature of method (Pennycook 1989) is relevant again here, but equally, in my judgment, now is not the time to deal with it. See below under Reflexivity and Chapter 7.

EDUC 70020 Assignment

Describe a teaching *situation* of which you have experience and analyse it in such a way as to highlight a particular aspect of that situation that you think merits the *focus* of your attention in terms of classroom methodology. (You may focus on a goal that you would wish to achieve, a problem that you would wish to solve, an opportunity that you would wish to take, a need that you would wish to meet, or any one of a number of such possible focuses.)

Present an appropriate *response* to this aspect of the situation. You must justify your ideas with regard to the literature and you must explain explicitly how these ideas will be put into practice. Both your arguments and your procedures must be clearly appropriate to the situation that you have described. We recommend that the detail of this *response*, both with regard to justification and implementation, should take up approximately half of the assignment.

Finally, you need to *evaluate* the success of your response. If you have had the opportunity to try out your suggestions, draw evidence from your experience. If you have not had the opportunity to try out your suggestions, explain how you could evaluate their success and suggest criteria that you might use.

Give your assignment a title that clearly communicates its content and purpose. Orient your title (and the whole assignment) towards action rather than only topic.

The assignment should be 3,500 words long (plus or minus ten per cent). **Please include a word count at the end of your text**. References or any appendices that you wish to add are not included in this count.

FIGURE 5.2   The MA assignment

Making larger-scale connections

When I launched into the doctoral research that my experimentation with Hoey's relational analysis turned into, I was not aware of the mode of working called action research to which I was to become committed (Edge 2001a). When I did begin to become aware of it, however, I realized that this was one of those occasions where I had been moving towards something without knowing that it had a name and a well-developed literature.

The archetypal pattern of action research is a spiral (e.g. Kemmis & McTaggart 1988), in which affordances are discerned through the careful observation of fully contextualized action and are reflected on until a plan is formed and then implemented in an attempt to improve the quality of experience available to participants in that context. Once again, the need to escape a problem-only type of focus has become an issue and the emergence of appreciative inquiry (Ludema et al. 2001) has provided the basis for the positively-focused approach to pedagogy already referred to above.

I came to see that the Action–Observation–Reflection–Planning–Action spiral of action research was an expression in research terms of the Situation-Focus-Response-Evaluation pattern that I had taken from Hoey in terms of discourse organization. The two patterns interweave like the teeth of a zipper, or perhaps even like the double helix of a DNA molecule in the sense that they express in reinforced fashion a genetic code of cultural inheritance. Thus, while involved in Action in a specific Situation, one Observes carefully until one has established a Focus. One then Reflects and formulates a Plan, which one puts into Action and Evaluates before deciding whether to stay with this Focus or develop another.

In bringing these two patterns together to the attention of my MA teacher-learners, I reinforce the significance of both and bring out an underlying coherence in '*the Western world's concern with problem-solving and classification*' (Hoey 1983:178). I have discussed the parallelism of these patterns further in Edge & Wharton (2002, 2003) and in Edge (2008b). What I want to bring out here is the way in which reflexivity can reach out to escape the confines of what seemed originally to be a simple theory/application dynamic. Here the two domains of research methodology and discourse analysis are brought together by the presence of a common, culturally-approved pattern to make up the two parts of a unitary whole that can also separate in order to communicate with each other. This is reflexivity in action and awareness makes it available to us as an enhanced tool for our development as teachers and teacher educators.

Reflexivity

The core of this chapter has been concerned with the idea of applying theory in teacher education – the first A of my CATRA acronym representing the necessary elements of teacher education processes. I have also commented in passing on how reflexivity can function in this context. In this section of the chapter, I summarize and expand on these reflexivity functions.

First of all, we note that the theory chosen was one explicitly concerned with categorization and problem-solving, which thus consciously aligns itself with these archetypically Western cultural preferences that the theory itself identifies. My strong positive response to this type of analysis was caused by its explanatory power. In choosing this theory and making it an important plank of my teacher education approach, I inevitably created a context for my teacher-learners that shaped the sets of options that they had available. They needed to become intercultural discourse analysts and develop metacognitive awareness of reading strategies in order to benefit most from what I was offering. Here, then, we have a straightforward case of what, in Chapter 2, I called prospective reflexivity. My advances in technical rationality shaped the teacher education that I offered.

What is more, this reflexive effect works at a broader level than only with regard to learning a particular type of analysis. To do this work at all requires the teacher-learner to want to take on the role of analyst in a way that might be quite unfamiliar and perhaps also not welcome. In the 'final vocabularies' (see Chapter 1) of many British teachers, for example, terms such as *theory, intellectual, academic* are marked as negative. Perkins (2002), a USAmerican moving into TESOL from a medical background is struck by the same phenomenon. Of her former work in healthcare, she writes (ibid.:98):

> Professional journals were read. It would be an embarrassment not to know what was going on in the field. Precise terminology from our field was expected in conversation.

She describes taking this mindset into TESOL as '*running into a cultural wall*' (ibid.):

> Theoretical basis? Not a common topic of conversation. I have learned that it is OK to ask a colleague for ideas for classroom use, but *not* OK to ask them *why* they do what they do . . . Many teachers seem to be of the mindset that theory and practice are indeed separable. Teachers tend to downplay what they know. I have never before met professionals that shied away from understanding their own field.

We shall return to this theme in the next chapter, but the point that I want to make here is that each teacher education choice of mine creates a context (i.e. a set of options to choose from) for my teacher-learners. Sometimes, I am doing little more than asking them to do what I tell them and show them, but often that involves doing what I have found useful (and attractive). If 'I' step back from this everyday scenario and establish a relationship with the interactions between my teacher-learners and 'me', I feel a concern that this relationship is only one step away from constituting a call for what might be seen as an identity change: Be the kind of person that I am (and your life will be better).

Working in this way also creates its retrospectively reflexive effects as the work that I do shapes my own continuing development. I have outlined above three such effects. First, in what we might call vertical reflexivity, I am motivated to experiment with linguistic theory itself. Second, in what we might call horizontal reflexivity, I copy over the application to a related area of my work. Third, in what we might call expansive reflexivity, I recognize patterns and make connections across previously unrelated areas of my knowledge and experience.

The danger of the *vertical/horizontal* metaphor is clear in that it suggests that informing areas of theory are placed somehow 'higher' than practice. This is not the intention. In order to explore the dimensions of reflexivity as well as I can, it seems worth holding on to this useful spatial metaphor without wishing to claim its hierarchical implications, even if one notes that, in terms of social status, they also represent a well-established reality. With regard to what I have called expansive reflexivity, this takes on more significance in Chapters 6 and 7.

This section on reflexivity has necessarily concentrated on ways in which my choices have contributed to my own development and potentially constrained the avenues of development for others. I do not want, however, to leave this last point lowering in its negativity. My enthusiasm for the application of relational analysis in teacher education contributes to its effectiveness and helps others benefit from it. This element of *continuity* should not go unnoticed. Furthermore, as others take up the work and develop their own specific enthusiasms and uses, their work comes back reflexively to shape my own continuing development.

To take just one example of this phenomenon, Cheng (2006) writes of how her own abilities have been enhanced by awareness of the SFRE pattern and its signalling. Here she is on the topic of '*reading purposefully*' when faced with huge numbers of articles that appear relevant to a topic in which she is interested (ibid.:11):

> I did not realize how valuable the title might be until I could recognize the clause relation and in turn the signal for the pattern by analyzing the title. With the awareness of what the article is about in the light of the analyzed title, I can realize whether the content is what I am expecting and then determine to read it or not. Selecting what suits me is more significant than searching as I am living in a world with overwhelmed information.

A common critique of teacher-learners from some cultural-educational backgrounds different to the Anglo-Saxon is that they do not read 'critically' enough. Indeed, this need to encourage evaluation of what was read was an integral part of my early work with the Problem/Solution pattern. What Cheng taught me was how analysis of the semantic pattern of text organization supported her own reader evaluation of the pragmatic significance of what she was reading. This comes through clearly in her comments on one article that she had read (ibid.:12):

> The article is quite well-structured and seems to provide teachers with effective techniques to encourage students to talk with others. The problem I find is where the criteria or evidence are. When it comes to Evaluation, criteria or evidence are the main elements which the worth of suggestions can be judged by, or demonstrated with. However, the author concludes the article by just repeating her own thoughts without revealing either criteria or evidence to consolidate her arguments. Being conscious that the part of Evaluation is weak, I become doubtful about the techniques she tenders. To sum up, all these principles allow me to analyze and to criticize at the same time.

She also reports (ibid.:14) that she finds it possible to engage this developing critical faculty in relation to her own writing, where analytical use of the SFRE pattern:

> allows me to become a critical reader of my own product, scrutinizing it through different perspectives.

Through her becoming technical in this way, Cheng also opens windows of critical perspective that change her, that expand her horizons. This is an example of expansive reflexivity. I learned about (underwent) this through working with Cheng. I had not seen it so clearly before.

So I, in such reports and responses, see teacher-learners discerning positive affordances for their individual development in the contexts that I have helped them create. This is both enlightening and empowering for me. I also continue to live, however, with the suspicion that 'I' advantage most those people who think and respond like 'me'.

Reflexive memo 5.6: It would have been equally possible to write the previous three sentences in reverse sequence:

> So, I continue to live with the suspicion that 'I' advantage most those people who think and respond like 'me'. In such reports and responses as Cheng's, however, I also see teacher-learners discerning positive affordances for their individual development in the intellectual contexts that I have helped them create. This is both enlightening and empowering for me.

Through the necessity of sequencing these propositions, one produces either one rhetorical effect or the other. In this instance, I wish to produce neither. Both thoughts exist in equilibrium.

In this chapter, I have focused on the applying-theory aspect of teacher education, the first A in my CATRA acronym. By itself, as Schön, Wallace and Boxer have warned in their different ways (see Chapter 2), the pursuit of technical rationality carries the consequent risk of instilling a feeling of impotence in teacher-learners. The first criterion that one seeks to meet, therefore, is that teacher-learners are clearly taking hold of a certain application of theory and deriving benefit from it. What matters for teacher educators and teacher-learners is what happens next.

The issue then is whether this activity of application triggers a rise in awareness. Are some people motivated to copy over the application to a related area of work in what I have called an experience of horizontal reflexivity? Do they begin to experiment with the informing ideas themselves, in a mode of vertical reflexivity? Do they recognize patterns and make connections across previously unrelated areas of their knowledge and experience in what I have called expansive reflexivity? Do they see what is happening not only as a single set of procedures to be copied over, or ideas to be pursued, but also recognize that what we are dealing with here is just one example of the broader move of applying theory? It is in this mindful trying and undergoing that a shift into a broader experience of *becoming technical* is to be found.

It is experience of this kind that I have tried to document in this chapter, while also exploring issues of prospective and retrospective reflexivity in my own work as a teacher educator. It is important that I do not confuse my own experience with that of others – the autobiography with the framework. Applying *this* theory was a significant step in *my* becoming technical. Learning about this application, and learning to exploit it is one possible key to the process of becoming technical for my teacher-learners. I hope that fellow professionals will identify their own affordances.

In the next chapter, I turn to what it can be useful to regard as a dimension of teacher education complementary to becoming technical in a broader conceptualisation of becoming theoretical: *theorizing practice*.

6

THEORIZING PRACTICE AND BECOMING THEORETICAL

Introduction

In the previous chapter, I used the expression, *becoming technical*, to capture one dimension of being a teacher educator and I identified *applying theories* as the key parameter of activity characterizing this dimension. I suggested that along with the demonstrable effectiveness of the application of some particular theory, what was required was recognition of the broad potential of applying theory, and of the possible reflexive consequences of that parameter of work, whether horizontal, vertical or expansive.

I took the term 'technical' from the *technical rationality* that Schön and Wallace (see Chapter 2) contrast with *reflective rationality*. I now want to draw on the potential of reflective rationality to construct understanding through reflection on practice. Rather than contrast rational/reflective in a displacive way, however, I want to augment the applying of theory with the complementary parameter of *theorizing practice* and say that when one is operating in both ways, one is involved in a broader process of *becoming/being theoretical*. This development has further reflexive consequences of its own.

Before taking those steps, I need to take a little time to mull over a few different uses of the term *theory* that are involved in this discussion, and to clarify what I mean by it.

On theory

Many disciplines inform the teaching of English, one of them being linguistics. Such disciplines develop their own theories – general, abstract statements that account for the data of their field according to their own criteria. These statements will differ in the extent to which they seek to describe the way things are and/or to explain why things are the way they are. In Chapter 5, I worked with one form of linguistic theory, Hoey's relational approach to discourse analysis. This is a usage of the term, *theory*, that I stand by.

In Chapter 1, I raised my objections to a different use of *theory* as it occurs in the well-worn expression, '*It's OK in theory, but it doesn't work in practice.*' This use of *theory*, to mean something not of the real world, something unreliable, something from the domain of people who deal in arcane speculation or in sealed laboratories and who do not really understand actual environments is very much with us in our everyday lives. A favourite example of mine that I jotted down at the time is:

> Theoretically, these showers should arrive tomorrow evening, but prac- tically, they might already turn up in the afternoon.
> *Suzanne Charlton, BBC 1 television weather forecast, 19 May 1996*

So, should one take one's umbrella according to the theory, or according to the practical possibility? Is the difference just one of likelihood? It really is difficult to see what type of theory is being invoked here. The point is, I think, that *theory* is seen as something divorced from what actually happens. Things which are '*all very well in theory*', are, by implication, unlikely to work out in everyday practice, when the '*theory*' is '*applied*'.

In TESOL, this use of *theory* expresses a justified frustration with the ways in which the results of controlled experiments have frequently been touted as underlying truths that would be reliable if only applied properly, or if only one could learn to iron out unfortunate human idiosyncrasies. At the same time, however, this line can also be used to excuse the speaker from moving on from unquestioned, conservative practices. This use of *theory* is one that I like to encourage teacher-learners to question and to move away from.

A third use of *theory*, and the one that most concerns us in this chapter, involves the concept of a statement with which the speaker articulates his or her best understanding of what is actually going on. With this statement, the speaker says, '*These are the data of my experience and this is my best shot at accounting for them.*' The important issue is not one of the complexity, or even originality, of what is formu- lated. The importance lies in the individual (or group) attempt to take responsi- bility for putting into words the current state of awareness and understanding with which one is operating. In essence, in the act of articulating as best one can a statement that accounts for the data of one's field, this act of theorizing is of a kind with the first use of theory that I sketched above. There are differences of generalizability and differences of status involved, and I return to these below, but let me first give an everyday example of the kind of action I mean to invoke here.

For years, when students told me that they did not understand a set of instructions, or that they were confused about what they needed to do, I would explain again, possibly in simpler terms. Sometimes this was successful. Sometimes, the response was one of, '*Yes, I know all that, but I still don't see . . .*' Sometimes, my second explanation would introduce doubt into the minds of students who thought they had understood the first time. I came to find that, rather than explaining a second time, I got better results if I said to a 'confused' student or students, '*Tell me what you think you have to do, and I'll tell you if you're right.*' The result is that the student focuses his or her attention on making every effort to express what s/he thinks is going on, and I get to understand exactly where his or her difficulty lies, perhaps also discovering where my instructions have been unclear. If I now try to articulate what I learned here, in other words to theorize my practice, I would say:

> Under the circumstances described above, it is more effective to ask a student to tell me what they *have* understood than to explain again something that they say they have *not* understood.

That's my theory.

Returning briefly to the questions of generalizability and status that I raised above, I make no claim as to how generalizable my theory is, so this cannot be a weakness. I offer it for what it is worth to others. In most cases, I would expect teachers' theories to be shaped by the constraints and affordances of the contexts in which they work. The more these *local theories* are articulated, the more chance we shall have to understand better how the particular impacts on the general, or how particular understandings might help us formulate a useful general statement.

With regard to status, this is one of the shifts that teacher educators, reflective and reflexive, are committed to bringing about. Precisely because we do not accept the role of the teacher to be (only) the technically skilled applier of other people's theories, we wish to see teachers taking up the status of theorizers. Here, *theory* takes on a positive, democratizing meaning, one that entails a sense of striving and of taking responsibility. In this sense, it reconnects with the Deweyan concept of experience that we have been working with, of trying and undergoing, as well as with the idea of reflection as a major instrument in turning that experience into knowledge.

Furthermore, rather than settle into the implicitly static noun-ness of *theory*, we should remember that it is the active, developmental gerund of *theorizing* that lies perhaps closer to our interests. This is a major parameter of action along which teacher educators wish to engage, and along which they wish to encourage engagement by teacher-learners. This is a major dimension of being and continuing to become where we wish to operate. To a large extent, this is as much a question of attitude as anything else, of not being satisfied either with what is, or satisfied with evaluating other people's theories, but of wanting to make sense oneself.

In the terms of the writers who are never far from my mind while I work on these ideas (Rorty 1999:120):

This notion of a species of animals gradually taking control of its own evolution by changing its environmental conditions leads Dewey to say, in good Darwinian language, that '*growth itself is the moral end*' and that to '*protect, sustain and direct growth is the chief ideal of education*'.

Moreover, all of the above seems to me to be of a piece with Canagarajah's (2006a:30) suggestion that:

> it is not the comfort of solutions that matters but the vigilance of the search, not the neat product but the messy practice of crossing boundaries, mixing identities, and negotiating epistemologies.

However, rather than press on down this postmodernist route, with its accompanying risk of disappearing up my own reflexivity, I want to establish a firmer grip on lived experiences of theorizing practice as I have been aware of them. I shall first go back to my roots.

Reflexive memo 6.1: I have just experienced (again) a strong sense of connection to the Boxer-inspired matrix presented as Figure 2.1 in Chapter 2, with its quadrants of teaching styles. It now strikes me that just as the revelatory style relates most directly to applying theory, the emancipatory relates more to theorizing practice as a step on the way towards the conjectural style of autonomous work. This presents me with something of a paradox because, while I have already acknowledged my tendency to favour the revelatory mode, I have also always thought of myself as favouring the theorizing of practice over the applying of theory. I have, perhaps, identified a mismatch between my espoused theory and my theory-in-action. This demands more work, but I can't do that here. It is an affordance to note.

Roots

Pre-service teacher education

In Chapter 4, I referred to teacher education experience in Turkey and procedures designed to help teacher-learners 'become methodological'. In addition, my colleagues and I also devised procedures that aimed to help teacher-learners relate effectively to grammatical and other linguistic information available to them. The *status quo* position saw teacher-learners in their last two years of training being given courses on syntax and phonology, and then asked (or left) to apply this knowledge to their teaching. Our innovation was to prepare for and complement these future courses during the first two years of training by confronting language issues in their teaching materials and pursuing linguistic explanations in the reference materials that we had. So, we would look at a piece of teaching material and ask such questions as, '*What exactly is the point that we want to get across here?*' or, '*What would you say if the learner asked you the difference between X and Y here?*' Teacher-learners would take on specific tasks, inform themselves and report back to class. As well as giving purpose to the learning of explicit grammatical knowledge, this procedure allowed us to talk about how their previous teachers had explained such things, how a teacher might explain them, and the important difference between explaining something fully based on one's extensive knowledge and the sensitive discipline required to tell a learner only as much as they needed to know. (Since those days, fortunately, more easily accessible reference texts (e.g. Swan 1995) have made this kind of work more straightforward to carry out.)

As with the early methodology training I described in Chapter 4, one outcome was that by the time teacher-learners came to their formal lectures on syntax and phonology, they had received a conceptual and terminological preparation that had arisen out of their professional concerns. They were attitudinally open to the idea that such information could be useful and they were less affectively threatened by the challenges that faced them.

Most importantly, in the context of this chapter, teacher-learners became accustomed to what I then (Edge 1988a) called '*reference out*' to theory, as distinct from '*application in*' to practice. The significance of this is captured by Olsen (1977:79, 87):

> Means are not optional routes to the same goal; they are optimal routes to different goals.
>
> . . .
>
> Hence, the choice of a means of instruction, like the choice of a content, must be based upon a consideration of its social and personal consequences.

Teachers, as their careers develop, are unlikely to continue to study linguistics and practice a pedagogy of 'application in'. They are very likely to continue to be faced by issues of language complexity in the face of which a practiced ability to 'refer out' will serve their pedagogy very well. In this sense, the attitude to sources of information and to informing disciplines, along with the reference skills and interpretive abilities that we encouraged, I now see as forming an early manifestation of the later development of an inclination to begin with practice and then to seek out such theoretical information as might inform it.

In-service teacher education

As my work as teacher educator continued through the late 1980s and the 1990s, I became increasingly involved in Masters-level distance education with experienced teachers working in their own contexts and I experienced an immediate fit between this way of working and the overall discourse of teacher education itself.

The traditional (!), academy-centric perspective had always seen its 'distance'-learning students as being removed from the centre of learning, but my colleagues and I saw the teacher-in-context as the centre of learning, with the academy at some distance from it. Rather than transmitting knowledge to teacher-learners, therefore, for them to learn and apply, we saw ourselves as working to help the situated teacher-learner explore, discover and articulate what they had learned. So, instead of taking teachers out of their professional contexts and bringing them into the academy in order to lecture them on the importance of situated learning and the dysfunctions of a theory/application discourse, we worked to support (as I still do) the development of *situated* action researchers.

In line with this, the written assessment of participants' work (as outlined in Chapter 5) ceased to be based on the writing of essays on topics and came to be based instead on reports on contextualized action and what had been learned from it.

I came to see how my earlier praxis involving 'reference out' and 'application in' related to the 'outside-in'/'inside-out' trajectories of Prawat's (1991) discussion of teacher empowerment and Nunan's (1993:41) use of the same terms with explicit reference to action research in TESOL. Prabhu's (1990) formulation of a teacher's developing sense of *plausibility*, along with the equally praxis-oriented literature of action research, whether in terms of general education (e.g. Altrichter et al. 1993, Reason & Bradbury 2001) or of TESOL (e.g. Edge & Richards 1993, Wallace 1998, Burns 1999) all served to strengthen the emphasis on the theorization of practice as an alternative discourse to that of the application of theory. One felt a welcome change of discoursal direction from theory/application to exploration/articulation.

By the time I edited a collection of action research papers for the TESOL organization, I was formulating my thinking in the following way (Edge 2001a:6):

> I believe that we have reached a point at which we accept our responsibility to raise our awareness first of what our current practice is, and then, on the basis of that awareness, to set our directions and seek the information we require. The thinking teacher is no longer perceived as someone who applies theories, but as someone who theorizes practice.

Throughout the 1990s and the first decade of the twenty-first century, I have found this perspective providing a metaphorical wind beneath my wings in several dimensions of my professional life. With regard to the Master's programme I referred to above, I was able to express this visually in a poster that, the substantive content of which I have to admit, I still read with some satisfaction today, more than ten years later (see Figure 6.1). The opening line of the poster was also to form the basis for a discussion to which I return in Chapter 9.

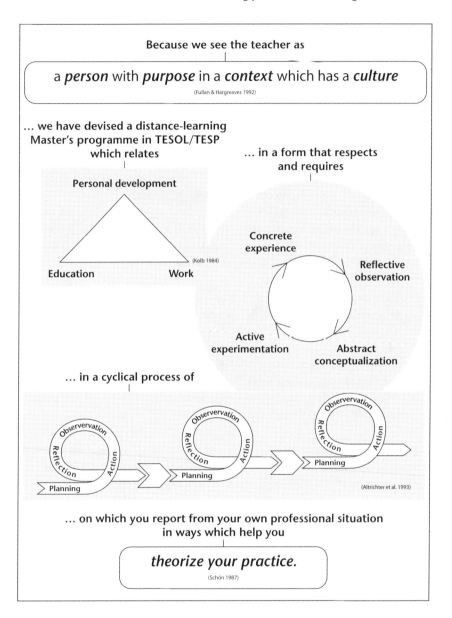

FIGURE 6.1 An MA course poster

This vision, pictured at programme level, also had to be realized in terms of individual and group experience. One early exercise embedded in foundation module materials was a direct addressing of participants' expected prejudices regarding such words as *researcher, theorist, academic* and *intellectual*. The overall task looked like Figure 6.2.

I have listed below some terms that I find it useful to think about at this stage. Before you read on to discover what I have to say about them, please do take the time to jot down your own responses to the words. What do they mean to you? Are they roles of yours/aspects of you? What do you think of when you hear these words? How do you react?

FIGURE 6.2 A foundation module task

At this point, it could be interesting for readers to reflect on the kind of response that you would expect from colleagues, or teacher-learners with whom you work, to these terms. In the materials, I drew attention to such uses as that of *theoretically*, already given above by our weather forecaster, before going on to make the arguments that pertain to the theme of this chapter (Edge 1998:22):

> The type of theorist which we want to encourage is the person who struggles to articulate statements which make sense of that person's own experience. Theory, in this sense, is the understanding which arises from practice, and the theorist is the person who gives voice to it. Theory is evaluated according to its usefulness in helping a person account for what is happening, and in planning future action. That is why we are interested in the specifics of a local situation, and why our participants need to be researchers in order to formulate local theory.

Another favourite quotation of mine from that time involves the following use of *academic* in a report on a soccer match, to mean something like, unimportant, irrelevant, insignificant with regard to what actually counts in the world:

> Blackburn raised their game from a canter after Wise put Chelsea ahead after 35 minutes. At once, Sherwood headed in the splendidly direct Wilcox's centre from the left and before the hour was up McKinlay, with a cleverly taken header, and Fenton with a volley had effectively settled it. Spencer's late reply proved academic.
>
> *Frank Keating*, The Guardian, *6 May 1996*

An example that I used in a later revision of these materials, however, now provides rather less light-hearted exemplification of the same usage. Interviewed about his reaction to a report by the Audit Commission that British tanks had ground to a halt, soldiers' boots disintegrated, their rifles jammed, and communications systems had not functioned well during military exercises in Oman, the political journalist, Andrew Gilligan, commented:

This makes speculation about Britain's possible role in a war against Iraq actually rather academic.

Today. *BBC Radio 4. 2 August 2002*

The point I wanted to make here was expressed as follows (Edge 2003c:23):

> But *academic* is also a word to which we want to lay a claim. One of the purposes which we hope you will embrace as long-term TESOL professionals working on a higher degree, is the ability to take part in the kind of well-informed exchange of opinion which can add to the body of knowledge available for TESOL. We are committed to high academic standards of information and argument, also to the ethical importance of acknowledging the sources of ideas that we employ and being sure that we have permission to use any data that we collect. In these senses, and for these reasons, *academic* itself is a word that we want to appropriate and make positive in these ways.

Reflexive memo 6.3: I realize now, in retrospect, that this exercise was a straightforward assault in terms of what Rorty (see Chapter 1) calls one's *final vocabulary*. This engenders very mixed emotions: some along the lines of satisfaction at recognizing previously hidden lines of coherence running through my praxis; but also a sense of frustration at my ignorance, at not having been informed about possible connections, possibilities, affordances earlier.

Some of these key vocabulary items received further activation through classroom tasks that participants were asked to carry out (and my sincere thanks for permission to quote responses from those named below). One such item was *researcher*, in the sense that participants were asked to record themselves teaching and comment on what they heard, perhaps discussing the extract with one or more of their students. The effects of consciously transforming everyday experience into a process of *trying* and *undergoing* as a proto-action researcher begin to be apparent in reports such as this one, which might be seen as emphasizing the element of *trying*:

> I did not expect that much would emerge from discussing the tape and my interpretation of it with my student. However, his explanation and justification of why he interrupted me so loudly at one point illuminated something about his classroom performance which influences to his detriment the way teachers think about him and is possibly a hindrance to his progress. From this emerged something I can follow up with him in the future.
>
> *Richard Paiaraudeau*

Further comments arose as participants were completing the foundation module and were asked to evaluate their experience on the Master's course thus far. They were invited to comment explicitly, if they so wished, on the concept of *becoming theoretical*, in the sense of learning to theorize their practice. Bartlett's response seems to me to emphasize the element of *undergoing*:

> I no longer feel daunted by books with titles such as, *Discourse Analysis*. Rather, I feel myself wondering whether I will find a useful reference to code-switching in the classroom.
>
> *Jenny Bartlett*

A third voice brings out what, in Chapter 5, I called the expansive potential of such work, leading the participant out to view wider horizons:

> My notion of 'theory', which I suppose I have been carrying round with me since the RSA Dip, defined it more as an externalized body of knowledge to be imposed *upon* practice, so it is profoundly empowering to realize that pedagogic theorizing actually arises *out of* reflective practice with one's own local context. The value of this insight cannot be overstated, for the rejection of universal, totalizing theories seemed to connect with so many areas of the literature that I subsequently read.
>
> *Justin Richards*

I find such statements of growth and liberation moving, and draw great satisfaction from having played some kind of a facilitative role in making them possible. With repeated thanks to the above course graduates, I feel no embarrassment in invoking at this point a metaphor of spreading wings.

Wings

Arguments that I have put forward regarding the importance of consistency, coherence and continuity in teacher education insist that the theorizing of practice needs to play an explicit part in my own professional development. This is not a challenge that I intend to duck, not least because therein lie the threads that I hope will weave themselves together to support my own sense of congruence. That is not to say that I am about to reveal any dazzling new theories, but I will show you what I want to mean by the expressions, *theorizing my practice*, and *being/becoming theoretical*. Let me begin by picking up an earlier thread arising from conditions of work.

I have described how my jobs led me from face-to-face teacher education to a full-time involvement with so-called *distance* education, and how I came to prefer to refer to this as *situated* teacher education – already an example of theorizing. This process has continued as my current job has brought me to work with experienced teacher-learners who study full time, on site, at my university, and others who study part time, in context, around the world. Furthermore, the use of a virtual learning environment (VLE) means that both groups of course participants can communicate and collaborate with each other, while interacting with me, with the materials that I supply and recommend, and with the sources that they seek out. This experience has led me to think further about the concept of *distance* itself and about its role in my work. As my thinking develops, I share it with new course participants on the VLE home page of the methodology module with which the programme begins. Here is an extract from the course rationale as it now stands, with the expression '*a methodology course*' used to replace our rather arcane course numbering system (see Edge 2010a):

> For full-time students, this period of study probably fits into their long-term professional life most positively as a 'time-out' for reflection and renewal. For part-time students, this period probably functions best as an intensely integrated experience of work and study. You will have your own thoughts on those descriptions and, again, you are invited to share them.
>
> For all course participants, the concept of 'distance' (and how we deal with it) is essential to the experience. Part-time course participants in context around the world are distant from Manchester and from fellow participants. Full-time course participants in Manchester are distant from their students and colleagues and from the teaching contexts in which what they learn must make sense. I, as course tutor, am distant from everyone's teaching context. With in-context participants, I can at least address you directly in your contexts. With on site participants, I can at least address you face-to-face. For in-context participants, the e-availability of resources has enriched your study possibilities enormously. For on site participants, you have similarly enhanced possibilities for communicating with your colleagues in the contexts that you have left. For both sets of participants, you have the potential in this space to communicate and collaborate with each other. For everyone, a major requirement is to remember that we are interested in the development of ideas in action, and action always needs a context in order to be meaningful. We are all in some kind of context. We are all at some kind of distance.
>
> Given the importance to the course of various forms of distance, then, the one central metaphor underpinning the rationale behind this course, the one image that I want you to hold on to, is of you, yourself, the course participant, as the centre. You are the centre of operations which must succeed in bringing about a productive synergy between the experiential learning available to you through your teaching context(s), remembered, experienced and imagined, and the intellectual learning available to you through this course and your further study. We are all working in what my colleague, Susan Brown, has called our '*context in mind*'.
>
> The three elements that I believe to be essential to the success of these operations are:

- action and interaction to power the learning,
- communication to turn learning into knowledge; and
- goodwill to get us through the hard times.

All of the above, or another tutor's version of it, could be said just as well of any other course unit in this MA programme. A difference with regard to a methodology course, however, is perhaps that it makes more sense to spell these things out. This kind of meta-commentary seems appropriate on the grounds that a methodology course is necessarily reflexive in nature. That is to say, it is a course on methodology, so whatever it does or says rebounds back on itself in some way with regard to its own methods. And on me. Hmmmmmm. Unavoidable, I fear.

A further effect of this particular theorizing of my practice has been my realization of how far I had allowed my pendulum to swing when articulating my (2001a) thoughts about '*the thinking teacher*' that I quoted above. In order to state the importance of theorizing practice, there is no need to dismiss the usefulness of applying theory. This is another example of the 'displacive' style of argument that can waste our creative energies. This realization has led, in turn, to the attempt in my CATRA framework to include both Applying and Theorizing and to suggest that they are complementary parameters of action that contribute to an overall dimension, including but exceeding the *technical*, of *becoming theoretical*.

I draw a second example of theorizing practice from a more specific area of my work, that of Cooperative Development – the area that I find more motivating and satisfying than any other. Here, rather than my theorizing being a process of working to understand my experience in a bottom-up kind of a way, I discovered a ready-made concept in another frame of reference that helped me take my own thinking forward.

Cooperative Development is a discourse framework for pursuing professional self-development in collaboration with one's peers. It is based on Rogerian principles of self-actualization and of non-judgemental understanding (Rogers 1980, Rogers & Freiberg 1994). I have been working in this mode and developing the framework since 1989 and have written about it quite frequently (e.g. Edge 1992, 2002a, 2008b), as have others (e.g. Boshell 2002, Mann 2002, Boon 2005, 2007, 2009, de Sonneville 2007, Butorac 2008, Bibila forthcoming).

I have no space here to argue the case for Cooperative Development or give examples of it in action, although I do present a working example in Chapter 8. I hope that I can simply explain enough here to give a minimally comprehensible version of what is going on as a basis for what I want to say about continuing theorization. In this description, I capitalize terms that have specific meanings in Cooperative Development.

As simply and briefly as I can put it, then, two people agree to work together in the complementary roles of Speaker and Understander in order to support the professional self-development of the Speaker. They undertake to follow a set of rules that makes their exchanges (for the period of the Cooperative Development session) very different from the discussions, critiques and ideas-exchange of more usual peer collaboration. Let me be clear: this work presents no argument *against* the usefulness of discussions, critiques and ideas-exchange. Indeed, I believe that it is fundamentally important that people learn how to construct and to conduct an argument, how to defend their beliefs and how to stand up for their rights. Cooperative Development, however, is meant to provide something different, to create brief spaces where unfamiliar constraints apply and novel affordances might be discerned. It offers a challenge/opportunity to extend one's repertoire for those motivated to learn the discipline of working with non-judgemental discourse. It will not be of interest to anyone who insists that an interaction can be complete only once they have delivered their own opinion and/or evaluated the opinions of others.

Speakers identify an element of their praxis that they want to work on. Knowing that their statements will not be judged or contested, they then Explore that topic in a non-defensive manner, hoping to make a discovery significant enough for them to devise a plan of action arising from it. Understanders work to support this trajectory. They put aside their own ideas, opinions and experiences in order to accept and empathize with what the Speaker has to say. Their initial purpose is to help the Speaker clarify exactly what the Speaker wants to mean from the Speaker's own perspective. They check their Understanding by Reflecting back to the Speaker what they have Understood, cognitively and affectively, in order to have this version confirmed, or corrected, or expanded on by the Speaker. Speakers thus rehear what they have said, interpreted through the sensitive re-articulation of a supportive colleague. They confirm, correct, amend or expand. They make every effort to drive the process of Discovery forward, channelling the energy of their non-defensive thinking into the matter of language. And when things work out, Speakers do make discoveries that they can use to take their work forward in terms of Action.

I say, 'when things work out', because there is no simple causal mechanism here. Speaker and Understander work together to construct a context in which the Speaker might discern affordances that otherwise would not be available. There are no guarantees of immediate solutions to given problems, or of new ways, or new ends. There is potential.

As well as Reflecting, Understanders have other response-types available in order to support the Speaker's work. The most important of them are Thematizing, when the Understander asks the Speaker if s/he sees any common theme between points that s/he has separately made; Challenging, when the Understander asks the Speaker if s/he sees any inconsistency between points that s/he has separately made; and Focusing, when the Understander asks the Speaker if s/he wants to choose any specific point that s/he has made in order to go into it in more depth. In all of this, the Understander is sincerely trying to Understand, not to guide, and the Speaker knows this.

The Speaker experiences the novel pressures of expressing opinions and making plans without knowing how the hearer would respond to them if they occurred in a normal conversation. The Understander experiences the novel pressures of withholding personal ideas and opinions while accurately and non-judgementally representing those of someone else. None of this is easy, but it creates a dynamic that can lead to individually-empowering discoveries for the Speaker and an enhanced sense of collegiality and common purpose between the colleagues involved as they become accustomed to working in these different roles as a developmental unit.

My recent thinking about this work (Edge 2009) has been helped considerably by exchanges that I have been engaged in among a cross-disciplinary group of colleagues who meet to discuss readings in sociocultural theory, drawing on the core intellectual nexus of Vygotsky (1978, 1986), Bakhtin (1981) and Leont'ev (1981), as interpreted and developed in the West by scholars such as Lave & Wenger (1991), Wertsch (1991, 1998), Engestrøm, R. (1995), Wenger (1998) and Engestrøm, Y. (2001). These sources have been supplemented in TESOL terms by Lantolf & Appel (1994), Lantolf (2000), Thorne (2005), Johnson (2006, 2009) and Lantolf & Thorne (2006). The kind of theorizing that I am involved in here, then, is of learning to see one's practice through a lens provided by others, and then learning more about one's practice by articulating it in those new terms.

Johnson's (2006:237) elaboration of the '*more general sociocultural turn in the human sciences*', sets the scene well (ibid.:238):

> Learning, therefore, is not the straightforward appropriation of skills or knowledge from the outside in, but the progressive movement from external, socially mediated activity to internal mediational control by individual learners, which results in the transformation of both the self and the activity.

While we recognize the familiar rejection of the outside-in trajectory of transmissive learning, we also note the absence of a simple replacement by 'inside-out'.

When Johnson writes about the construction of legitimate, situated understanding toward self-defined purposes, it (ibid.:241):

> emerges out of a dialogic and transformative process of reconsidering and reorganizing lived experience through the theoretical constructs and discourses that are publicly recognized and valued within the communities of practice that hold power.

This formulation has the subtlety to encompass outside-in and inside-out trajectories of learning, as social behaviours are internalized to feed individual psychological learning and this learning is externalized as social behaviour. We are once again in the domain of hermeneutic cycles of thought and action which result *'in the transformation of both the self and the activity'* – harmonizing with the internalizing and externalizing nature of reflexive experience identified in Chapter 3.

Wertsch (1998:43) also highlights this reflexive connection in a way highly relevant to Cooperative Development:

> the introduction of a new mediational means creates a kind of imbalance in the systemic organization of mediated action, an imbalance that sets off changes in other elements such as the agent.

Johnson (2009:109) makes the connection explicit:

> Overall, Cooperative Development creates a unique kind of mediational space and a unique kind of discourse within which self-exploration and the articulation and re-articulation of ideas can emerge.

In this instance, however, another type of 'theorizing' is also in play, and it highlights an old danger. Johnson (2009) makes two extensive and positive references to Cooperative Development (pp.25–29 and 105–109), which I am very happy to read. In so doing, unfortunately, she also shows how easy it is for grand theory to sweep all along before it without necessarily pausing to pay attention to the actual experiences of which it claims to be providing an account.

No one who has seriously attempted to listen carefully to another human being and then to check that they have fully and sensitively understood what that person wanted to say is likely to refer to the process as *'simply parroting back'* (ibid.:26). Johnson (ibid.:105) then poorly represents the notion of Challenging as being concerned with *'ideas or opinions acknowledged and affirmed by the Speaker that the Understander finds difficult to accept'*. If this were the case, the whole non-judgemental framework – the *'unique kind of mediational space'* – would collapse. In her discussion of data from Mann (2002:108ff.), she fails to distinguish between the Speaker being not well Understood (the point that Mann makes) and the Speaker being criticized (the point that Johnson wants to make in favour of the importance of *'constructive critique'*) in a way that subverts much of what she has written. As is so often the case, when divorced from action and experiential understanding, 'theory' finds its own way forward to achieve its own ends from vantage points uncomplicated by experience.

My interest here, however, is in the theorizing *of* experience.

One question that has intrigued me about Cooperative Development is how best to represent the idea of the Speaker and Understander as certainly being engaged in a type of dialogue, but simultaneously comprising a unified source of ideas and plans for action, driven and refined by complementary uses of creativity and sensitivity. I found a way forward in the concept of the *dyadic subject*, which Wells (2007) introduces with reference to the scaffolding strategies of teachers in teacher–student exchanges during discussions and problem-solving tasks. There is what he calls (ibid.:173ff.) *intermental* work and *intramental* work going on between teacher and learner as they combine as one subject working towards goals '*that are often emergent in the action*'.

My situation is fundamentally different in that teaching, in which a person who usually knows helps a person who does not know, belongs to a very different world from Cooperative Development, in which it is the person who knows, the Speaker, who is supported by the person who does not know, the Understander. Nevertheless, as a way of conceptualizing a single, but dialogic, source of ideas and plans, the *dyadic subject*, as a concept, is extremely helpful to my thinking and therefore to my praxis.

One example of such usefulness arose in an exchange that took place recently between a doctoral student and colleague blogging about styles of research interviewing. The question came up of the extent to which an interviewing style as Understander would be possible or desirable. In my contribution, the use of the concept, *dyad*, was useful to me in emphasizing the conceptual unity entailed by the Speaker/Understander relation, from which it would not be possible to detach one member:

> It seems to me that if an interviewer wants to understand what an interviewee thinks about something, then that interviewer may well want to behave in a non-judgemental, empathetic way in order to elicit that information and collect those data on the topics that interest the researcher.
>
> To be an Understander, however, is to be part of a dyad committed to working on the Speaker's development. The Speaker will choose what is to be worked on and will be committed not to reporting what they have thought thus far, but to developing their ideas in the direction of a plan of action. In complementary fashion, the Understander is committed not to finding out what the Speaker has thought thus far, but to helping the Speaker move that thinking along. A person being interviewed is not a Speaker. Without an aware, committed Speaker, there cannot be an Understander.

With regard to the continuing theorization of Cooperative Development, I have found myself working in the light of Wells' (1999:334) comment that the very essence of sociocultural theory is that its products arise from specific historical and spatial circumstance, and that, therefore, with regard to Vygotsky:

> in appropriating his ideas and putting them to use, we should also be willing to transform those ideas so that they can be of greatest use in meeting the demands of our own situations.

It is in this spirit that I am also working to reformulate sociocultural theory's probably best-known concept, the *zone of proximal development* (ZPD), for my own purposes. Given that the purpose of Cooperative Development is to produce plans for meaningful action, rather than only promote learning, one can envisage the goal of the Speaker/Understander dyad as being to increase the scope for a teacher's meaningful action. It is attractive to develop this idea of the Scope for Meaningful Action (SMA):

> The SMA can be understood as a set of affordances created by the expanding state of awareness emerging for the Speaker from the articulations and re-articulations achieved by the dyadic (Speaker/Understander) subject of its intramental and intermental interaction.

The SMA expresses the extending reach of the dyadic Subject in its language work towards action, that is, what we might call its *action-in-discourse*. What is learned here can provide a basis for the Speaker's meaningful next move in terms of putting a plan into action, what we might call his or her *action-in-context*. Both what is learned though action-in-discourse and action-in-context can prove developmental for the Speaker in unpredictable, but not random, ways. In this cyclical relationship between action-in-discourse and action-in-context, one sees clear parallels with the hermeneutic cycle of action research and other expressions of reflexive learning and of trying and undergoing that have been our topic throughout this book.

It is not my intention to pursue these, or other sociocultural theorizations here. I recognize that I may well already have written either too much or too little. My point is that such work stimulates me. My suggestion is that if one approaches new areas of thinking (in my recent case, sociocultural theory) with the security of practitioner knowledge, and if one is prepared to take the appropriate risks on the periphery of a new community of knowledge or practice (Wenger 1998), one can achieve entry into unfamiliar discussions from which one's praxis can be significantly enriched. This is the experience that I have wanted to exemplify here. I am painfully conscious of how thin my report has been. Let me repeat that while I have here been most interested in the principle and process of theorization, I present a genuine example of a dyadic subject extending a Speaker's SMA in Chapter 8.

Over the course of this section, Narcissus and Icarus fused. I began with my roots in Cooperative Development and ended up spiralling away on my dyadic subject into my Scope for Meaningful Action. Theorizing one's practice carries an in-built risk of making a fool of oneself, of flying too close to a theoretical source of heat that will melt the wax in one's wings while one is peering intently at one's reflective practice. So be it.

I am prepared, at this stage, to let Icarus take the chances that he always will, and to leave Narcissus to continue his terminological reflections alone. A couple of paragraphs ago, I made a claim about clear connections between my then topic and the overall theme of this book. It is time to regroup around this claim. I hope that I have said enough about the theorizing of practice, the T in my CATRA acronym, to allow me to re-engage with my overarching theme of reflexivity.

Reflexivity

In Chapter 5, I suggested that Applying theory could be seen as a form of intervention *into* one's praxis. In this chapter, I have presented Theorizing as the articulation of what it is that one has learnt *from* one's praxis. Together, the A and the T combine to form the hermeneutic process of becoming/being theoretical. You will have recognized the familiar phenomenon by now: a unitary whole that can be seen as divided into two elements that communicate with each other.

It is, as life goes by, not possible to insist on a discrete boundary between the processes of applying theories and theorizing practice. Once a developing teacher, or teacher educator, has engaged with the hermeneutic cycles of discovery and growth in terms of thought and action, Applying and Theorizing interact, they may become seamless along the theoretical dimension. I intend my examples from Cooperative Development to exemplify the kind of fusion that I mean.

On the other hand, the *as-if* categorization can still be useful and the initial trajectories of inside-out and outside-in do remain meaningful. They may be more or less appropriate in different circumstances, and, in any given set of circumstances, they may seem more or less attractive to particular individuals. The task of the teacher educator is to experience both trajectories, to make both available, and not to let 'the theoretical' become divorced in the minds and actions of the teacher-learners with whom he or she works from what they might wish to call 'the practical'. To pre-empt some of the argument of Chapter 8, as the time seems right, here is Rorty (1999:xxv) on the topic:

> There is no deep split between theory and practice, because on a pragmatist view all so-called 'theory' which is not wordplay is already practice.

In the spirit of coherence, consistency and continuity, I hope it is clear that I and the Masters students that I quoted were all seeking to engage in the transformative processes referred to by Johnson above and seeking thereby to achieve congruence.

The professional is personal and, for some of us, as whole people-who-teach, such theorizing of practice is one form of personal, as well as of professional, renewal. This very process of theorizing is at least as important to me as the necessarily interim theories that I formulate to account for the data of my experience. By the same token, it is the theorizing process that I now see as the goal for the teacher-learners with whom I work. It is only in part that I encourage theorizing because it will produce useful personal theories. It is at least equally true that I encourage the production of personal theories because it is the process of theorizing itself that I hold to be useful. When I see this viewpoint explicitly acknowledged and taken up by educators whom I admire (Nunan & Choi 2010:4), the Narcissus in me smiles, of course, and Icarus is encouraged to fly higher.

Working at the boundaries of my understanding of sociocultural theory, I recognize the dangers of trying to soar too high and having the sun melt the credibility in my discourse. I fear the embarrassment, but still want to see a little further. I believe that I encourage such behaviour in my Masters and doctoral students, just as I did when working previously with my undergraduate teacher-learners. In fact, it is of a piece with attitudes I tried to foster as a full-time language teacher – how else to proceed but to risk the embarrassment and try to communicate a little more? Well, there are other ways, of course, and I have consciously tried, on those occasions when I remembered, not to disadvantage those who preferred different paths.

It remains the case, however, that if you study with me, you are less likely to be advised specifically how to teach than you might be with other teacher educators. If we work well together, you will learn how to use Hoey's approach to discourse analysis and you will learn how to be a Speaker and an Understander in Cooperative Development. This is a pretty idiosyncratic mix, one that you would probably not get anywhere else. Should I be spending more of the little time we have together introducing a more standard review of teacher education practices from one of the standard collections? I refer to them, of course, and we engage with them in dedicated critical reading sessions. Nevertheless, I cannot escape the fact that, for better or worse, you have got me, and I do spend some of our time teaching who I am (becoming). The effects of my retrospective reflexivity reach out prospectively to influence your affordances as you reach out to create them.

To round up this chapter, then, I turn to a quotation from the domain of activity theory (Bedny & Karwowski 2004:150ff.) that captures a vision of the self that my Narcissus-persona is hoping to understand better, along with a vision of activity that inspires my Icarus-self to take another risk. I hear echoes of this in the work that I have referred to above and it expresses for me the essential role of *theorizing practice*, the T in my CATRA acronym, as an element of the reflexive development of one's praxis and oneself:

> Through activity a person simultaneously transforms or creates the external world, while obtaining knowledge about that world which, in turn, through reflection, catalyzes change in the subject.

In the next chapter, I pick up a theme that was aired only briefly earlier, in Chapter 3 and again in Chapter 5, where I floated the idea of an *expansive reflexivity*. I do so in conjunction with what I have called the process of *becoming intellectual*.

7

REFLECTING AND BECOMING INTELLECTUAL

Introduction

I skirted the term, *intellectual*, in Chapter 3 and it is now time to return to it. I do so initially in the form of some meta-comment on the placing of this chapter in the book – a task that has caused me a deal of difficulty.

I have organized my five central chapters around a general process of *becoming, being* and *continuing to become*. I have suggested that this process can be seen along five dimensions: *methodological, technical, theoretical, intellectual* and *pragmatic*. Language is necessarily linear, that is one of the ways in which it fashions us. We retain, however, the freedom to choose our own sequences, this being one of the ways in which we fashion ourselves. In a book dedicated to reflexivity, therefore, my sequencing of the above dimensions deserves some comment.

One of the structural tensions in the book is that I am using an autobiographical narrative to build a framework. Once that framework is in place, however, I want you to forget about the linear sequence in which I introduced its elements. All the above dimensions and their potential affordances are there, and interacting, from the beginning. The task for teacher educators is to make them accessible from the beginning (for themselves and for teacher-learners) without insisting on the details of anyone's individual developmental trajectory.

In the sequence thus far, then, I placed *becoming methodological* first (Chapter 4), because of its chronological precedence in my own narrative. There, I focused on classroom activity and the need to unpack, with my undergraduate teachers-to-be, the significance of their apprenticeship of observation, their current experience and their future aspirations. *Becoming technical* came next because of the need to inform action with thought. That is not to say, of course, that the methodological work was thought free. Quite the reverse, it is in becoming methodological that one begins the thinking that takes one beyond merely imitating and into the creative dimensions that follow. My autobiographical sequence involved first learning to apply theory (Chapter 6), then learning to theorize practice (Chapter 7). Then came the realization that a more complete understanding and experience of becoming *theoretical* involves creating praxis bi-directionally through the application of theory *and* the theorization of practice, sometimes to the extent that the two merge in interaction. (How foolish would we be to allow our traditions of adversarial, displacive discourse to force us into unnecessary either/or choices?)

With *becoming intellectual*, however, we run into another structural tension in the book. I am running these various forms of *becoming* in parallel with my CATRA acronym for forms of action in an overall approach to teacher education: Copying, Applying, Theorizing, Reflecting and Acting. *Copying* and *becoming methodological* match comfortably enough, and *Applying* and *Theorizing* work well to capture the two elements of *becoming theoretical*. Between *Reflecting* and *becoming intellectual*, however, I am claiming a different kind of relationship from one of working synonymy. Reflection itself is clearly at the heart of reflective practice, as it is of action research, and this sense of a process whereby we forge meaning from experience and also employ that meaning to help us plan new experience was the celebratory topic of Chapter 2. The picture I want to sketch here, however, requires a broader perspective and takes up the issue of what I have previously (see p.75ff.) called *expansive reflexivity*.

Rather than referring only to a willing engagement with ideas and thinking, I mean *becoming intellectual* to be understood as a process of discerning and articulating connections that may seem to lie outside the obvious needs of the TESOL teacher education process. *Becoming intellectual*, in this sense, involves stepping back from the picture of theorized methodology thus far presented. It opens up a perspective on a broader landscape outside the frame of that picture. It is, in a way, reminiscent of Kegan's image of an individual stepping back from a relationship with another individual in order to take up a relationship to the relationship itself (Chapter 3). In that sense, it suggests what Kegan calls a higher order of consciousness. I want to invoke the social commitment side of Dewey's (1916) educational vision, echoing Giroux's (1988) use of the term, *transformative intellectual*, in the sense of teacher educators who (Aronowitz & Giroux 1985:37):

> take seriously the need to come to grips with those ideological and material aspects of the dominant society that attempt to separate the issues of power and knowledge.

Not that I mean *intellectual* to be understood only in rational, cerebral terms. Once one engages this broader picture, the affordances may be discerned in many forms – the affective, the ethical, the ideological, the spiritual and others.

Narcissus 'steps back' to observe the youth on the riverbank. He sees the water, smells the forest, feels the sun blink out as large wings pass overhead, hears footsteps and the clink of metal on metal, senses danger, becomes aware of an inkling of responsibility. Reflecting-in-action, he wonders where this leaves the still transfixed 'him' that 'he' sees and must now rejoin.

More immediately and less fancifully, the teacher educator as intellectual steps back from situated, professional thought/action praxis in order to see beyond it, while remaining ready to re-engage with that praxis, nourished with hopefully enhanced insight or overview.

As an ESOL teacher educator, I find that I have, over the years, come to speak and to publish (I hope with appropriate humility) on the topics of international conflict, the suppression of linguistic diversity, cultural politics, religion, terrorism, military occupation, state-sponsored murder, and, on two occasions, astonishingly, have even come very close to expressing an opinion on the meaning (or otherwise) of life itself. In the Roots section of this chapter, I ground some of these issues in my earlier TESOL experience – events that I noted at the time, but the significance of which escaped me. Under Wings, I pursue what I have subsequently come to see as the significance of such episodes. To use the terminology of earlier chapters, I hope to discern the affordances for coherence in what I earlier perceived only as incidents. In the final section, I take these patches and sew together a statement of reflexivity that seeks to justify my asking you to read these stories now.

Reflexive memo 7.1: Any attempt to embrace the intellectual in the Anglo-Saxon culture of which I am a product is by definition suspect. The comments by Perkins (2002) reported in Chapter 5 about the anti-theoretical stance of USAmerican ESOL teachers are relevant again here. In other cultures, this may be less of a problem. My approach is clearly open to the charge of narcissism, so I feel a need to remind my readers that I do not accept the illocutionary force of 'charge' in this context. I reassert that it is the rehabilitation of Narcissus that is at issue. Let us entertain the possibility (hinted at in Graves, see Chapter 1) that he stared so long not because he was so delighted by what he saw, but because he wanted to understand the *me* before him, and its relationship to the seeing *I*.

Roots

Politics

For me, the contextualization of TESOL in international politics and conflict was there from the beginning. My first job, as I have already reported, was as a United Nations Association volunteer teacher in Amman, Jordan. This was in September 1969, two years after the Israeli invasion and partial occupation of the country.

Palestinian resistance had emerged in the shape of Fatah, which was launching raids into the occupied territories from the east bank of the River Jordan. Israel retaliated with air and artillery attacks on Jordan. King Hussein deployed the Jordanian army to bring Fatah under control. Before my first full academic year was over, this situation had escalated into the conflict that became known as Black September and I had been evacuated by Red Cross convoy to Beirut and then by the RAF via Cyprus back to England. Once there, I was struck by the effectiveness of the USAmerican- and British-accented performances of the Israeli spokespeople on British television, and by the usually halting, or translated, statements of the Arabs that went down so badly in my home country.

The suppression of linguistic diversity has also been a part of my everyday TESOL experience. During my time in Singapore, between 1978 and 1980, the government there ended Malay-medium and Tamil-medium education at primary level. Primary education was to be carried out in either Mandarin or English. The government will have calculated that any loss in human development for individuals, or for minority communities, would be offset by the advantages gained for the national economy and, arguably, by the economic advantages eventually accruing to the members of those minority communities themselves. The significance of this example to me is that it is a reminder, too, that the broader topic involved here is not English, but power and perceived advantage. It just so happens that in this passing phase of history, English is the language most often involved in such developments. And, of course, this is our passing phase of history, the only one that we will have.

Overt quasi-governmental interference in professional matters has been another feature of my TESOL experience. In 1981, two weeks after I had taken up a position at an overseas university's School of Education, we were visited by a representative of the British Overseas Development Administration, which was funding my post. With the whole English department gathered, including three full professors and the Head of School from the French section, our visitor asked me what I had achieved so far. As I started to describe my teaching duties and plans, he interrupted with a wave of the arm and said, '*You are not here to teach students, you are here to train these people.*' It cost me a lot of energy to make up for the goodwill lost in those few seconds. More insidious, however, was that I was later told that the section of my report detailing this incident was removed because our ODA visitor was a senior figure and it would be unwise to jeopardize further funding unnecessarily.

At a later date, I submitted a short piece to *ELT Journal* raising concerns about the Iranian government's incitement – by way of a religious ruling (fatwa) – to murder the author, Salman Rushdie, an incitement which had already led to the actual murder of his Japanese translator, Professor Hitashi Igorashi. I wondered how, in a values-based field such as TESOL teacher education, one could work with people who applauded such actions as part of their values base. As I learned from later correspondence, publication of the piece was objected to by the British

Council representative on the *ELTJ* editorial panel, on the grounds that the public prestige of the British Council and Oxford University Press might be put at risk. She represented the position that such a question might only be raised, '*if a piece of similar length in favour of the fatwa is also published*'. I commented subsequently (Edge 1994b:19):

> This valuing of balance with regard to the killing or not killing of writers may be thought appropriate as BC/OUP editorial policy, but I cannot find in it values coherent with my work in teaching and teacher education.

On being informed that the *ELTJ* Board of Management and the Editorial Advisory Panel wished to keep discussion to '*pedagogic and professional matters*', I knew that our understandings of pedagogy and profession were no longer shared.

Ideology

In the high and heady days of full-blown communicative language teaching, I lacked enough of a conceptual framework in the field of cultural politics to help me analyse the unease that I felt about the methodological tsunami that was washing around the globe and which I had been riding for most of my working life. I do, however, remember asking a question (Edge 1987:308) that received no response at the time, but never really went away:

> ELT has pressed on as if a characterization of communication as found in (more or less) 'the Western world' is the basis of communicative learning theory. But not even the massively ethnocentric world of ELT as represented by publishers, language schools and academics in the dominant areas of the United States and Britain would probably go so far as to say that this mode of communication just happens to coincide with the mode by which human beings learn languages. Does communicative language learning theory, therefore, suggest that to learn the language of the Tzeltal, one communicates like a Tzeltali and neither asks nor answers direct questions (Hymes 1972:16)? In order to learn the Burundi language referred to by Albert (1972, cited in Coulthard 1986:63), perhaps, learners would speak in order of seniority. The claim, in this case, could be that it is the individual features of use of each language which hold the key to the learning of that language. Is this the claim? In the forward rush of English teaching, I do not know that the claim has ever been clarified.

In the same piece (ibid.:308ff.), I now see myself moving closer to the kind of formulation that I was seeking:

> a lot of the methodological advances made under the heading of communicative language teaching have involved task-based, problem-solving

activities in which learners are encouraged to identify a problem, seek out relevant information, and cooperate with their peers in order to reach consensus on an appropriate solution to the problem. This is clearly not a value-free mode of behaviour, but one which is valued in certain geopolitical situations at a particular period of history. Not to put too fine a point on it, it is the sort of behaviour which would get you locked up in a lot of places. But this hasn't stopped a lot of people touring the globe and selling such methods as the basis of communicative language learning.

Are we convinced that learners will best learn a foreign language by behaving in ways that are both alien to their educational culture and pro-scribed in their everyday life? Why . . . isn't the astonishing memory capacity of some Arab learners being more usefully harnessed to their language-learning purposes? Because memory has so little to do with language learning?

Native-speakerism

During a brief visit to Japan in the 1980s, I became involved in discussions regarding the respective roles of the Japanese teachers of English and the (overwhelmingly young, inexperienced, unqualified) native speakers of the major dialects of English who were being brought into the country in large numbers as part of the government's Japan Exchange and Teaching (JET) programme. To a large extent, the Japanese took care of the formal teaching, while the foreign assistants provided spoken models of the language. My thinking at the time (Edge 1988b:155) was:

> When I stood in front of a class of Turkish schoolchildren, there was clearly only a very restricted sense in which I could act as a model for them in social, cultural, emotional or experiential terms, with regard either to their past or their future. The person who could act as such a model would be a Turkish teacher; and, if we believe that reference to the social, cultural and emotional experiences, awareness and aspirations of our pupils is important in learning, then this is the ideal model.

I was told that I was confusing *learning* model with *linguistic* model. I regret to report that I was not quick enough at the time to say that the embodiment of language and learning was not best understood as a confusion. Neither then (nor now), however, did I mean to criticize either group of teachers engaged in a very challenging operation.

Racism

Racism in its most cheerfully open form illuminated my brief experience as a would-be textbook writer during the early 1990s. I was advised by a representative of a major British publisher not to include dark-skinned characters in the course-book I was working on because the Japanese wouldn't buy it. This was not to be understood as racist, heaven forfend, merely market realism. There would surely be no point or purpose in wanting to write, or publish, a book that no one in a key market would want to buy. Perhaps fortunately, it turned out that textbook writing was really not my forte.

Religion

As late as the 1980s, I was completely naïve about the relationship between TESOL and Christian missionary work. Turkish students would tell me that they knew of schools where English teaching was merely a front for proselytizing and I would tell them that they should not believe such tales. A brief published mention of this phenomenon (Edge 1996b), in which I assumed that all people of goodwill would agree with my 'straightforward' position on the unacceptability of sailing under one flag while serving another master, made clear that the intermingling of TESOL and Christian evangelism was established beyond my wildest . . . dreams. The fact that simply raising the issue would be seen as aggressively provocative by some came as a huge surprise to me.

Looking back on these themes, however, how is one not to raise questions once one has become aware of them? Each seems to demand a place in the discourse of TESOL professionals. Politics: is it true that the understanding of internationally volatile situations is affected by an audience's expectation to be addressed in polished English? Ideology: is it true that our very teaching methods are a form of cultural imposition? Native-speakerism: is it true that the accident of one's birth and mother tongue(s) will have a decisive effect on the kind of employment one might apply for, or the rates of pay or job security one might expect? Racism: is it true that selling TESOL sometimes follows racist principles? Religion: if some colleagues are engaged in covert proselytizing, so might anyone be. Is this acceptable? Do you mind falling under suspicion?

You may dispute my examples. You may regret the absence of any mention of gender, sexual orientation or ecology. So do I. My point, however, is that such issues, and time for reflection on them, deserve embedding in the core TESOL teacher education curriculum. They are central in terms of the intellectual work to be done and necessary in terms of the pragmatics of what that intellectual work brings home. These are the directions in which I now wish to turn, holding to the themes that have impacted on me.

Wings

One might argue that the requirement for intellectual work has nothing specifically to do with TESOL or teacher education. Any responsible citizen might want to develop views on such issues as those evoked above, and might wish to live a more aware life through so doing. Absolutely right. And because this desire to live an aware life is the prerogative of any responsible citizen, it is equally available to the TESOL professional. As with everything I have written in this book, none of this is essential, it is all available. What I have further suggested, however, based on a self-regarding review of my working life so far, is that these issues of international relations, language suppression, censorship, religion, cultural politics, native-speakerism and racism are not simply random topics on which one may wish to have an opinion. They have always been actively present as influential elements of the context in which TESOL professionals operate. In a way somewhat bathetically reminiscent of the role of furniture in a classroom (Edge & Garton 2009:71), if you do not consciously exercise control over it, you might not notice that it is ever so subtly exercising control over you. In this section, then, I want to fill out a little my discussion of where TESOL thinking has flown in the meantime, as it relates to those working experiences recorded above.

The ur-text with regard to formulating the shadow-side of TESOL was Phillipson (1992), now updated as Phillipson (2009a). This was followed soon afterwards by Pennycook (1994), whose (1989) article in *TESOL Quarterly* had given fair warning of what was to come. I shall indicate further readings as I continue, but a review of the literature is not my aim. My purpose is to demonstrate the meaning that I want to give to the expression *becoming intellectual* as it relates to reflexivity in teacher education.

Politics

In the briefest terms, we know that before we TESOL practitioners start to ask our questions about students' needs, larger forces have brought about situations which create those needs. Those forces are not neutral, but the product of other people's decisions and actions over time. We know that a fundamental reason why English is in such great demand around the world is the historical transition that saw one English-using empire of military and economic dominance (the British) succeeded by another (the USAmerican).

A personal example of the contradictions and dilemmas of such dominance now shoulders its way forward. In the mid-1990s, just after the Soviet Union had fallen apart and the states of central and eastern Europe were establishing their independence, the publisher of one of my books phoned to say that they were going to make a special effort to launch TESOL methodology texts in that part of the world because of the complete lack of up-to-date publications in the area. Teachers were crying out for them and they would be sold at reduced prices so as to make them available to as many people as possible. She was phoning to tell me that my book had been selected as one of those to be used in the launch. I was very pleased and a little proud.

A year later, I made a brief working visit to Hungary. An economics lecturer who was showing me her city said:

Even those of us who did not think ourselves naïve have been taken aback by the way the West has behaved. The industries that were more or less functioning have been bought up and some then simply closed down. Those that have retained some independence, such as our publishing houses, are having to struggle in the face of a glossy Western product that is being dumped here at unrealistic prices in order to drive our publishers out of business.

I felt less good, and this is one reason why I have come to feel that the following position is no longer tenable, although it is taken from a book (Holliday 1994) which also demonstrates a great deal of intercultural concern, as well as professional expertise. Holliday (ibid.:216) presents the whole TESOL endeavour as a negotiable commodity in a free market:

'Making friends and influencing people' seems to me perfectly respectable as long as the trade is clear and meaningful. The concern with cultural or linguistic imperialism is surely reduced in the event of fair and meaningful trading.

As with so many statements that are made with reference to free markets and fair trade, a more careful analysis tends to lead to the conclusion that international markets are powerfully controlled, and international trade deeply and structurally unfair. This is a view that Holliday (2005, and see Chapter 9 of this book) has more recently come to share and to develop, but the argument lingers on.

None of this is to say that people are overtly forced to learn English. There is no need for such force. People (individuals and countries) choose to learn English in their own best interests.

But the use of such expressions as '*choose*' and '*in their own best interests*' is not simply the same as saying '*because that is their unconstrained wish*'. This is where the concept of *hegemony* comes into play, in the sense of an ascendancy which people accept and live with, and thereby actually support with their own actions. That is to say, people accept the need for English, given the current state of power relationships in the world, and, by learning English, they support the state of affairs in which a knowledge of English is essential.

In this light, and in the context of Iraq since 2003, one can make out the possibly legitimate perception of the TESOL professional as a kind of '*imperial trooper*' (Edge 2003b) – someone who appears after the fighting is over in order to help residents of the occupied country adjust to the way things are going to be from now on, someone to open up new opportunities for them under the new dispensation and educate them '*in their own best interests*'. (In essence, the metaphor of the imperial trooper might stand for TESOL's role in the whole globalization of capitalism phenomenon, but for present purposes we can stay with the more literal interpretation.) In 2006, I published a collection of papers entitled,

(Re)Locating TESOL in an Age of Empire (Edge 2006b). What concerns me here and now is the way in which the collection was reviewed by Waters (2008) and Phillipson (2009b). In brief, Phillipson, a seminal writer in the linguistic imperialism tradition, reviewed the book very positively, focusing his main critique on two contributions. In one of these, Brumfit (2006:47) argues in cautionary fashion that:

> Sympathy of the strong for the weak can form the foundation for a new imperialism: the powerful tell the weak what to feel and what to aspire to.

In the other chapter in question, Woods (2006:208) argues in favour of the teaching of English for military purposes, on the grounds that:

> English is both needed and justified for effective inter-operability when troops from many different countries are working together to keep the peace or to provide humanitarian assistance following a natural or man-made disaster.

Waters, who maintains (2007a) that a distorted sense of *'political correctness'* has become the defining *'spirit of the times'* in TESOL, reviewed the book overall negatively (Waters 2008), singling out for praise exactly the two chapters referred to above.

This should serve to remind us that it is not only our fundamental professional situation that is intensely political, so is our discourse about that situation (which comprises a reflexive part of it): frequently ideologically motivated, shaped by adversarial position-taking and committed to persuasion. This world of discourse, taken for granted by those of us who shape it and are shaped by it, has its own rules of operation. As legitimate inhabitants, we may work to exploit those generic expectations and to develop them. As whole-people-who-educate-teachers, however, we have a more complex set of responsibilities.

First, we should not feel obliged to represent ourselves as anything other than who we are. Indeed, I believe that we should be as transparent as we can be in representing ourselves exactly as we are. Second, however, the greater success we can achieve in stepping back from the positions that we take up in order to be aware of what they are, and to illuminate them by non-dismissive contrast to others, the more likely we are in our teacher education roles to live up to the challenge posed by Menand (2001:431) in his survey of the American Pragmatic tradition:

> We do not permit the free expression of ideas because some individual may have the right one. No individual alone can have the right one. We permit free expression because we need the resources of the whole group to get us the ideas we need. Thinking is a social activity. I tolerate your thought

because it is a part of my thought – even when my thought defines itself in opposition to yours.

When I take up this reflexive stance with regard to my own ideological positions, I know that I have to inform my teacher-learners about Brumfit's reservations just as much as I do about Phillipson's accusations. And out of the possibilities created, I also, in another twist of reflexivity, have to demonstrate that these deliberations matter in terms of how I intend to act.

Ideology

This is perhaps the area that raises the most immediate questions about the connections between our own everyday actions as teachers and teacher educators and the larger contexts in which we work.

The continuing immediacy of these issues in terms of classroom behaviour was brought home to me in the context of an MA TESOL Methodology module that I was teaching while writing the first draft of this chapter in October 2009. In the discussion space of the virtual learning environment, one course participant (permissions have been granted) posted the following:

> One problem that I have always encountered throughout my teaching of grammar and its effect on language acquisition is that students are over-sensitive towards peer correction. Therefore, they focus on the grammatical knowledge which they gain consciously and which often leads to the students being inhibited and reluctant to express themselves.

Very soon, a response came in from South America:

> I see an interesting point there. However, I would like to say that one very positive aspect from peer correction is the fact that students are actually learning from each other. Nevertheless, I do know that students' feelings get hurt when peer correction is not well guided. What you can do is establish criteria for peer feedback and that way you can have constructive and meaningful assessment sessions among students themselves. We should train our students into a more cooperative learning atmosphere. We should tell them from the very beginning how to deal with partners' mistakes and how to approach possible corrections.

More suggestions about how to handle peer correction came in from China, Japan, Korea, Russia, Thailand, Turkey and Vietnam. To give the flavour, here is just one of them:

> I was just thinking whether sometimes anonymous peer feedback would be a solution, at least to help students get used to it and see the benefits.

> Similar to when we collect language used by students when monitoring them and then elicit correction from students without telling them who said or wrote that.

At this point, I intervened in order to link this exchange to our earlier, general discussion of brief articles by Bax (2003a, 2003b) on the importance of prioritizing context, and Harmer (2003) on the countervailing importance of methodology. During that earlier period, we had also familiarized ourselves with Kumaravadivelu's (2001) parameters of *particularity, practicality* and *possibility*. My intervention referred explicitly to the last participant contribution above, but related to them all:

> Notice that your potential 'solution' follows a decision that the *possibility* of methodology is more important than the *particularity* of context. I am not saying that I disagree.

This drew the following reflection:

> Hm, interesting that you should say that, Julian. It made me pause and think

> I thought I was taking the context into consideration and therefore suggesting ideas (methods if you want) that might work within this context. Reading what I have written, I can see what you are getting at. I suggest ways that will make the students accept peer feedback because I believe that this methodology is beneficial. It might, of course, be the case that in some contexts peer feedback is not appropriate/beneficial at all.

The issue at stake here is the one that I flagged up in Chapters 4 and 5, with reference to Pennycook's (1994:152) linking of the '*promotion of particular teaching approaches*' to the '*promotion of particular forms of culture*'.

The abiding question for the teacher educator is: to what extent are we actually arguing about how to introduce ways of language teaching that we know to be universally effective and to which learners must therefore somehow be introduced, or adapted? To push this a little further, to what extent are we proceeding on the unspoken assumption that learning anywhere would be more effective if all societies were just a little more like us, where 'us' represents an overlapping alliance of Westerners, Whites, Anglo-Saxons, Europeans, or wherever one decides to draw the group borders? In essence, whoever is in power. Once one reaches this question, it appears not to be so very different from the question as to why, at the time of writing, so many Westerners, Whites, Anglo-Saxons, Europeans (or however one decides to draw the group borders) are killing and being killed by Afghanis in Afghanistan. Is there (not) perhaps, mixed in with the overt and covert geopolitical truths, an unspoken assumption that Afghanis would be better off if they were just a little more like 'us'? And thus, in their own best interests, we proceed.

You may find this outrageous. Rajagopalan (1999:201) sets out explicitly, '*to argue against this currently fashionable trend, marked, in my view, by a certain misguided spirit of penitential self-flagellation*'. Waters (2007a, 2007b, 2009), as I have already mentioned, refers to 'political correctness' run wild. I try to stay level-headed, and still I cannot help but wonder at the way in which Hedge (2000:110), for example, opens her chapter on the teaching of vocabulary with the following, very well-known, quotation from Lewis Carroll's *Through the Looking Glass*:

> 'When *I* use a word,' Humpty Dumpty said, in a rather scornful tone, 'it means just what I choose it to mean, neither more nor less.'

> 'The question is,' said Alice, 'whether you *can* make words mean so many different things.'

I rather think that this might be seen as a very partial quotation. As many people know, the exchange continues with the following line, which is arguably the point of the exchange:

> 'The question is,' said Humpty Dumpty, 'which is to be master – that's all.'

In similar ways, issues of power and dominance and liberation run all through language and communication, whether we are talking about the sound of your accent, the look of your handwriting, the accuracy of your grammar, the books that you read, or the connotations of the words that you choose to use. We may decide not to focus on these issues in class, but we should not forget that they are lurking in the background of just about any lesson that we teach, especially if we choose to describe our teaching as 'communicative', and we mean by that something more than the classroom-bound performance of teacher-designed tasks.

I find it easy to agree with Rajagopalan's (1999:205) assertion that, '*it is in the nature of human languages, all of them, to be riven by power inequalities*', and still to feel that TESOL tends to turn away from these aspects of communication rather too easily and comfortably. And when we do face up to them, there are no easy answers. At the procedural level, the importance of reflexivity in this aspect of teacher education is never to lose sight of the pedagogic interplay between the particular and the possible, the established tradition and the new idea; never to presume that one is simply better or worse than the other, and never to think that there is a formulaic relationship to be plotted in one context that can be transferred elsewhere.

At the ideological level, teacher-learners have to be brought to consider the different interpretations available of the varying factors that motivate and underpin the teaching procedures on offer. This would have to include, to take a counterexample, interrogating the underpinning of a methodology based on repetition and rote learning, controlled and monitored by a teacher whose authority may not be questioned. So much of what passes for principles of learning and teaching bears a striking resemblance to the philosophical traditions and social structures favoured by those in control.

For the teacher educator, congruence has to be established, and continuity offered, anew, in each situation, on each occasion.

Native-speakerism

With regard to its own generic dichotomies, as distinct from TESOL-specific manifestations of broader issues such as race and politics, TESOL is divided more than anything else by the native speaker/non-native speaker distinction between its practitioners, for which the best-known acronyms are probably NEST (Native English Speaking Teacher) and NNEST (Non-Native English Speaking Teacher). Phillipson (1992) discusses what he calls the native-speaker fallacy – at its simplest, that the native speaker is the better teacher – and different aspects of this discussion can be followed through Medgyes (1992, 1994), Leung et. al (1997), Braine (1999), Cook (1999, 2000), Liu (1999), Milambiling (2000), Lazaraton (2003), Matsuda (2003), Kamhi-Stein (2004), Nemtchinova (2005), Llurda (2006) and Park (2006).

I should like to highlight a number of points that stand out for me as relevant to our theme.

First, while any sensible commentator will point out that boundaries between groups of people referred to as native or non-native speakers are either deliberate theoretical fictions (Paikeday 1985), or extremely nebulous descriptions (Rampton 1990), the so-called distinction does hang around and we are all constantly called on to respond to it.

Second, this area gave me an excellent learning experience with regard to listening to the inside story. I used to argue against the use of NNEST as an acronym, because I saw it as wrong to define people in negative terms, i.e. as a *non*-native. From Matsuda (2003:15) I learned the following:

> If anything needs to be changed, I do not think it is the term, *nonnative*. Rather, the assumption that *native* is somehow more positive than *nonnative* needs to be challenged.

The point is well taken, even if I do find his counter-examples of 'non-toxic' and 'non-smoker' a little too aggressive for comfort. I have also learned from him to think in this way. Being now in my sixties, I get annoyed when people tell me that I am not old. Of course I am old. If anything needs to be changed, it is the assumption that a perfectly reasonable descriptive term such as *old* needs to be interpreted in a negative way. And so professional learning has reached out to increase coherence with my private life.

Third, it is all too easy for a facile in-TESOL discourse to centre around prototypical representations of well-trained, ambilingual, professional NNESTs versus monolingual, untrained and linguistically naïve NESTs, with a self-congratulatory expression of preference for the former being the standard outcome. These characters do exist, but so do many other combinations of linguistic, pedagogic and intercultural ability.

Fourth, it is argued that NNESTs and NESTs bring different strengths to the profession, all of which are needed. (See Medgyes (1992) for a brief encapsulation of this position.) Interesting, then, is the question as to whether these different strengths should be seen as implying that NESTs and NNESTs would be well advised to pursue different styles of teaching in order to teach at their best. I do not know that this question has been properly addressed in the literature.

Fifth, and extending the above point, while I do not question the argument that we should judge speakers and teachers of a language by their abilities rather than their background, we have to avoid a situation where we do not address directly and as effectively as we can those situations in which the *de facto* teachers of English in a given setting are indeed operating at a low level of linguistic ability. Apart from trying to help people improve their standard of English, are there ways of teaching that are particularly suitable for such teachers? Would the development of such distinct ways simply confirm a perception of them as second-class citizens in our community? We have to take care that our insistence on recognizing the dazzling linguistic abilities of some NNESTs does not embarrass us out of considering such issues, which have nothing to do with the classic NNEST/NEST set-piece arguments.

Sixth, the most pernicious effects of the NEST/NNEST distinction are not to be found justified in our professional literature, but embedded in the economic realities and public prejudices of TESOL provision. To address those prejudices and realities, TESOL professionals need to develop new ways of addressing that audience of politicians, school owners, administrators, mature students and parents who combine in their ignorance to disadvantage NNESTs worldwide.

Finally, and sadly, below the radar of awareness, native-speakerism continues unabated among well-meaning TESOL professionals. On an annual basis, I meet experienced, well-travelled ESOL teachers at the beginning of an MA programme for whom the generic superiority of the native speaker has never been questioned. This acceptance operates on both sides of that fuzzy border. One British teacher told me recently, after a session on the topic, '*I've never been so embarrassed as when I looked round that [seminar] room again and realized what I had inadvertently been saying about my classmates.*' I remember also an Indonesian teacher saying to me, with a fierce glint in her eye, '*I never thought of that before: all this English teaching – it doesn't depend on you. It depends on us!*' Among ourselves as TESOL professionals, at least, we need to work constantly to improve levels of awareness and self-awareness.

The reflexivity of the matter lies in our ability to discern where division is potentially useful to the development of the whole, where it is not, and in our capacity to act on those decisions.

Racism

It is possible to distinguish the NEST/NNEST discussion from that of racism, as I am doing here, but that is not necessarily the same as saying that one can always keep them apart. Holliday & Aboshiha (2009), for instance, argue that beneath the skin, if you will excuse the metaphor, the two may share more genetic code than we would like to admit.

Curtis (2006) recounts a telling experience of his early days as a lecturer in Hong Kong. New students who had signed up for classes with Dr Andrew Curtis would enter his lectures, see him, assume that they were in the wrong room, exit, and quietly creep back later, having ascertained that, yes, despite their expectations of what he should look like, the lecturer was indeed Dr Andrew Curtis. As he comments:

> Every day during my five years in Hong Kong, I encountered responses to me based on my appearance. Some of these responses were positive, some were negative, but the vast majority were simply incorrect.
>
> *Curtis 2006:21*

Javier (2010) also reports the difficulties of establishing her acceptability to students as their English teacher, while belonging to what she terms a '*visible ethnic minority*'. Put simply, being Canadian, looking Filipino and teaching English in China brings its own complications. Her students needed to see an embodiment of their mental schema of a native speaker of English in order to be able to hear the English that they required. This, however, left Javier needing to emphasize her native-speaker status in order to make her teaching maximally acceptable to her students – a position which she found ideologically dissonant with her thinking on NEST/NNEST distinctions, as discussed above. Here again, although in different terms, questions of native-speakerism and racism overlap.

From the obverse perspective of the effects on students of being stereotyped, Kubota (2002:90) argues that racism is '*woven into the very fabric of our institutions*' and that classically liberal attempts to bypass such racism in effect only turn a blind eye to its continuing influence. The exchange of comments (and accusations) between Atkinson (2002) and Kubota (2002) reveals how fundamental differences can be and how personal academic discourse can become. Kubota (2006) and Kubota & Lin (2009) provide a further range of treatments of the theme of racism in TESOL.

To experience oneself as unseen, or unseeable. To be manipulated into inimical positions because of how one is (not) seen. To see the racism in the behaviour of people who deny it. To be accused of racism by people who do not understand one's behaviour. These issues are indeed woven into the fabric of TESOL experience. If we do not each, individually, feel their impact, still we are called on to raise our awareness of them by reading reports such as those cited above and by establishing the themes with teacher-learners, who may well have stories of their own to tell.

TESOL, one of the most thoroughgoingly globalizing operations of our time, cannot afford not to explore its potential for racism. The reflexivity of the matter lies in our readiness not to emerge from such explorations unchanged.

Religion

I recognize that this is another very sensitive area. I also wonder sometimes if it was not a mistake of mine to publish comments on religion in TESOL in the same article that I used to make political and ideological points (Edge 2003b). However, I did, provoked initially by reports such as the following (Yeoman 2002) in the era of the explicitly evangelical George W. Bush presidency of the USA:

> Love notes that before he went to western Indonesia to proselytize among Sundanese Muslims, he went back to school and earned his credentials to become an English instructor. That way, he says, he had an excuse to be in the country. 'I could look someone in the eye and say, "I am an English teacher," ' he explains. 'I have a degree and I'm here to teach.' That, he says, is the model for winning converts in the Islamic world: Find another pretext to be in the country. Build friendships with the locals. Once you've developed trust, then it's time to try to gain new believers. But don't reveal your true purpose too early.

For those motivated to pursue the immediate consequences, then the initially relevant references are Edge (2004), Griffith (2004) and Purgason (2004). Since then, a broad collection of views has been gathered together in Wong & Canagarajah (2009). There are strong statements of English teaching as a form of Christian mission, exemplified by Robison (2009:263):

> To be a Christian is to believe that the greatest good achievable is to know God through Jesus Christ; and Christian teachers who are genuinely concerned for their students lack integrity if they do not desire that they also come to know God.

Whether this work is done overtly or covertly, Robison finds, is best decided according to circumstance, where '*justifiable prudence*' (ibid.:256) may recommend the latter.

Other perspectives include Pennycook's (2009: 60) almost despairing post-modern lament:

> to have to engage with ancient organized religions in their new incarnations, with claims to the existence of an almighty being still, after so much, seems such a desperate regression.

There has also been a specifically religious response to the perceived dangers of evangelical TESOL in the development of TESOL Islamia, whose website can be accessed at: http: www.tesolislamia.org

Browsing the website in November 2007, I was struck by the following:

What is the ruling on learning English nowadays?

Praise be to Allah. People vary with regard to how much they need to learn English. The Prophet (peace and blessings of Allah be upon him) commanded Zayd Ibn Thaabit to learn the language of the Jews. Zayd Ibn Thaabit is reported to have said: 'The Messenger of Allah (peace and blessings of Allah be upon him) commanded me to learn the language and writing of the Jews for him. He said, "*By Allah, I do not trust a Jew to write my letters for me.*" So I learned it, and no more than half a month passed by before I had mastered it. I used to write it for him if he wanted a letter written, and I would read it for him if a letter was sent to him.' Learning English is but a means; if you need it you may learn it, and if you do not need it then do not waste your time with it.

It is a fundamental tenet of research that data do not speak for themselves; they have to be interpreted. It is not clear to me how the idea of a fatwa (religious ruling) on permission to learn a language is meant to function, or how the example given is meant to be helpful, but I have not myself pursued these questions with those running the website and I refrain from interpreting these data at the present time. I leave those tasks to readers motivated by the prospect.

In the same way that a discussion of power and language in general has no unchanging connection to English, my reference to the two religions above is intended only to exemplify the more general phenomenon of spiritual certainty. Among such general phenomena, of course, there exists space aplenty for individual variation. Karmani (2005), for example, offers a distinction perspective on what is afoot here. Where reflexivity enters into teacher education is in the need to raise our awareness of these attitudes and motivations moving among our larger community, along with the need to check whether, the more we know, we feel an obligation to alert our teacher-learners to what is going on.

All across these issues of race, religion and politics, my point has been that they demand our intellectual and ethical engagement while we struggle to determine their pragmatic significance. This engagement is essential because of the role of English in the contemporary world (Kumaravadivelu 2006a) and because of what we English language teachers see ourselves as contributing to that world (Brumfit 2006). As we build the English-language bridges and barriers, the effects of which we sometimes disapprove of, and as we reflexively become the adaptive population of the environments that we create, Reflection, the R in my CATRA acronym, insists on its place.

Reflexivity

I have a precarious sense of error and of empowerment, a sense of having arrived at where I wanted to be by a path that I had not seen. I set out in this chapter with some concern that what I meant by *becoming intellectual* might '*lie outside the obvious needs of the teacher education process*' (see p.99). I did so, however, also in agreement with Denzin's (2009:39) assertion regarding the obligation of scholars, which I interpret as being equally relevant to teacher educators:

> I believe scholars have an obligation to write their way into their historical moments. The failure to do so makes us complicit with the histories that too often go on behind our backs.

For some of us, there is a more literal interpretation of this obligation, as the role of the *public intellectual* beckons. Kumaravadivelu (personal correspondence) puts it like this:

> A 'public intellectual', as I understand the term, specifically refers to the professoriate who have been successful in communicating with the general public, as against, narrowly, to faculty/students. His/her role is to communicate with the public in a way that they can understand complex issues.

Kumaravadivelu himself takes on this role on an occasional basis, publishing pieces for his regional community in Southern California, and providing perspectives of which many readers of the *San Jose Mercury News* would not otherwise be aware. I know of pieces by him, for example, on religious tolerance (2003b), the USAmerican ban on Al-Jazeera television broadcasts (2006b) and Californian school reform (Kumaravadivelu & Krishnaswamy 2009).

For those of us, however, who remain more circumscribed by the world of teacher education, there is also a sense in which there are historical moments with which we develop a relationship of mutual shaping. I have indicated some of mine above. And as this realization sinks in (not for the first time), my sense of redirected effort comes with it. What can I have meant by saying of intellectual work '*even when it exceeded the boundaries of demonstrable relevance to praxis*', above? Perhaps the key to my problem lies in the word, *relevance*. By seeking relevance, I assumed a separation that does not exist. Once again, we are in a territory where it can sometimes be useful to indicate the possibility of category boundaries, such as personal/professional, and sometimes to use them, but where one should not be too surprised if those boundaries dissolve. This is the case here. There is no need to demonstrate the relevance to teacher education of the broader intellectual work – the 'reflecting', as I have used the term specifically in this chapter – done by the teacher educator, because the reflecting itself, when done by the teacher educator and by teacher-learners, becomes by definition an integral and inescapable part of teacher education. The extent to which we engage with issues such as those touched on in this chapter, the ways in which our engagement impacts our praxis, the ways in which our praxis impacts our context and elements of that context respond – this is the stuff of expansive reflexivity.

As a teacher educator, I allow my intellect to roam free in terms of what it perceives, and thus to make possible the affordances that it might discern. As in the terms of Zohar's (1991:183) concept of the quantum self, we '*pluck reality from multiple possibility*', and, through self-reflection and articulation, use our freedom at the service of our creativity. This is absolutely fundamental to the overall growth of the teacher educator. Just as professional development for teachers must take account of the whole-person-who-teaches, so it is with teacher educators. One cannot divorce the intellectual from the praxis of the whole-person educator. I should have seen that immediately. Fundamentally a pragmatist, I necessarily depend on my intellect in order to see what it brings to the table; and what it brings to the table, I will use.

Reflexive memo 7.2: I feel now, immediately now, as I write, a powerful sensation of the empowerment that I mentioned a moment ago, arising from the realization of error. And in this moment, I experience a sense of belonging to a tradition that sees being proved wrong not as a defeat, but as the beginning of the next step forward. And then comes a direct link to the sense of '*working class intellectual*' that I invoked in Chapter 3. And at the same time an echo of Leonard Cohen's (1992) advice to recognize that the cracks that we discover in all things are also ways in which light can enter.

In opening this chapter, I wrote of the difficulty of sequencing what I had to say about becoming methodological, technical, theoretical, intellectual and pragmatic. At times, I thought that *becoming intellectual* needed to go last, because of the requirement that it sometimes exceed the pragmatic. I am now satisfied that this was wrong. In my present state of understanding, *becoming pragmatic* is the larger goal, and the intellectual serves it, as do the methodological and the bi-directional theoretical processes that we have looked at in previous chapters.

In that sense, I see this process of *becoming intellectual* as conforming still to my adaptation of Rorty's guiding axiom, that if something has nothing to do with practice, then we do not need it in our theorizing. The intellectual element of this '*having to do with practice*' lies in seeing connections, making links, articulating the affordances that the whole-person discerns and through which one tries to move oneself towards a sense of congruence in living and working.

To be concrete, if crudely so, what role does it play in your selection of a candidate for a teaching post if that person:

- Is ethnically different to you?
- Has an accent noticeably different to yours?
- Explicitly states a sexual orientation different to yours?
- Declares themself to be motivated to share a religious faith different to yours?
- All of the above?

Are your responses unchangeable? Under any circumstances? How relevant is Carr & Kemmis's (1986:43) insistence on the centrality of *reflexivity* to the very nature of social and professional life?

> Social life is reflexive; that is, it has the capacity to change as our knowledge and thinking changes, thus creating new forms of social life which can, in their turn, be reconstructed. Social and educational theories must cope with this reflexivity: the 'truths' they tell must be seen as located in particular historical circumstances and social contexts, and as answers to particular questions asked in the intellectual context of a particular time.

Here is where becoming intellectual sits in my sequence of becoming methodological, technical, theoretical, intellectual and pragmatic. I should never have doubted.

Throughout this discussion, I have mapped a role for reflexivity in our ability to become aware of our adaptation to the environments that we create – what we are prepared to undergo and what we insist on trying. It would be self-defeating for me to suggest what anyone's stance should be on the large-scale issues raised in this chapter. That was never my purpose, although I have not backed away from indicating positions of my own.

My purpose has been to insist that teacher education must raise these issues. My purpose is to argue that teacher educators can benefit from awareness-checks regarding their own attitudes and actions along lines of consistency and coherence. I argue also that a part of their responsibility is to engage on these issues with their teacher-learners, thus offering continuity with regard to their development in the profession.

I have undertaken to continue this progression of *becomings* with a chapter on *becoming pragmatic*. I do so in the light of the quotation from Menand (2001) above regarding the need to listen to as many perspectives as possible. This credo of acceptance will always leave us with the question of how to respond to those who see the credo itself as a sign of weakness, as an opportunity to claim space for their conviction that they have the only true answer, the correct way, the best method, and who discern an affordance for its imposition. We shall have to deal with that separately.

8

ACTING AND
BECOMING PRAGMATIC

Introduction

Once again, I need to begin the chapter with a consideration of my title. *Acting*, I hope it is clear, has here nothing to do with drama or simulation. I mean, *being involved in action*. We are constantly called upon to act. Inevitably underinformed, only sometimes mindful of the risks involved, lacking in certainty or over-confident, optimistic or fearful, sticking with routine, determined to experiment, or relying on our ability to improvise, frequently oblivious of unintended consequences, we act. While theory strives for simplicity, action remains resolutely complex, multi-dimensional, and embodies the beating heart of our learning.

OK, as far as '*beating heart*' is concerned, you can take it or leave it, but whether we consider reflective practice, action research, sociocultural theory, craft, copying, applying or praxis itself, there is no meaning without action, and, with action, meaning is inevitable. These are the meanings that count, the meanings that we express through our actions. Action is the medium through which we demonstrate what we have learnt and through which – mediated by reflection – we continue to learn. In teacher education specifically, our actions are the test of our coherence, our consistency and of the provision that we make for continuity – of our overall congruence.

From its occurrence in the title of this chapter, and especially after my deliberations in the last chapter, one would have to conclude that I am placing *becoming pragmatic* in some way higher in my implied hierarchy of professional development than my other *becomings*. One would be correct.

In its everyday use, I know, *pragmatic* means something like down-to-earth, matter-of-fact, practical (Collins *Thesaurus* 1984:516), something apparently divorced from theory. Some sample lines from the Cobuild Concordancer create a similar impression:

- . . . and so I, everything to me is real practical and real pragmatic and real now.
- . . . as this year of nineteen-ninety-six unfolds, it is the very pragmatic, practical, materialistic side of your nature which is . . .
- . . . you're selfish at all. I think you're being extremely pragmatic and realistic and good for you.

However, just as praxis is not simply practice, pragmatic, in the sense that I wish to invoke, is not simply practical. I turn again to Rorty and the philosophical tradition that his work continues – the American Pragmatism of Dewey and James, Pierce and Mead (Thayer 1970, Brogan & Risser 2000, Menand 2001).

A unifying purpose of the pragmatists was to forge (Thayer ibid.:viii):

> a theory of the reflective and experimental operations of intelligence in conduct responsive to needs and directed to rendering future experiences increasingly malleable to human growth and satisfactions. The concentration of analysis was on the possibilities of human action in a contingent and changeful world and on the functions of thought and language as ways of discovering the world and more clearly discerning the goods attainable in it, as well as making any enjoyment of these more luminous and complete.

The wording of this deserves some comment. I take *experimental* in the first line to index more the modern meaning of *experiential* than any idea of controlled experiment. *Goods attainable*, in the penultimate line, I take to refer to a wider range of benefit that only those of material comfort. Beyond those caveats, the central force of the passage lies in its evocation of *a contingent and changeful world*, and of the need for a philosophy of integrated thought, language and action that was not only *responsive to needs* but dedicated to *discovery* and to *human growth*.

Dewey (1931/1970:32ff.) presents Pragmatism in this way:

> as an extension of historical empiricism, but with this fundamental difference, that it does not insist on antecedent phenomena but upon consequent phenomena; not upon the precedents but upon the possibilities of action. And this change in point of view is almost revolutionary in its consequences.

The revolutionary element lies in this future-orientation. If we test our ideas not by their ability to account for what has already happened, but by their consequences (ibid.:33):

> the world will be different from what it would have been if thought had not intervened. This consideration confirms the human and moral importance of thought and of its reflective operation in experience.

At the same time, Dewey insists (ibid.):

> the conceptions of reasoning have only a secondary interest in comparison with the reality of facts, since they must be confronted with concrete observations.

He then (ibid.:32) sums all of this up with the masterful aphorism:

> A theory corresponds to the facts when it leads to the facts which are its consequences by the intermediary of experience.

Reflexive memo 8.1: I find in that last formulation of Dewey's a '*more luminous and complete*' counterpart to my own colloquial, *If it doesn't work in practice, it's not OK in theory.* Beyond that, I find that this tying together of past and future through experience, as shaped by thought, language and action, clarifies in American Pragmatism a philosophical underpinning of praxis that strikes me as both powerful and elegant. Thirdly, as a meta-comment on this memo, it should be clear that what I have been doing in this last section is also an example of my attempting to theorize my practice, this time by reaching out beyond my comfort zone in ways that can be satisfying, but are also dangerous. I refer to secondary sources and edited extracts. What if these interpretations of mine mislead you? What if I make an idiot of myself? These are the fundamental challenges of Narcissus and Icarus. I can only refer you to that last line of Dewey's, by which I am content to be judged, and to Chapter 9, where some judgments fall.

It is in the above sense that I bring *acting* and *becoming pragmatic* together in my title for this chapter. I see them as encompassing our craft, our theoretical and our intellectual/ethical capacities in this hermeneutic cycle of thought, language and action, where ideas have consequences and will be judged in terms of their outcomes, as we embody them in praxis. Learning to discern the nature of such repercussions is the very essence of reflexivity and suggests to me that a developed awareness of reflexivity is an essential element of pragmatism.

Becoming pragmatic, then, is my big picture. At this point, it is high time that I re-engaged more explicitly with the praxis of teacher education.

Roots

I return then, to the framework of Copying, Applying, Theorizing, Reflecting and Acting that I sketched out in Chapter 2. Back then, CATRA represented my attempt to fly. By now, it has become my roots. Adopting this change of perspective, and having used my as-if analysis and categorization to clarify the five dimensions that I identified, I now want to look at examples of them in combination. By exploring such interactions, I hope to explore further some of the complications of *acting* and of *becoming pragmatic*.

In my first flight under Wings, below, I explore a recent experience in which Copying and Theorizing have interacted. In my second flight, I explore a recent experience in which Applying and Reflecting have interacted.

Wings

Copying and theorizing

I have always insisted that Cooperative Development can only function in a non-hierarchical, peer-group environment (e.g. Edge 2002a:270). More recently, however, I came to wonder if it might not have a place in doctoral supervision. There is sufficient space there, I thought, where people need to find their own way, for the non-directive role of the Understander to be sincerely tenable, despite the overall responsibility of the supervisor. With the right candidate as Speaker, it must be worth trying. (Please refer to Chapter 6, pp.90–92, for a description of how the Speaker/Understander dyad functions.) I present below a brief account of one such experience, an exchange of nine turns of E-mail Cooperative Development (EMCD) between myself as Understander and a doctoral student of mine, who I shall call Kolo, as Speaker. To preserve anonymity, I have changed other names and I give no detail of geographical or cultural setting. For my immediate purpose, they are not relevant. I have edited the exchanges down in order to show the essential data in a form that will fit the requirements of this chapter. Kolo has approved this representation of our work, which draws on one of several EMCD exchanges (in differing roles) between us.

★ ★ ★ ★ ★

Kolo was researching in-service teacher education. Taking an action research approach, she devised a part-time course which acted as the main vehicle of her intervention and her data gathering. Course participants had had little previous training and were used to teaching as they had been taught, or following instructions from teachers' books.

Kolo began her first message by saying:

I am starting this EMCD session without knowing exactly where I want to go.

She was sure, however, that the general area was that of the relationship between 'the personal and the professional' in her research.

At one level, she said:

> I have at times worried about my relationship with participants getting too personal – I felt this might somehow affect the trustworthiness of my research.

This was relatively easy for me as Understander to Reflect back to her as:

> As a research student, you have a methodological concern about the possible effect of your personal relationships with your course participants on the trust-worthiness of your research.

In her next message, Kolo confirmed this:

> On the one hand there is the issue of trustworthiness, which was my original source of worry.

but she went on to explain that she had since thought this matter through satisfactorily. She refers in particular to Ashan and Rabba, two teachers who had made great developmental progress through their participation in the course and whose work she was keen to support:

> I would conclude that it is only natural that the personal blends with the professional – it is all part of the same thing. Besides, it might even be an advantage for me as a researcher because I not only have access to the professional but also to the personal level, something which was not a given for me at the start. These deeper levels of involvement have allowed me to see how in Ashan's and Rabba's lives the personal shapes the professional and vice versa . . . This is where I still stand on the issue, I think.

She closed, however, by saying:

> So at the moment, I am not sure why this is still a concern, I think there is something there I am still not articulating properly. But enough for today! I will wait and see what you understand so far.

In expressing my understanding, I Reflected the explicit message that I had heard, and then invited Kolo to continue with the preferred Focus for further work that I understood her to have implied:

> Intellectually, with regard to issues of research methodology, you have resolved your doubts about this. Something remains, however, that disturbs you and you are not sure what that is. Is that right? Is that something that you want to focus on right now?

Kolo picked this up immediately in a way that highlights the potential for self-development when the Speaker hears/sees what she has said Reflected back to her and has the opportunity to review it and take her thinking on from it. I have underlined phrases that signal this process:

> Yes, I would like to pinpoint what it is that I find unsettling, but I don't really know how I can do that. <u>Though just now, as I was rereading the last part of your message, this caught my attention</u>: '*Intellectually, with regard to issues of research methodology, you have resolved your doubts about this. Something remains, however, that disturbs you and you are not sure what that is.*'
>
> <u>As I read this now, the word 'intellectually' is making me think a bit further.</u> I think I have probably solved my intellectual concerns, but I might still have other concerns of a non-intellectual nature, maybe affective?
>
> <u>What I mean is</u>, if I have in fact solved the methodological issue that was worrying me, maybe what I haven't solved is the affective part. Maybe what I find unsettling is the fact that these people with whom I expected to establish a simple, straightforward (?) researcher–participant relationship have ended up considering me their friend. They feel they can trust me with their personal problems, not only their professional ones. Sociable and friendly though I consider myself to be, I might be finding this hard to cope with, not at a professional but at an affective level. The next question is 'why?' Not sure . . . Maybe I worry about not being able to cope, to fulfil their expectations? This needs more thought.
>
> Am I making sense? I am not so sure the Intellectual–affective dichotomy is correct, but it seems useful to make some progress.

I Reflected this back to her in the following way:

> I hear you wondering whether a simple intellectual/emotional dichotomy is the right way of analysing your situation. It is more that you were prepared for a researcher/participant relationship, and expected that that itself would have intellectual and emotional aspects, and you saw/see how all that works in research terms.
>
> What has happened, however, is that Ashan and Rabba have escalated the relationship beyond that research-based one to one in which they see you as a friend/helper/consultant in whom they can confide personal issues that have nothing to do with the research, or teaching, and for which they, to put it crudely, 'want something from you' in ways that a friend might, and to which, for a friend, you might be happy to respond. But you are not sure either that this unexpected relationship is one that you altogether want, or that you can necessarily live up to its demands in ways that will satisfy Ashan and Rabba.

At this stage, Kolo dug more deeply into her own emotional response to the situation. Again, she confirms the accuracy of the Reflection and discerns the affordance that will enable her to move on from it:

> <u>As you say</u>, I expected to be part of a researcher/participant relationship (with its intellectual and emotional aspects), and then what actually happened with Ashan and Rabba was that the relationship developed beyond the research.
>
> <u>I think you are also right when you say</u> '*to put it crudely, "want something from you" in ways that a friend might, and to which, for a friend, you might be happy to respond.*' <u>I think this is a key aspect</u> – the fact that for a friend I might be happy to respond yet somehow I'm not sure that this really is a friendship, crude as that may sound . . . The truth is my friends are a top priority in my life.

Kolo then explained the strength of her dedication to her friends, and how different this was from her relationship with Ashan and Rabba. This is where her openness and commitment to non-defensive Speaking enabled her to move her Exploration forward. The Exploration led to Discovery in the sense of achieving a much clearer analysis of the causes of her continuing unease – this being the goal of the Focus that the (Speaker/Understander) dyadic subject had established.

> There is a lot of affective support, to put it somehow, but to me this is an inherent part of the professional, and is being confused with a friendship.
>
> In that sense, I can see how I might be uncomfortable about two things: a) the term being loosely used to describe a relationship in which the affective part of the professional is being labelled a friendship; b) the risk of not being able to live up to the demands of this friendship. I sound horrible, don't I? I'm not saying I don't want to be friends with them, not at all, but I think that right now we are not there yet.
>
> In terms of my research, this seems an important step. I can now see that my relationship with Ashan and Rabba is more complex than I thought. This complexity has been worrying for me on different levels. Firstly, the superficial or easily seen methodological level, and now this personal level which affects my beliefs (I don't know what to call it).

And in a side-comment on the process, peripheral to her core topic, but central to my theme in this chapter, Kolo said:

> I think that if it wasn't for EMCD I might have never learned this about myself and my research relationships.
>
> If someone had said to me, '*You feel they're asking too much of you emotionally, and you're not prepared to give so much because you don't consider them your friends,*' – I would have said, '*That's not true, I really like them, and I'm always ready to give people emotional support.*' I would have easily convinced myself of that.

Exploring further what she had learnt, Kolo identified more specifically her own role in the building of differently understood relationships:

> As I see it, I have been very open and happy to offer unconditional professional support, and I suppose the confusion may result from the fact that they have never had this sort of relationship with a tutor before. Their idea of a tutor is probably that of the jet-in-jet-out expert who is not familiar with their local realities nor is interested in being so. Also, the traditional tutor is not involved in action research or in the politics of their professional lives, let alone in the issue of exploring possibilities. And I have tried to do all this with them. In that sense, I may have confused them, so to speak.

She then reviewed interim developmental outcomes for herself in the following ways, affective, cognitive and with regard to Action:

> On the one hand, there's peace of mind. Like with many other concerns in life, I think once you get to a new level of understanding you are bound to feel better. I now realize this was making me feel guilty. Guilty because they said they considered me a friend and I didn't feel the same way, and guilty because I didn't understand how exactly this whole issue was affecting my research, and I was afraid I might be doing something wrong research-wise. But all that is gone now. This is an affective consequence, maybe?
>
> The other consequence I see is more behavioural. It relates to how I am supposed to act, or how I want to act from now on, given that I have reached this new level of understanding.

At this stage, I asked Kolo if she wanted to go on to work on these behavioural consequences, which she did. Here, we move towards the close of a natural Cooperative Development cycle, in which Exploration had led to Discovery and Discovery on to Action. With Ashan and Rabba, she subsequently began carefully to modify her responses in order to delineate what she called 'boundaries' within which her support was being offered. Looking ahead, she made sensitive adjustments to her ongoing project in order to send the same message to all participants:

> Last week I went on with my plan to establish boundaries, so I emailed all participants and clarified the 2010 situation. This felt good!!
>
> This is probably a good time to finish this EMCD session. I feel it has been so profitable – not only because it helped me understand them, myself and our actions better, but also because I also put into practice the new understandings at the same time.

★ ★ ★ ★ ★

I have never found that reports of work in Cooperative Development come anywhere near capturing the sense of engagement and excitement that the work can generate. This is true again in this case. Nevertheless, I hope that a careful reading of the edited text above will reveal the discoveries that Kolo's exploration made possible for her, and that further reflection will bring home the significance of those discoveries without my having to elaborate them individually any further.

I presented this EMCD session with Kolo initially because it seemed a good example of what I mean by Copying, by thoughtfully taking an established procedure from one setting to another – in this case, taking Cooperative Development from a context of peer collaboration to one of supervision, a context where I have previously argued that it does not belong. Beyond that, I wanted to use it to exemplify an interaction in praxis between Copying and Theorizing. I believe that it was the discovery of the concept of the *dyadic subject* (Wells 2002, Chapter 6 in this book) that gave me the intellectual insight and affective strength to trust Cooperative Development in a supervisory relationship. I felt that if the strength of being engaged in a dyadic subject with Kolo seemed sufficiently genuine, then that shared agency would, at the very least, do no harm. In the event, I believe that we have here a clear example of the dyadic subject working successfully to increase the Speaker's Scope for Meaningful Action (see pp.94–95).

Beyond those initial intentions, however, and beyond experiencing another example of the power of non-defensive Speaking, supported by non-judgemental Understanding, I also learned more.

First, I became aware that my previous position on the unsuitability of Cooperative Development outside strictly peer-group relationships is *not* one that I want to give up. It provides a very useful guideline. Like any useful guideline, it is necessarily restrictive. What I have *not* learned through working with Kolo is that I would now extend the guideline for the appropriate use of Cooperative Development to include doctoral students. What I *have* learned through working with Kolo and one or two other doctoral students is that, beyond my peer-group guideline, there are individual calls to be made. That is a much more messy area. What is criterial to success is not the formal status of the participants outside the Speaker/Understander relationship, but the functional parity of the participants when in that relationship and their capacity to engage as a dyadic subject. I realize as I write this conclusion that this insight was partially available to me almost ten years ago when I wrote of a very successful group development experience (Edge 2002a:134):

> all colleagues were of equal status in so far as their roles as autonomously developing professionals were concerned. The fact that one member was director of the unit was not salient in these meetings.

My motivation at that time was in part defensive. I wanted to make as clear as I could what I saw as the most appropriate conditions under which people might try out Cooperative Development for themselves. In this sense, the guideline remains in place. What I am doing now is celebrating another step forward for myself, both with regard to awareness and to procedure. Of *course* (I now say) what counts is the quality of the Speaker/Understander dyadic connection and this may be found (or not) in what are otherwise symmetrical or asymmetrical relationships.

Second, I have come to realize more than ever before the extent to which Cooperative Development, with its commitment to personal reflection at the service of professional action, has reflexivity woven inevitably into its warp and weft. Kolo entered her research keen, as she put it:

> . . . to behave ethically as a teacher educator, and I understood this ethical behaviour as not 'jetting out' once the course was over. I would have felt bad if I had just finished collecting my data, wrapped up the course and disappeared from their lives.

This desire shaped her research effort. What she experienced, however, what she tried and underwent, led her to reassess her own behaviour in this particular context and to refine her research relationships along lines structured by explicit boundaries.

She herself comments on the session explicitly:

> I believe this is a clear example, in reflexivity terms, of how the research is affecting me and how it's making me learn more about myself as an individual, not just as a researcher.

So, through what I first took to be an instance of Copying in a methodological mode, I furthered my continuing process of *becoming methodological* by understanding more clearly the conditions facilitative to this style of work as a teacher educator. Beyond that, I furthered my continuing process of *becoming theoretical* by employing the concept of the dyadic subject as an intellectual tool with which to develop my praxis. And beyond both of those, I also grasped more explicitly than I previously had the direct involvement of Cooperative Development with the processes of reflexivity. My sense of congruence is enhanced and I believe that, in terms of continuity, Kolo's experience of working as part of a dyadic subject will also contribute to a passing on of values that we both prize.

Reflexive memo 8.2: While writing the above section, wanting to capture the moment without sounding too fey, the phrase, *the struggle for authenticity* (Grimmet & Neufeld 1994) kept coming to my mind. On revisiting my notes, I found the following (ibid.:223):

> The struggle for authenticity is a struggle of endless mediation between contradictions that we face in our moral choices. We suggest that teacher development occurs at the silent or humming points of mediation between such binary opposites as problem versus solution or between what is imagined as bad versus good practice. We are interested in the energy of the *versus*.

How complementary, I thought. In that part of my work that I have just been describing, I am interested not in the energy of the *versus*, but the energy of the *with*, not in the power of fission, but in the power of fusion. At the same time, the quotation is an excellent introduction to the next section of this chapter. And at this point, another realization dawns. The two complex examples of my work that I have chosen encapsulate my praxis along a yin/yang category line that I had not previously seen: the fusion of the dyadic subject and the fission of Problem/Solution patterns. This allows me a vision of my praxis as a unitary whole that can be divided into elements that can communicate with each other – a situation in which reflexivity can be encouraged.

Applying and reflecting

In Chapter 5, I described how Problem/Solution analysis of methodology texts has been continuingly useful across a range of teacher education activities, principally connected with reading and writing. The categorization involved uncovers semantic and pragmatic features of discourse that regularly prove helpful to teacher-learners, whether or not they are features in which those teachers have been subconsciously socialized. Whether one draws informing theories from linguistics, or any other discipline, or from educational theory itself, however, one inevitably favours course participants who either have, or can develop, a facility with the type of abstraction, categorization and linear thinking that such theories demand. I have already raised the possibility that such thinking is culture-based, indeed, the usefulness of Hoey's work with Problem/Solution patterns arises from the very fact that it helps teachers recognize and manipulate the culturally-favoured patterns of language use that comprise so much of the Western-oriented discourse of TESOL.

I took up the theme of cultural politics in Chapter 7, in the light of which discussion my own position here is that if one has identified a way to facilitate access for teacher-learners to the discourse modes of power, one takes on the responsibility to offer that access. The additional responsibility is to be sure to present such access as an opportunity for teacher-learners to extend their repertoire, and not to be seen as in any way displacing something inferior with something superior. The deep resonance of this work for me is with the elaborated codes (Bernstein 1971) that I was called on to master in order to proceed with my own education beyond boundaries not previously crossed by residents of Granville Street, as described in Chapter 3 (p.27).

When introducing Problem/Solution patterns to teacher-learners, I naturally try to use contemporary materials. When teaching in January 2010, therefore, the title of the first article in the latest issue of *ELT Journal* (Zhang & Head 2010) immediately caught my eye:

Dealing with learner reticence in the speaking class

What I want to describe in this section is how the Applying of a relational analysis to this text (as introduced in Chapter 5) led directly to Reflecting on its cultural-political significance (as discussed in Chapter 7). This experience was an extension of the undergoing that Cheng had facilitated for me (Chapter 5, pp.76–77). My purpose is not to join one side or the other in debates about political correctness or educational colonialism. I want to show how inevitably intermingled the pedagogic and the sociocultural are and to argue that to proceed without due acknowledgement of the decisions that are being made diminishes the extent to which we can fully engage in congruent teacher education in TESOL.

One of the central strengths of Hoey's relational analysis is the identification of how the organization of a text is signalled on the surface of its discourse. Let me take you through this one, in SPRE terms, beginning with the title. Best of all, of course, would be if you were to read the whole article yourself.

As readers, we initially encounter *dealing with* and, if there is a something that we have to deal with, we know, simply from our general semantic knowledge as human beings, that that something is very likely to be some kind of problem.

'What is it that we are having to deal with here?' we ask as readers, and immediately we run into *learner reticence* as a candidate for our predicted problem. As language teachers, we recognize from our professional knowledge that learner reticence can indeed be a problem in a number of ways.
'Do the writers have any particular aspect in mind?' we ask.
'Yes, indeed,' the writers reply, 'The way in which learner reticence can get in your way "in the speaking class." '

Fine, we feel ourselves seriously addressed with regard to our content schemata.

Meanwhile, in terms of formal schemata, we have constructed a semantic pattern of discourse organization that we expect the text to fulfil:

SITUATION: In the speaking class.
PROBLEM: Learner reticence.

RESPONSE: Dealing with [it] – to be spelled out as the main purpose of the text.

EVALUATION: Positive evaluation of the response is implied by the use of 'deal with' itself, because if you deal with a problem, it is no longer there.

With regard to the pragmatic significance of what has happened so far in this particular instance of textual communication in a professional genre, we recognize that the writers have specified a Situation and a Problem and promised, should we be interested, to report on at least one successful way of dealing with that problem. There is a generic implication that this direct speech act of reporting can also be understood as an indirect speech act of suggesting a way of dealing with the problem that can be useful for us, the readers.

It has taken me some time to spell all that out. I am not suggesting, of course, that these processes are as linear, sequential or long-winded as my description. I do suggest, however, that something like this is what is going on as far as the competent reader is concerned. Similarly, whether consciously or not, this is what these highly competent writers set out to achieve by their selection of the idiomatic gerund, abstract noun phrase object, and prepositional phrase of their title.

If we move on from the title with this Problem/Solution schema in mind, we find that the abstract (Zhang & Head 2010:1) reinforces our expectations. I have reproduced it here with numbers inserted for ease of reference:

[1] This paper describes an oral English course for non-English majors at a university in the People's Republic of China. [2] In the first year of the course, the students were very resistant to participating in group-based speaking activities, and their end-of-year results were disappointing. [3] In the second year, the teacher decided to involve the students actively in designing their course and planning activities which would meet their needs and reasons for wanting to speak English. [4] The aim was to increase their motivation and overcome reticence by getting them to talk about what and how they wanted to learn. [5] It was expected that both their confidence and their ability to speak English would improve through more personal engagement with the course. [6] The effectiveness of this approach was assessed using self-evaluation forms, classroom observations, and tests which showed significant progress in the students' speaking.

Without going into too much detail, a relational analysis might proceed along the following lines. S1 is initially outside the SPRE pattern in that it is *about* the text rather than part *of* it. Nevertheless, it goes on to provide a lot of information about Situation (Setting), answering such questions as:

What kind of course are we talking about?
What kind of student are we talking about?

What kind of institution are we talking about?
Which country are we talking about?

S2 introduces Problematic aspects of the Situation, signalled by *resistant* and *disappointing*.

S3 tells us the teacher's Response. We infer that this is the Response due to the temporal sequence (*first year, resistance/disappointment – second year, teacher decided to*. Also, we see S3's *meet their needs and reasons for wanting to speak English* as directly addressing S2's Problematic *resistant to participating in group-based speaking activities*.

S4 confirms our inference, providing the End (*aim*), lexically realized by *to increase their motivation and overcome reticence* (where *reticence* stands for *resistant to participating*) and the Means (*by getting them to . . .*). Notice the grammatical signalling here, achieved through an infinitive of purpose (*to increase*) and the instrumental subordinator (*by*). Notice, too, the repetition by paraphrase between S3 (*involve the students actively in designing their course and planning activities*) and S4 (*getting them to talk about what and how they wanted to learn*). This confirms our earlier inference regarding the S2/S3 Problem/Response relationship.

S5 both justifies the Response and establishes criteria against which it should be judged (*expected/improve*). The Problems of S3's *reticence* and S1's *disappointing results* are to be replaced by (their working antonyms) *confidence* and *ability* and this End is to be reached by the Means of *more personal engagement*, which is itself a paraphrase of S2's *involve the students actively* and S3's *what and how they wanted to learn*.

S6 provides detail of how this whole *approach* (i.e. what we have been told in S3–S5) was Evaluated (*assessed*) and tells us that Evaluation was very positive (*significant progress*), with *the students' speaking* referring directly back to S2's Problematic *speaking activities*.

The abstract fairly represents Zhang & Head's article as a whole. The central section of the article, under the sub-heading (p.3), *A case study of how problems of reticence were addressed*, provides good procedural detail of the Response element of this SPRE pattern. Evaluation, when it comes (p.8), is conclusive, in that the students:

> acquired a better understanding of the learning process and were more self confident in developing the skills they needed to progress towards their own goals in speaking English.

While the term, *case study*, acts as a reminder that the authors are not making explicit suggestions that readers should necessarily follow in their footsteps, it is reasonable to infer that the authors think that useful lessons might be learnt that could support interventions in other contexts where similar problems arise. Their closing sentence (p.8) corroborates this inference:

> Overall, this study supports the view that learner reticence can be overcome by an approach which gives learners more say in the design of their course and allows them to create their own opportunities and activities to practice speaking.

The next section of this chapter needs to tread carefully, and I ask to be understood carefully. My aim is to provide a second analysis of the above article that will bring out a parallel reading of it. My intention in so doing is not to attack either the article or the work that it represents. My intention is twofold. As far as my wider readership is concerned, I hope to provide some common ground on which different factions in the discussion of TESOL methodology (e.g. Bax 2003a, 2003b vs. Harmer 2003; Waters 2007a, 2007b vs. Holliday 2007) might stand in order to have fruitful discussion, rather than point-scoring exchanges. More narrowly, but central to the design of this book, I hope to show how interaction between the *applying theory* and *becoming intellectual* strands of my work have generated useful growth in my praxis.

As I have explained, I turned to this article initially in order to provide contemporary professional data for a class in discourse analysis. I was drawn to it by the explicit Problem/Solution signalling of its title. As I read the article, however, in reader/analyst mode, a very different SPRE pattern emerged, shadowing the authors' explicitly intended one, and just as clearly signalled, in Hoey's seminal terms, on the surface of their discourse.

Let us look again at the Problem that is signalled in the text (Zhang & Head 2010:1):

> In the first year, classroom activities designed to improve their speaking skills such as role-plays, simulations, and group discussions aroused resistance among some students, who considered them a waste of time.

We are told (ibid.) that central to the teacher's espoused theory is '*the concept of a negotiated syllabus which is determined jointly by teacher and students*', an approach '*accommodating their different ideas and learning preferences*'.

However, the teacher's actual Response is not to negotiate an accommodation with the students' ideas and learning preferences, but to regroup around devising a different way of putting her own beliefs and preferences into practice (ibid.):

> The teacher believed that reticence to participate in speaking activities was preventing her learners from making progress and achieving the outcomes intended for the course.

In other words, the teacher appears to hold two beliefs, in (1) the need for situated negotiation and (2) the supremacy of a particular methodological approach. In the event, to judge from her theory-in-action, the former is to give way to the latter. Students will be consulted, but only inside the frame of the teacher's preferred methodology. I repeat, my purpose here is not to dispute the efficacy of that methodology, or the teacher's right to decide, but to clarify what is going on – possibly below the radar of the teacher's awareness and certainly not articulated in the writers' report.

Research is cited in favour of the teacher's beliefs, but background knowledge tells us that Swain (1985) is based on research done with immersion techniques for schoolchildren in cognate languages in an at least notionally bilingual country. These principles may transfer to non-English majors at a Chinese university, but if we are to be convinced of that, more argument would have been helpful, or, at least, an indication of who these '*other researchers*' (evoked in Zhang & Head 2010:2) actually are.

What then follows in the central section of the article might be seen, from the perspective of TESOL as cultural politics, as a set of thoughtful procedures aimed at making Chinese learners behave more like Western learners, in order to help them fit better into the Western-derived learning theories in which the teacher believes.

Well, we might say, it all comes down to what works, in the end, doesn't it? And the writers make a good job of evaluating their work from various perspectives. Results seem overall very positive. But what is it, we might still ask, that is being evaluated? According to which criteria is the work being seen as successful? Against that background, two points stand out.

First, the statement, beginning '*The teacher believed that . . .*' (ibid.7) is more or less a paraphrase of the same statement on p.1. In other words, the teacher is not providing evidence of having learned anything about how to accommodate different learning preferences, but demonstrates that she has learned how to mould learners effectively to suit her teaching preferences.

Second, we are told on p.8:

> In particular, the stronger students (those who scored higher on the first test) achieved dramatically higher scores in the second test.

So, the students who were already fitting in well with the teacher's preferences were further advantaged when those preferences were more efficiently implemented. It is difficult to see this outcome as a fully satisfactory Response to the initial Problem, that some students resisted participation in these activities and '*considered them a waste of class time*' (ibid.1).

These two readings diverge completely in the penultimate sentence of the article, in which the writers identify what they discern as an affordance for future research. With regard to the more successful students, they write (ibid.8):

> It would be interesting to undertake a closer examination of how they used the opportunities provided by the more learner-centred approach, and what specific strategies they found most helpful.

The overshadowed reading that I have tried to bring into the light would discern an affordance in the performance of the weaker students, seeking a closer examination of the learning opportunities that they had been denied and which specific, valued strategies they felt they had not been able to deploy.

Once more, my aim here is not to attack the work that has been done. My aim is to demonstrate that methodological decisions such as the ones made here do have ideological implications and that, given all the discussion that there has been in this area, it will no longer quite do for us to proceed as though issues of cultural politics were a sideline to be pursued only by those fringe cranksters who get off on that kind of thing.

If a teacher educator believes that language learning processes have been identified that are common to human beings above and beyond their social and cultural backgrounds, and, further, that language teaching procedures have been developed that facilitate these processes, then that is a position that needs to be argued. The methodological task before us then, as exemplified in this article, is how to make students around the world fit into that facilitative template. In this scenario, the fact that 'learner autonomy' essentially involves training learners to behave more like the citizens of those countries where these processes have been identified is something that needs to be acknowledged.

What also needs to be acknowledged is that an alternative version of what is going on is available.

If a teacher educator believes that what the above article describes is a typical exercise of hegemonic power, in which the chief agents are probably not even aware of the roles that they have taken on in imposing their own naturally acquired and/or consciously learned system of cultural values and social norms, then these views can also be stated. What is then required, however, is an explanation of why such approaches have proved popular and successful in so many different contexts. Is it only through the exercise of hegemonic power? Is it only through the conviction of certain teachers? Is there nothing of general value here to language acquisition? Allied to the same argument, are working examples being brought to light in which more local, native, autochthonous, traditional (chose your own epithet) approaches are proving satisfactory?

Most of all, perhaps, I believe that the ideology-deniers and the ideology-only voices of our profession need to get together and affirm that it is never either/or, it is always both/and. The enhancement of participatory communication has surely brought something useful to our language learning classes, and another part of what it has done is to increase the influence of dominant Western social norms and to favour those learners who find it easy to adapt to those norms. Until we can agree on that, it will be difficult to move forward. If we can move forward, perhaps along the lines of situated, hybrid approaches, we shall still need to remember that it is not of our nature, or of the nature of the world in which we live, to produce a source of light without simultaneously producing a source of shadow. The role of critical thinking, as I understand it, is to keep reminding us of that fact, without demotivating us from trying to produce more light.

Refocusing rapidly on the purpose of this section of this chapter, it has been to exemplify an interaction in my own work between aspects of what I have called *applying theory* and *becoming intellectual*. What began as an exercise in discourse analysis engaged an area of broader intellectual concern. This was not a case, I wish to emphasize, in which I approached a text with a predisposition to beat ideological points out of it. It was a case where the application of the discourse analytical theory itself brought to light an alternative reading of the text. Necessarily, I would argue, this connection then became a part of the seminar work with my teacher-learners that followed. In this way, my sense of consistency and continuity felt satisfied.

Reflexivity

In closing my accounts of action in this chapter, I have evoked again the concepts of coherence in expressing my personal values in my work, of consistency in explicitly practicing what I preach, and of continuity by offering my teacher-learners developmental opportunities in line with the values that I prize. I have repeatedly identified these as aspects of the congruence through reflexivity that I seek to realize in teacher education.

It remains very clear to me, however, that there is only a very thin line, and perhaps even a changing line, between what I am describing here and what Zhang & Head might claim lies behind their approach to language teaching. They bring themselves recognizably into class and offer learning opportunities based on values that they prize. All I would say in response to that is that it would be helpful to make clear that these decisions of what is to be valued are conscious decisions, and that they are aware of the shadows that their light creates. This is where an openness to what I have called expansive reflexivity might help us all to communicate more effectively.

Any sense of continuity for a teacher educator must engage with the likelihood that one is favouring teacher-learners who share important common features with oneself. Prospective reflexivity will always tend in this direction. My CATRA framework is not an abstractly conceived category model populated by logical exponents, it is an autobiographical construct populated by my experiences. My work in reflective practice, discourse analysis, Cooperative Development and action research seems to indicate an affinity for loose organizational frameworks that demand a certain discipline but retain fuzzy boundaries. My efforts are likely to favour teacher-learners who respond well to the same kind of phenomenon. My successes here will encourage me. Retrospective reflexivity will threaten to complete a self-supporting cycle of solipsism. My challenge is to be attentive to this tendency and to create a developmental context in which both the more fiercely organized and the less strictly disciplined can also discern their affordances, along with others who differ along other parameters.

Among the interacting and individually differentially balanced possibilities of CATRA, I hope to make such repertoires available. With the goal of *becoming pragmatic* as the end of this central run of chapters, I am setting a target that allows space for all the previous *becomings* to jostle into and join up. Not as established states of *having become*, of course, but as continuing processes of *being* and *becoming*.

In all honesty, however, and along with every effort to respect and empathize with difference, it is probably inevitable that an approach to teacher education that prizes reflexivity as I have characterized it, that seeks congruence and continuity as I have defined them, will favour teacher-learners who are inclined in similar ways. In tune with the legacy of Dewey and Rorty as I understand it, then, my work at its best will favour teacher-learners who share:

- an acceptance that the world is interpretable in multiple ways, that our '*final vocabularies*' (see Chapter 1, pp.9–10) set limits to our understanding, just as they make it possible;
- a concern to act *reasonably* rather than *rationally* or *reactively* (see Chapter 3, pp.44–45) in specific situations;
- an interest biased towards the unreliable human activity of learning (achieved experientially, intellectually and expressively, cognitively, affectively and kinaesthetically) rather than in the structured abstractions of knowledge (see pp.119–120);
- a disposition to look to the future for the justification of their conclusions and consequent actions (see pp.120–121).

To become pragmatic, in this sense, is not to acknowledge the down-to-earth limitations of one's ambitions, but to aspire ambitiously to be deeply rooted in the specifics of the human condition and still seek to fly. Both Narcissus and Icarus need to be enlisted. Only awareness will see us through.

And always one must remember, in the struggle for self-acceptance, that it is not wrong to have high ideals, not wrong to have lofty ambitions, and not unlikely that one will make mistakes. I spoke above about the inevitability of light creating shadows. In my next, and penultimate, chapter, I intend to pursue some of the shadows that flit about in my own narrative. I hope, by taking the time and trouble to look at this negative print, to enlist those shadows, too, in helping us see a little more of what it is that we are up to.

9

SHADOWS

Introduction

An earlier title of this chapter was, 'When things go wrong.' Perhaps it would have been better to stick to that more literal version, but I was attracted by the metaphorical possibilities of 'Shadows': it captures the point made in the previous chapter that shadows are the inevitable result of light and that unintended consequences abound. It implies an area of darkness where we do not see clearly what is going on. It evokes the possibility of shapes left behind when a person is no longer present. I want to touch on all of these.

Moreover, still trapped in meta-comment, it has just struck me, even now, as I write the first few words of the first draft of this chapter, why it is that I cannot approach it on a Roots and Wings basis. I had thought, as previously, to write about certain occasions and events, to reflect on what I have learned from them, and to seek out the elements of reflexivity that seem worth noting – why did some things happen because it was I who was involved, and how did those events help shape me and the I that emerged?

However, I have just made a new connection. Of course, my writing has always arisen directly from my work. I have always seen this as a strength: write from experience, pursue theorization, but/and don't make general claims. That relationship, however, is not a roots-and-wings one. That is to say, my attempts to fly have taken place just as much in terms of the lived experience in the field as in terms of the written experience in the literature. What happens '*in the field*' and what happens '*in the literature*' are two aspects of what I might call my '*area of operation*', but it is not the case that the latter is simply a report of the former, nor that the former is simply a launching pad for the latter. Both need to be rooted; both need to fly.

The relationship between my work in the field and my work in the literature is of the reflexive kind that a person would expect to find in what is fundamentally an action research-oriented area of operation. The action feeds the writing and the writing feeds the action and the thinking runs through it all, trying to link both together and undergoing change as it does. Icarus is there in both mediums, seeking forms of flight and a further view. So is Narcissus, staring, reflecting, trying to see deeper and understand more.

Moreover, when Narcissus looks down into the water, it is perhaps his Icarus-reflection that he seeks. When Icarus soars to his highest point, the furthest view he can achieve is perhaps into himself. Has reflexivity always been about this connection? The flight is not separate from the roots – this is a strange metaphor to interpret.

What has become clear to me at this point is that this chapter demands a different, if related, organizing principle to its predecessors. There have been things that have gone wrong in the field, in the physical world of projects, courses and employment, and things that have gone wrong in the written world that we refer to as 'the literature'. When the two types of tribulation come together, as well they might, as both occur in the reflexive teacher educator's area of operation, the resulting crash is the heavier. We shall come to that eventually.

In the meantime, I shall organize this chapter initially around the distinction that has emerged from the above discussion: 'in the field' and 'in the literature'. I shall then bring the two together before closing with more reflection on reflexivity.

In the field

From an early point in this book (Chapter 3), I have evoked Dewey's characterization of experience as a unique combination of *trying* and *undergoing*. Without losing that concept – reflexive, of course, in its own right, as it divides a unity into mutually-shaping parts – I would like to overlay it with another. Partly in an attempt to add a little lightness to a chapter that risks becoming rather dark, I wish to evoke the epigrammatic wit of the ever-insightful Oscar Wilde (1892): '*Experience is the name everyone gives to their mistakes.*'

I would not want to commit to that definition but, as we smile, we might also note that although we often refer to the importance of learning from our mistakes, we write more or less exclusively about our successes. The misconceived project, the bungled interview, the failure to liaise with supervising teachers during a school placement for trainees – these do not occur as the focal points of our reports. My intention, then, is to move 'things going wrong' more centre stage. The difficulty lies not so much in finding examples, but in choosing which ones to highlight. To those people familiar with failures of mine that I do not mention, and with which you feel I should be confronted, I ask your forbearance and assure you, with due acknowledgement to Jackson Browne (1973), that I have not forgotten them.

In Chapter 4, I recounted several aspects of the teacher education work that I was involved with in Turkey in the early 1980s. It was also the stage of my working life at which I started to write about what I was doing, leading to a series of articles, particularly in *ELT Journal*, that I have already referred to. In that sense, one might say that it was where I learned to spread my wings a little in the literature.

In the field, however, things did eventually go badly wrong. I discovered, too late, that while the British Council had advertised the post that had attracted me as one with responsibility for the design and implementation of an undergraduate teacher education course, for in-service professional development work with colleagues, and for some direct language teaching, they had negotiated with the university on the basis of its English Department being provided with a native-speaker teacher, who could also help with materials development if they so required. Because my personal preferences led me to close collaboration with my immediate colleagues in the staffroom, rather than to close conferencing along the corridors of power, it took me too long to understand the differently perceived situation that I was in.

After two years of collaborating to introduce popular and successful innovations with regard to language teaching and methodology training, and with two Turkish colleagues returning from Britain after MA courses selected to help them take the project forward, I believed that we had in place an example of sustainable educational development to be proud of.

As the third year began, however, the plans that had been laid were vetoed and one of those returning colleagues was transferred to another department. At this point, I was enraged by the professoriate's reneging on the agreements that I considered that we had made, and my superiors at the university were enraged by the presumption of their guest worker, whose eccentricities they had thus far indulged, and by the effrontery of his suggestions for changing their curriculum. I resigned, leaving the project, if there was one, to founder and leaving myself unemployed.

From the outset, I had fundamentally failed to take account of the inevitably different motivations driving the various participants in this scenario. In fact, it was probably only ten years later, when reading Johnston & Peterson (1994:71) that I properly recognized what had been going on:

> The stakeholders in a program all have an interest, of one kind or another, in the program; but it would be naïve to assume either that these interests all centre exclusively around improving the quality of learning of the learners, or that the interests coincide at all. It is only when this fact is confronted that the true nature of a program can be perceived, and only when this happens that it is possible to understand exactly what can and cannot be changed, and how.

I had failed to grasp that once my post was filled, the major stakeholders were happy. The British Overseas Development Administration had another project running. The British Council had furthered its own self-interest by eliciting funds from the ODA at home and simultaneously raising its profile in a local context overseas. The university had its free, extra staff member. From that point onwards, the perspective of '*improving the quality of learning of the learners*' was not represented at high table and the only news that anyone wanted to hear was good news.

At the very least, even if they had on this occasion exceeded even my expectations with their priority-reversed job description, I should have known how the British Council functioned, like any organization, to justify its existence. I should have known that the hierarchical power structures of a traditional university in an ex-imperial society would move only glacially, and even then only under the influence of top-down pressure. At the time, I felt as though I had been betrayed by the usual suspects, the British Council and the encrusted power-hierarchies of old-and-in-the-way institutions, but that is not the reflection that I see now, if I look more closely and deeply into what is reflected back to me.

I allowed the 'working-class intellectual' attitudes that I referred to in Chapter 3, allied to my comfort at working on the chalk-face, to restrict the effectiveness of what my colleagues and I could have achieved. I combined this ideological superficiality and level of professional comfort with a mixture of intercultural insensitivity (why would *any* university authorities allow a junior foreigner to reshape their curriculum?) and micro-political naïvety (one has to talk to all interested parties, not just the ones one finds it easy to get along with, in order to clarify the objectives one does have in common). In so doing, I unwittingly and unintentionally conspired to undo the potential long-term effects of what had been a hugely positive educational experience for colleagues and teacher-learners alike. In addition to that, of course, I left the power structures in place, perhaps even enhanced.

If I needed a way to forgive myself, I might blame this waste on my youth. While that may be a contributory reason, it does not provide an excuse. I do at least, however, recognize procedural mistakes that I made, and from which I have learned.

Reflexive memo 9.1: At this point in my telling of this Icarus story, my Narcissus self sees a dual image reflected back to me. What I describe above is certainly valid as I work to make meaning now from what I tried and what I underwent at that time. In addition, however, I also see a reflection of the young man who was there then, trying and undergoing (and also having a wonderful time of life in Turkey). It is as if one were to drop a pebble into a pool and, as the ripple spreads across the reflection that one sees, the two self-images (me now/me then) alternate. But then, instead of two images arising from these historical episodes, the reflection kaleidoscopes as more events crowd in unbidden. Let me explain.

Reading Bartlett (1932) on *remembering* was foundational in my doctoral studies in the mid-1980s, immediately after leaving Turkey. Last semester (October 2009), I was teaching an MA class about the use of schemata in reading and I referred to Bartlett. Last week, we were discussing the use of deductive and inductive strategies in grammar teaching, and I used the expression '*effort after meaning*', acknowledging that I could not remember whose expression it was, perhaps Bruner?

One of the MA course participants googled 'effort after meaning' immediately after class and emailed me to say that the source was Bartlett (1932). As I followed up, I came to see (remember?) that Bartlett's usage was broader than the one I had attributed to the expression. Whereas I was suggesting that a conscious effort to work out a grammatical rule by studying relevant language data and formulating a generalization to account for it (i.e. inductive rule-formation) might assist the learning of grammar for some people, Bartlett's usage also includes the unconscious, schema-building processes that the human brain carries out subconsciously in order to assimilate and accommodate new information via meaningful association.

An important part of Bartlett's message was that remembering is not a reconstructive process, but a constructive process, built around what he hypothesized to be a granule of affective trace somehow chemically encoded. Remembering is something that we do *now*.

The implicit challenge that arises for me is to hold my gaze long and steady enough for the ripples of each pebble to pass – Turkey – PhD – Bartlett – MA class – schemata – so as to allow me to fix on clear and meaningful images from which I can learn, in full knowledge that the significance of the effort after meaning is that it, itself, generates the pebbles that drop into the pool. Is it any wonder that Narcissus remained transfixed?

Returning to how one deals with events in the field, Clarke (2007:181) comments on the creative ambiguity of the expression, '*changing schools*':

You may be faced with the choice of changing the school where you work, or changing schools so that you can do your work.

Over the years, I have probably explored the latter alternative to excess, and this has no doubt been influenced by the fact that I have never been fully integrated into an education system in the way that most teachers and teacher educators are. In Jordan, Germany, Egypt, Singapore, Lebanon and Turkey, I was always a foreigner who would move on. The move from Turkey took me to doctoral studies in Britain and, surprisingly, because it had not been my intention, into university posts in Britain, where I have worked as a teacher educator for most of the past twenty-five years. I do work in the British education system, then, but my teacher-learners are spread all around the world, or are from all around the world, and my commitment to the importance of situated learning leads me to look for ways to understand the contexts on which they are reporting rather than explore my own national scene, even to the extent that I am woefully under-informed about the teaching of English among immigrant communities in Britain.

There was one point at which it seemed that I might change this lack of situatedness, albeit rather late in the day, but that was not to be. I constantly tell the teacher-learners with whom I work that the important question is not, 'Did it work?' but 'What can I learn from this?', so it behoves me to keep that in mind. Let us explore this more recent scenario next.

In 2003, a long and fruitful period of work in Britain was drawing to a close as a variety of institutional pressures and personal trajectories led to a closely-knit group of colleagues moving on in different directions. I had, in fact, thought about moving along on three previous occasions. On two, I had not been offered the post I applied for, on the other I had. In all three cases, I had been pleased, in retrospect, to stay where I was. Nevertheless, I had for some time been wondering if, as I frequently put it, I 'had one more move in me'. By now in my mid-fifties, I was not interested in reliving the experience of earlier years on short-term contracts, but was attracted by the idea of a long-term move to another country to see out my professional life.

The opportunity arrived with a post in Australia. I was offered a dual role that I might have written for myself. I was to be Research Director of a Centre committed to furthering action research in the country's many institutions dedicated to teaching English to Australia's highly variegated immigrant, refugee and asylum-seeking population, while also holding a post of Associate Professor in the TESOL section of the host university's Linguistics Department. I foresaw an opportunity for fully situated educational engagement along with an opportunity to continue to pursue international connections. This vision was corroborated by colleagues on both sides of my dual-employment situation. I was flying.

Within weeks of my arrival, however, an irrevocable rupture had occurred between the Research Centre and the Linguistics Department, with old grudges and personal enmities folded into the mix of differing and emergent professional agendas. Colleagues withdrew from projects that I was in the process of putting in place and the central purpose of my post in institutional terms, to establish synergies between the research potentials of the Centre and the Department, crumbled away. Both sides offered me full-time employment on each side of this divide, but I felt bruised and somewhat let down.

Behind this professional picture, a personal narrative was also unfolding. With so much experience of living in different countries and cultures, I had under-estimated what it would mean to sell up and move, lock stock and barrel to the far side of the world, 'leaving behind' three parents in their eighties and a daughter in her second year at university. There comes a point at which a distance of separation exceeds the geographical, and the young man who went to Turkey was not the middle-aged man with family responsibilities, even though supported unfailingly on both occasions by the same wife. Probably, once again, this ought to have been obvious to me in advance, but I wanted to know if I had another move in me and I did what I wanted to do in order to find out.

It is a commonplace of our discourse in teacher education that the professional and the personal intermingle. We usually mean this in positive, creative and synergetic terms and those terms can be very positive indeed. The converse, however, is also true. Professionally speaking, I still had some shots in my locker, but I could not revive the sense of purpose with which I had set out. Personally, I buckled inside. I fulfilled my duties, but resigned at the end of the first year. Quite unlike my experience in Turkey, I left with strong feelings of professional failure and personal weakness, held together only by the knowledge that I had tried to do what I wanted to do, and that that is worth a lot.

The freedom of action that I had enjoyed throughout the years of moving on was thus maintained, although at somewhat increased cost. As I noted earlier, I have never regarded TESOL as offering a career so much as a sequence of jobs, in which I have been more fortunate than most.

These are two experiences from my time in the field, to which I return later in the chapter. In the meantime, of course, readers might want to take a break and reflect on experiences of their own where things have gone wrong.

In the literature

For the reflexive teacher educator, life 'in the literature' runs partly in interaction with one's life in the field and partly along lines parallel to it. In both cases, one is looking to meet the same criterion of personal congruence and meet variations on the same demands of consistency, coherence and continuity that we have already evoked. Here, consistency will involve ensuring that the professional action that one reports chimes with the principles that one articulates; coherence will involve the expression of whole-person values, characteristics and skills whether writing of personal or professional domains; continuity will involve writing about what one does as a part of one's purpose to encourage the next generation of teachers to write about what they do.

Unrecognisable reflections

It is sometimes very satisfying to bump into oneself in the literature. Not always, however. Sometimes, one finds that things have gone wrong in the most unexpected fashion, as one finds oneself constructed in ways that feel more or less unsatisfactory. In this section, I hope to give a taste of what this feels like, with reference to other people's constructions as well as my own. I invite those that I cite to comment, and I search for the reflexive upshot.

I was recently challenged, for example, with regard to my dismissal of the importance of power inequalities in second-language acquisition. When I failed to recognize this description of my position, the person doing the challenging referred me to the following passage in Norton (2000:108):

> At the 1999 TESOL Convention in New York, USA, Julian Edge and I (Edge and Norton 1999) debated the extent to which it is productive to incorporate notions of power into theories of SLA. The point I made at the time is that, if we avoid naming and confronting questions of power in social interaction, we may struggle to understand the language learning experiences of our students.

While I had to concede the reasonableness of the reader's inference of what my stance in such a debate must have been, I also had to point out that, from my perspective, the debate had actually been about teacher education. Specifically, the question debated was:

> If teacher educators seek to treat each teacher as *'a person with purpose in a context which has a culture'* (Fullan & Hargreaves 1992), do they augment this goal by adding, *'in a world where power is distributed unequally'*?

The summary of the session elaborated this question in the following way:

> The presenters are sympathetic both to the strand of humanistic, developmental psychology, and to the strand of sociopolitical, critical theory which are to be found in the contemporary discourses of TESOL and teacher education. They differ on some points of emphasis and positioning, and one of these will provide the basis for their presentation.
>
> One speaker will argue that the following formulation is both necessary and sufficient to guide the work of colleagues in teacher development:
>
> *'Each teacher is a person with purpose in a context which has a culture.'*

The other speaker will argue that this formulation, while compelling, needs to be elaborated as follows:

> *'Each teacher is a person with purpose in a context which has a culture, in a world where power is distributed unequally.'*

In counterpoint to Bonny Norton, the point that *I* made at the time was that, while the unequal distribution of power is indeed ubiquitous, it is the autonomous teacher who has the right to decide the extent to which this fact should be the focus of their developmental work: exactly herein lies the demonstration of the teacher educator's respect for that individual teacher's particular, contextualized, encultured *purpose* that the original statement set out to express.

What was clear from the interview data that Bonny Norton presented during the debate was that she deliberately led her informants to focus on the power inequalities of their situations. When challenged on this, she replied disarmingly, '*Well, yes, that is my research interest.*' I believe that, at this instant, we both thought that our point had been made: she, because her research had brought out the importance of power relations in language acquisition; I, because she claimed that her purpose as researcher should override any undiscovered putative purpose of an interviewee, or, in the context of this debate, of a teacher.

As far as our continuing life in the literature is concerned, of course, there we are, Bonny and I, situated in an introductory paragraph of an argument about second language acquisition.

I might also add that not only do I have very positive memories of the debate, but that I have, in the ten years that have elapsed, moved closer to Bonny's position. I still maintain that teachers have the right to focus their developmental activities where they will, and that this right should override a researcher's interested steering of them. At the same time, I do also assert that teacher educators have a responsibility to make sure that teacher-learners do not proceed blithely through their careers unaware of the significance of the unequal distribution of power in our work, as it resonates through issues of language acquisition, language policy, course design, methodology, teacher employment, and wherever else one looks. It was unsettling to bump into that shadow of a Julian Edge, but not unpleasant.

The next encounter is more difficult. It is in the nature of our literature that writers use the work of others in order to locate their own thoughts, ideally in order to move an argument along and, where possible, to take the field as a whole forward. These are skills that teacher educators try to help teacher-learners acquire as they become not only consumers, but also creators of this discourse world. The longer one lives in this world, of course, the greater the likelihood that one's work will become not the next step forward, but a staging post for someone else's future.

In Chapters 6 and 8, I talked about my continuing work in Cooperative Development, a style of collaborative self-help between peers on which I first published in 1992. The conceptual framework was already there at that stage, including the idea of a cycle during which a teacher as Speaker might hope to *Explore* a self-selected issue and thereby *Discover* something which could form the basis of consequent *Action*. Against this background, I introduced nine non-judgemental types of response that a colleague acting as Understander might use in order to facilitate the Speaker's development.

The work has been attacked occasionally over the years, usually by people who have misunderstood it, and never by anyone who has experienced it. I had not, however, expected to find myself playing the vaulting horse quite to the extent that I came across in Randall & Thornton (2001:77):

The previous chapter, then, identified three 'stages' of providing advice, and Edge (1992) suggested different macro-skills which were appropriate for each stage of the process.

The problem with the 'stage' approach is that it is overly simplistic; there is no one-to-one relationship between the skill or intervention type and the stage of the helping cycle. Attending and reflecting are skills which will be used all the time. Similarly, 'challenging' and 'disclosing' are interventions which could be used at any stage of the process. What is required is a framework for describing different interventions and then to look at their use in a complete cycle.

A hurried return across the years and pages led me to Edge (1992:13), where I found myself reassuringly explicit on the topic of 'stages' and 'skills':

> I have tried above to lay out the necessary conditions of respect, empathy and honesty. In Part 2, I describe the style of interaction in terms of the actual techniques or abilities that one needs to develop. I shall describe nine such abilities, grouped into three blocks of three. They are introduced in this sequence as it suits their presentation and explanation. There is no suggestion that this represents a rigid order to be followed in a cooperative interaction.

Nevertheless, my '*overly simplistic*' shadow wanders on through the literature, carried by Randall & Thornton's frequently excellent book, perhaps picking up the odd reference here and there, perhaps undermining the credibility of that area of my work in the field that means most to me. I was annoyed. Not to the extent that I thought it worth trying to take any kind of action, but it rankled.

My 'uncritical' and 'overly simplistic' shadows combine to powerful effect in Holliday (2005). Edge (1996a) was the article in which I had come closest to making an overt statement of personal/professional philosophy. For better or for worse, it is one which I can still read without too much embarrassment. I looked in vain, however, for my reflection in the following passage (Holliday 2005:75f) on ideology and methodology:

> Edge (1996[a]) has revealing things to say about this sort of thing. His claim that 'we have developed a culture of TESOL (which also reflexively encultures us) through which our values are expressed' (ibid.:11) is right in that the dominant professional discourse I am describing is indeed a reality which I and many of my colleagues are a part of. It does represent our professional and life values, which, as Edge (1996[a]:12) suggests, include 'diversity', 'inquiry', 'co-operation' and 'respect' – for the student, for the student teacher and for our colleagues. I, however, disagree with Edge who says that:

> *These values are made operational in the TESOL class every time a teacher says, 'I want you to get into groups'. Or, to put that more carefully, the strategic and contextual sensitive use of group work is the one way in which a teacher can communicate a respect of the diversity of learning process and learning outcome while encouraging co-operative enquiry. And it is as an expression of those underlying values that group work has emerged as such a widespread teaching technique in the realization of the TESOL culture with which I am most familiar.* (Edge 1996[a]: 13)

It is probably simplest to quote here what I actually did say. I have marked the most important point of change (Edge 1996a:13):

> These values are made operational in the TESOL class every time a teacher says, 'I want you to get into groups'. Or, to put that more carefully, the strategic and contextually sensitive use of group work **is one way in which** a teacher can communicate a respect for the diversity of learning process and learning outcome while encouraging co-operative inquiry. And it is as an expression of those underlying values that group work has emerged as such a widespread teaching technique in the realization of the TESOL culture with which I am most familiar.

The intrusion of the definite article in '*the one way*' leads to a serious mis-representation of what I wrote, and one on which Holliday turns a fair amount of argument regarding the imposition of inappropriate methods with hegemonic intent. In this context, I was struck also by his decision to cut the final line of my paragraph above, in which I say:

> This is not to iconize group work as either necessary or sufficient evidence for the presence of that culture. It is the values base that counts.

I say that this is significant because Holliday goes on (ibid.:83) to tie me into an example of how a specious sense of cultural superiority can be attached to methodological choice:

> 'Dependency' and 'hierarchy' in association with Confucianism are thus polarized against the 'independence', 'freedom', 'privacy', 'choice' and 'equality' of the Self of 'quintessential American values', which, as in Edge (1996[a]), are associated with group and pair work.

And this despite my own assertion (1996a:18):

> Nor are particular procedures, such as group work, ruled in, any more than other procedures, such as learning lists of vocabulary, are ruled out. Appropriateness to context is best judged by informed, sensitive insiders.

On this occasion, I admit to having felt a sense of grievance, probably because the issues involved had escalated from ones of professional technique to human values. Moreover, because we writers all use the present tense to allow our constructs to speak now – Edge *has things to say*; Holliday *goes on* – this immediacy is perhaps a part of the problem when things go wrong. The sense of grievance may go away, it may grow old, but its cause is preserved ever-new in the aspic of our generic style. Inevitably, then, there are emotional undertones that these shadows evoke as they pass in and out of our lives.

I am not called upon to own the Edge shadow who walks these particular pages, a figure out to represent quintessential American values by imposing group work on the world, but I have to acknowledge his continued presence and confess that he offends my sense of congruence, as well as interfering with my attempts to demonstrate coherence and consistency in my life in the literature, as well as to facilitate continuity by encouraging others to become involved.

On this occasion, I was motivated to write to Professor Holliday, who graciously acknowledged and regretted the misquotation, which he undertook to correct in the event of a second edition.

Reflexive memo 9.2: I recognize the danger here of appearing, or indeed, becoming, too precious, too delicate, too easily put out. That is not where I am going. I am trying to establish a sense of a literature in which TESOL professionals also live, where one sometimes looks in vain for a reflection that one recognizes, even as one is content to inhabit it as an environment in which one can fly. I do not suffer from the misapprehension that many people will notice or care about any published slippage of perception between Bonny Norton, Mick Randall, Adrian Holliday and myself. I note simply that there are shadows out there with my name on them that I neither recognize nor approve of. This can be frustrating, but it is not actually threatening. It is one's own misrepresentations that are threatening, and that is where I am going. Perhaps I have created unwelcome (to them) representations of Bonny, Mick and Adrian only to keep me company. The only way to deal with this possibility is to ask them how they feel about the journey and offer them a chance to speak for themselves. If they decline the invitation, of course, no one will read this last section. If they accept, they will be found at the end of this chapter, with no further comment from me. In either case, I shall go where I am going. Ah. Who would have thought it? [Smile.] A melodramatic chance to quote my favourite line from Shakespeare: *I have set my life upon a cast. And I will stand the hazard of the die.*

Richard III Act 5 Scene 4

The invisible man

I wrote earlier of 'life in the field' and 'life in the literature' as running, in one sense, along parallel lines. I have also referred to them, along a different dimension, as being in a mutually energizing, hermeneutic relationship of cyclical development. There are other possibilities: that a downward spiral in one domain can influence misjudgements in the other, for example, or that the flight of Icarus can distract Narcissus' attention from his roots. It is an experience along these latter lines that I intend to explore now.

Rather than rely only on data already in the public domain, as I have thus far, I shall tell rather more of the story than appears on the surface and risk a real subversion of my fragmented self. Much more subversive than the presence of shadows-in-the-literature that others have created are the illusions that one has created oneself.

I have already told the in-the-field version of my brief 'one last move' experience and indicated some of the stresses involved. There is more to tell.

One of the action research projects for which I was responsible, and one which I personally led, involved the training of groups of teachers in the skills of Cooperative Development, the approach to peer-supported self-development already described in Chapters 6 and 8, and referred to above. This included the use of Cooperative Development in two newly developing modes: by e-mail (EMCD) and by instant messenger (IMCD) – See Boon 2005, 2007, 2009). I carried out workshops in four regional centres, all of which were received well, in some cases enthusiastically.

An important element of the training materials comprised extracts from Cooperative Development exchanges that were used to exemplify specific discourse moves available to the Understander. As I was myself engaged in Cooperative Development work at the time with more than one colleague, I also introduced from those exchanges some data that seemed particularly effective, using pseudonyms throughout. In terms of the effectiveness of the training sessions, I believed that this was a good move. For me to have turned up in regional centres as the Research-Director-featuring-himself would, I judged, have been seen as self-regarding in its usual, negative sense. There is already, however, an underlying question as to whether it was a misjudgement to use my own data. I was swayed by the fact that I wanted the clearest examples of what I was trying to teach, wherever they came from – and these ones 'worked'.

At one point in one of the workshops, a particularly insightful participant pointed to the data on the screen in which the Speaker was struggling with a particular problem and said,

'*That's you!*'

'*You're right, it is,*' I replied.

Everyone laughed and we continued work. Uncovered in this way, my occasional presence in the data seemed to lend an extra authenticity to what we were doing. Cooperative Development was not simply a topic that I was talking about, or recommendations for what others should do, it was a professional experience that I was committed to. Narcissus was, in that sense, redeemed. These workshops were the highlight of my working life at that time. For those brief periods, I was flying. Icarus was, in that sense, released. Subsequently, one regional group in particular took the work on in very satisfying ways (Barber et al. 2005, 2006, Butorac et al. 2005, Butorac 2006).

I made two conference presentations based on these workshop experiences. These also went well. Again, the aim was to present Cooperative Development effectively as well as to report on the project, and it seemed appropriate to use the same data.

As writing about what I do had long been an established part of what I do, I wrote an article on computer-mediated Cooperative Development (CMCD) that appeared as Edge (2006a). This shift of Cooperative Development into the world of information technology was something that excited me. The way in which the available data allowed for a focus on the centrality of the affective in developmental discourse also excited me. The article demonstrates the media-shifts into synchronous and asynchronous communication very effectively, as well as showing how Cooperative Development can help the Speaker usefully clarify the affective aspects of a situation without slipping off into a misplaced 'counselling' session.

In ways that I can easily make clear, for reasons some of which I might be able to explain, and due to errors of judgement that I would not wish to attempt to justify, this article is a fatally flawed piece of work that undermines many of the values and practices that I have been trying to discover, understand, implement and live up to over my working life. Let us begin with the clarification.

When introducing the two data sets used in the article, I provide pseudonyms which disguise the fact that I am one of the participants in both cases. I explain some of the difficulties of editing and selection and go on to say:

> As analyst, I submitted my original analyses to the participants concerned, whose input has informed the analysis presented here. What is claimed in terms of warrant, therefore, is inter-subjective agreement on the selection of data and on its analysis and interpretation.
>
> *Edge 2006a: 211*

This remains true, inasmuch as I discussed the selection of data, its analysis and interpretation with my co-participants. The truth of it, however, is not the apparent reference to inter-subjectivity among three people in each case, but only between two.

In introducing the first pair, I say the following, without pointing out that *Adrian* is a pseudonym for myself:

> In this example of the work, the two participating colleagues are, pseudonymically, Adrian and Layla.
>
> *ibid.:211*

During the analysis of the data, I write as two separate personae:

> To an analyst's eye, Adrian's final line, with its past tense usage and expression of thanks might also be seen as indicators of a move to closure – a sign that Adrian has gone as far as he wants to on this topic. Adrian, however, reports that this was not the case, nor did Layla feel that this was a good place to stop.
>
> *ibid.:215*

The other specific example of this occurs one page later:

> Like myself as analyst, Adrian as Speaker is careful not to be seen to be claiming any kind of clinical diagnosis here, and warns against the dangers of amateur self-indulgence in this vein.
>
> *ibid.:216*

Similar points of principle can be made about the second exchange. Finally, in acknowledging the contributions of my colleagues, I also preserve the fiction of separation from the participants:

> Sincere thanks to the Speakers and Understanders concerned for their permission to use these data. Special thanks to Andrew Boon and Nur Kurtoglu-Hooton for their comments on an earlier draft of this paper.
>
> *ibid.:225*

When I take out the above extracts and present them in this light, I feel diminished and defeated. At its baldest, I was guilty of presenting an analysis of interactive data sets in which I was a participant (once as *Adrian*, once as *Joe*) in a way that disguised this participation, and which would lead any reasonable reader to conclude that I was operating only as a third-person analyst. In so doing, I transgressed the most fundamental requirements of transparency and reflexivity, thus undermining the credibility of the work itself and, by extension, other work done in qualitative, constructivist, and person-oriented traditions.

Reflexive memo 9.3: Once again, I recognize the danger of seeming to over-inflate the significance of my error. I am not saying that this affair was significant 'for the literature', nor were my co-participants upset, but, as someone who has to be responsible for his own actions, it was significant to me. Mistakes in the field, even if reported, belong to a past from which one can learn. Indeed, the report is probably the record of that learning. Mistakes in the literature, as I have already noted, remain ever-present. Perhaps even the fact that one has *written*,

> moreover, represents an attempt from one perspective to rise above action in the field, so the danger associated with falling is greater, the stakes are higher, the crash more painful.

Given the history of the piece, one explanation is that, in a grotesque piece of misjudgement, I transferred my arguably justifiable workshop approach to the article, where my intention was less to report on research as such and more to exemplify how the approach in question could function at the service of any type of ongoing reflective practice. The first lesson arising, therefore, naïve as it sounds, is to beware the genre-shifts required between reflective practice, professional development workshops and academic reporting, along with the different criteria that quite properly apply.

Further, I was at the time of writing struggling with a number of personal and professional difficulties already alluded to, some of which are highlighted in the *Adrian* data, and I believe I baulked at implicating or embarrassing the real people associated with those problems in a public statement. In retrospect, I now see that the fact that this misjudged granting of self-anonymity did not seem important to me was perhaps indicative of the conflicted state of mind that I was in, which was perhaps more serious than I then realized. It is so easily asserted that the personal and the professional intermingle. My warning here is to beware of the seductive power of the personal insight, even as one acknowledges its explanatory potential, when deciding whether or not, and in what form, to make it public.

Oddly, perhaps, while pleading guilty to an inexcusable representational blunder, I do wish to defend myself against a possible charge of a deliberate attempt to mislead. The identity of *Adrian* in the data set used was very apparent to a number of people in my acquaintance and I was very relaxed about this in a fair amount of private correspondence in which *Adrian* featured as the *alter ego* with whom I was struggling. It is, indeed, due to the discussions of one such group of ex-colleagues and friends that I have been helped to bring this matter into the public domain.

Some friends wrote supportively, one saying:

- those who know you well (as a colleague and friend) would know Adrian was you;
- those who know you in a professional capacity through your work could guess that Adrian might be you;
- those who do not know you much may not realize Adrian was you – but at the end of the day it does not matter which of the three above someone may fit in. What does matter is that the analyzed data show the power of CMCD.

I wanted to believe this, but it applied only to one of the discourses that the article expressed, and I fully accepted and accept the critique of the lack of transparency that others made clear. In terms of research methodology, the article might stand as a useful case for the study of the implications of such lack of transparency. Without transparency, there is no credibility; without credibility, nothing can be effectively demonstrated and no amount of 'actual' authenticity of experience or legitimacy of argument (Edge & Richards 1998) can be employed *post hoc* in order to put Humpty Dumpty together again.

In the field, *Adrian* was frightened, out of his depth and potentially destructive. I saw myself as needing to defeat him, or even exorcize him, as I put it at the time. I now entertain the possibility that his appearance in the article was part of an extended cry for help that I did not consciously want to make. In terms that I have learnt since (Mearns & Cooper 2005:87-95), I now believe that what I needed to do was to *meet Adrian* and reintegrate his/my fears into my ability to deal with them. This was also advice that I received at the time and could not heed.

My overall failure, in the metaphor of this current attempt to learn from experience, from what I *tried* and from what I have *undergone*, lay, after years of first-person research and writing, in not trusting Narcissus to speak for himself. Also in not consistently applying to myself the straightforward criteria that I would have applied to anyone else's work. Or in not deciding to keep silent and use other data.

Reflexive memo 9.4: I am still negotiating with myself how this story can best be told. Of course, what I might have learnt from the experience itself is that you either tell the whole story, or it's better not to tell the story at all. And yet there is that within me that says that you can never tell 'the whole story'. There is no such thing as a whole story. You can never say everything. You can only tell 'a' story to certain people at certain times for certain purposes, even if you are not always consciously aware that that is what you are doing, or are not sure what the purposes are.

My continuing difficulty is that, unlike the case of the impostors who walk through other people's texts with my name, but whom I do not recognize, here I do recognize myself where others cannot see me. My hope is that if they do see me, they will negatively evaluate my improper act of disguise, without missing the value of the professional work that it misrepresents, with regard to which I stand as discredited witness to the authenticity of the data and the interpretation, as also to the legitimacy of the argumentation regarding the efficacy of the approach that the data exemplify.

When things go wrong, they can mess you up. When you mess up yourself, it is so much worse.

Reflexivity

Working from the above experiences of things going wrong, what difference did it make to the teacher education achieved that I was the teacher educator involved? What difference did it make to the I who emerged, that I had those experiences?

The first general point to note is that all our mistakes and our misunderstandings, our misperceptions, misreadings and misinterpretations, are all as much a part of the reflexive, mutually-shaping world that we move through as are their more 'positive' counterparts. If we think of them as the 'dark matter' of our communication, frequently only deducible through their effects, we can no more afford to ignore them than cosmologists can ignore the dark matter in their own calculations. From this perspective, I am encouraged in my commitment to Cooperative Development and its efforts towards intra-personal and interpersonal clarity. I am returned, also, to my work on *ablocutionary value* (Chapter 5, pp.70–71), which suggests that we create those negative 'mis'-namings by insisting on a message-sending vision of language use that might not always be the most appropriate.

At one level, I note (but only after writing them) that both the experiences reported 'from the field' relate to occasions when I was trying to shape relatively large-scale operations. They both portray a character happier, and more effective, when working to inspire bottom-up development than when dealing with organizational strategy. I had apparently learned less that I had thought in the meantime. Given the probably age-related decrease in resilience that I have also recorded, it does not surprise me to find that I now have no ambition to take on any managerial or directorial role in institutional terms.

As I work further to formulate personally reflexive responses, a strangely well-formed quartet emerges, evoking the parameters of continuity, consistency, coherence and congruence that I laid out in Chapter 3 and have referred to since. This was not planned, but I have not struggled against it. It serves, perhaps, to demonstrate Bartlett's point (p.142) concerning the subconscious effects of schematic effort after meaning, while simultaneously reminding us of how that effort guides our interpretation of our experiences, no matter how grounded-in-the-data we strive to make our analyses.

The lack of long-term engagement in the same situation as that of my teacher-learners has been an ever-present influence, tipping me perhaps towards walking away rather than hunkering down for the long haul, or meaning that I work only at some remove from the experiential learning situations of my teacher-learners. The teacher education, therefore, has been partial and intermittent, injected rather than seen through. It relies, and makes great demands, on teacher-learners to get the point, to pick up the ball and run with it themselves. Even during my long stay in Britain, I have worked in four different universities and applied for four posts while in one of them. Continuity is at serious risk.

Connected to this, while I see myself as a teacher educator/researcher, my passion is for the teacher educator side of that partnership. This can tip me, in an insufficiently guarded moment, to choose the immediately effective, and what I believe to be useful in that sense, without sufficient regard for the lasting worth of what is transparent and true. Consistency is under threat.

I had to step back from my relationship with my *alter ego-Adrian* experience in order to create my discussion of it in text. Stepping back now from my relationship with that text in order to see how this new relationship looks, I would say that the personal and the professional do indeed intermingle incessantly, but that one's life is one's life and reflexivity should not mean an inability to distinguish between what is properly private and what public. I believe that I have come to understand that I confused these issues. That is to say, my desire to use powerful personal data towards professional ends ran foul of my disinclination to make public data that was intensely private. In the service of our emergent understanding of reflexivity, that is the contribution that I have to offer from this sad episode. In that sense, I hope that my prospective coherence is enhanced.

Trying to articulate this chapter has not been easy, and undergoing its consequences has only just begun. One difference that it has made to me is that it has made me see more clearly the connection between Dewey's *trying* and *undergoing* and my own version of two-sided reflexivity. *Prospective* reflexivity lives through what I *try*; *retrospective* reflexivity through what I *undergo*. At the same time, I have also come to see a union of Icarus and Narcissus much more clearly than I had before, through all the discussion of becoming methodological, theoretical, intellectual and pragmatic. In fact, I cannot now see them apart. I have a working intuition that the acceptance of shadows – rather than the hunting of ghosts – might have something to do with it. Most importantly, with the embracing of *Adrian*, I do feel an enhanced sense of congruence, even as I feel more at risk.

We all have different ways of facing up to things going wrong, and we take our support where we find it. As Earl Stevick so memorably put it (1982:201):

> Teaching language is only one kind of teaching, and teaching and learning are only two limited aspects of being human. I therefore hope, first of all, that you will take time to sit down and read again whatever philosophical or religious writings you have found most nourishing to you.

I acknowledge that I have also found such support in the fictional. For what it might be worth to anyone else, I refer you to the Litany against Fear, from the novel, *Dune*, by Frank Herbert (1965:3). It has at various times been pinned to my office noticeboard and I have frequently felt better after quietly murmuring it to myself. A small number of others of my acquaintance have also found it useful. I expect to turn to it at some point again while trying to deal with the existential threat posed by the fact that I am free to make my own decisions and act on them. You can find it easily at: http://dune.wikia.com/wiki/Litany_Against_Fear

In response

I am happy to say that Bonny, Mick and Adrian did take up my invitation, and I undertook to make no further comment on what they wanted to say.

From: Bonny Norton, University of British Columbia

It is sobering to think that more than a decade has passed since Julian Edge and I engaged in a debate about language teacher education and power at the 1999 TESOL conference in New York City. If I remember correctly, the session was well attended and the discussion lively and respectful. In responding to Julian's invitation to comment on my reflection of this event in my book, *Identity and Language Learning* (Norton 2000, p.109), the discussion will reach a wider and possibly more diverse audience, and no doubt take on new meanings.

In continuing this discussion, I do not wish to return to the substance of the 1999 debate. As Julian notes, our respective positions on the relevance of power in language teacher education represent differences of emphasis rather than disagreement. Instead, I wish to reflect on this trajectory of the debate with reference to the ideas on identity that I have developed over the past 15 years. I do this in the spirit of coherence, consistency, and continuity that Julian has discussed in his work, and in the spirit of critical language teacher education that characterizes my own work (Hawkins & Norton 2009). I thus welcome Julian's invitation as an opportunity to engage in critical reflection on the relevance of theories of identity to scholarly debate.

As Julian notes, my 2000 reference to the TESOL debate in 1999 took place at the beginning of a chapter on second language acquisition (SLA) theory. In this chapter, I made the case that theories of SLA would be enriched if they engaged with issues of power in social interaction, and if they incorporated theories of identity in language learning. Interest in identity, power, and language learning has now grown considerably over the past decade, and these ideas have been extended not only to language learners but also to teachers, teacher educators, institutions, and communities. (To name just three of many books, see Toohey 2000, Pavlenko & Blackledge 2003, Block 2007.) Julian's invitation has encouraged me to consider how such ideas might extend to the identity of the scholar.

The term "scholar" has many meanings, but for the purpose of this response, I define it as a professional who makes her or his work available to a wider public audience in oral or written form. In this view, a scholar could be, amongst others, a teacher, a teacher educator, a graduate student, a researcher, a policy-maker, or an administrator. In an extension of the terms of the TESOL debate, I take the position that '*Each scholar is a person with purpose in a context which has a culture, in a world where power is distributed unequally.*' With reference to this definition, and the ongoing debate between Julian and me, I wish to make the case that presenting one's work in a public forum engages the identity of the scholar in diverse and often unsettling ways.

Further, relations of power between the scholar and other participants in the exchange are relevant to the scholar's identity in this public space.

I have argued in my work that identity is multiple, a site of struggle, and subject to change. Further, I have made the case that identity references how a person understands his or her relationship to the world, how that relationship is constructed across time and space, and how the person understands possibilities for the future (Norton 2000, p.5). When scholars present our work in a public forum, we are engaging in a risky activity. The activity is risky because language and meaning, like identity and culture, are not fixed and stable. Rather, meaning is co-constructed by the speaker/writer and the listener/reader; it shifts across time and space; and it is sometimes deliberately distorted to serve particular purposes. Further, how and in what ways these shifting meanings impact the identity of the scholar is often determined by relations of power between diverse stakeholders within particular institutions and communities.

Cummins's (1996) distinction between coercive and collaborative relations of power makes an important contribution to an understanding of the relationship between identity, power, and scholarly exchange. He argues that coercive relations of power refer to the exercise of power by a dominant individual, group, or country that is detrimental to others and serves to maintain an inequitable division of resources in a society. Collaborative relations of power, on the other hand, can serve to empower rather than marginalize. In this view, power is not a fixed, predetermined quantity, but can be mutually generated in interpersonal and intergroup relations. By extension, relations of power can serve to enable or constrain the range of identities that can be negotiated in classrooms and communities. In this view, it is possible to argue that if the relations of power in a scholarly exchange are coercive, there is great threat to the identity of the scholar, and what I have called his or her *investment* in the scholarly exchange. (Norton Peirce 1995, Norton 2000). If relations of power are collaborative, there is less threat to identity, with concomitant shifts in investment.

As I read the three accounts that Julian has identified as having gone "wrong" with respect to his positioning in the literature, it strikes me that theories of identity provide much explanatory power. Indeed, I also held my breath when I saw reference to my own work in his chapter. Like many other scholars, Julian and I are both highly invested in our work, not only because we devote countless hours to research, writing, and publishing, but because our work is also a reflection of our personal values and professional goals. In Julian's terms, we are both centrally concerned with consistency with respect to action and principle; coherence with respect to personal values; and continuity with respect to future impact. If we have not been successful in making our work understood, or if it has been misrepresented in the literature, then our identity becomes a site of personal and professional struggle.

Further, it is important to note, given the centrality of language in our field, that debates amongst scholars are constituted in and by language (oral or written), and that language plays a constitutive part in the construction of identity within the context of these exchanges. Such exchanges provide powerful evidence that language is not only a linguistic system of signs and symbols, but also a social practice in which identities and investments are negotiated and renegotiated. In addition, it is not only the identity of scholars that is of interest to the field; teachers, learners, teacher educators, policy-makers, and administrators are also active in the negotiation of identity in diverse domains of personal and professional life. It is intriguing to reflect on the ways in which the debate between Julian and me might impact language teaching, language learning, and language teacher education.

I thank Julian for the opportunity to critically reflect on my work with respect to an interesting and important debate. It is my hope that collaborative relations of power have characterized this debate, and that we can look forward to further productive discussion on language, power, and possibility in the future.

From: **Mick Randall, University of Dubai**

Dear Julian

Sorry not to respond earlier. I did think about it and felt that there really was no response except to say, '*Fair cop, guv.*' I obviously mis-read or misinterpreted your work. I am deeply sorry that I have caused you grief. It was certainly unintentional and entirely due to my own sloppiness.

I don't know the book very well and as a writer and thinker I do not rate literature (whatever that is) very highly in the development of ideas. Thus, I tend to skim quickly, sometimes get the wrong end of the stick and then misrepresent people's ideas. On the other hand, I am scrupulous about making sure that any ideas are attributed, that's why I look through what others have written to make sure that I am not saying things which are attributable to them.

It is interesting that during my PhD viva I was accused of not reading a whole series of papers for a rival concept of word recognition (which was true, but I had come to the same conclusion completely independently – so they accepted it). What a cheek! Actually, I now use those ideas I hadn't read about as the cornerstone of my thinking, so perhaps they were right. I must learn to read.

From what I can remember, my interpretation of skills to be used in different stages came from a diagram (I tend to read and use diagrams as a principle

continued

means of understanding/explanation – they are more powerful to a partial dyslexic than text). Indeed, a colleague's only comment on my psycholinguistic book (don't bother to read it – you'd hate it and it's not that good) was that "*You're very good at diagrams.*" Damned with faint praise and all!

I think perhaps you could reflect on the way that what is written can be misinterpreted. I always rant about students using sources to defend their ideas. I keep pointing out that very often it is not what the author actually said or meant that counts, but that what they are quoting is their own interpretation of what s/he said. Call me postmodern if you like. I'm not a fundamentalist postmodernist, but even this movement has some truth in it – provided you don't take it too seriously (possibly a mild reflection on your chapter you sent me, the point of which I really couldn't see). Actually, it was this issue which initially decided me not to make a response, as I did wonder if you are taking yourself too seriously. Maybe this is also a comment on my attitude to self-reflection and personal development. I obviously buy into many of the ideas, but there is more to it than that (as you probably realize from my attempt to put down what I've learnt in my professional career as an advisor/trainer).

Julian, I do admire some of the ideas you have, even though I don't buy into them lock, stock and barrel. I am very sorry to have caused you grief. I am a dilettante as far as ideas go. I still teach with passion about counselling and feedback and do a lot of blasting on about aspects of sociolinguistics, English as a Feral language, the conflicted discourse of Higher Education, etc. to anyone who will listen. (By the way, I do like your re-locating book and often misrepresent (I am sure its authors will say) or re-interpret (my defence) ideas from within it to play the academic game. I have never plowed the single furrow like successful academics, so am sometimes flaky as far as accurate referencing goes).

I always remember your comment down in Bognor about my doctoral work – that I needed to get my head examined. Well, I didn't and it's too late now, but I still do cognitive psychology as my main drug.

This is not so much a formal response, but more a stream of consciousness outpouring to someone I often speak of as a friend – god, aren't academics posers? Hardly know you really!

Cheers, mate.

Mick

From: Adrian Holliday, Canterbury Christ Church University, UK

There are three issues connected with my citing or mis-citing of Julian's 1996[a] article. The first is that very clearly I did make a fundamental error in inserting a definite article, which is unforgivable; and I am pleased that he has acknowledged my acknowledgement of this. The second issue is to do with the nature of citing which is often complex and difficult to manage. It is relevant to note that my citation of his work is within the wider context of my (2005) book. This relates in an interesting manner to my second reference to Julian's article, where I associate it with 'quintessentially American values' (ibid.:83). Within the narrow confines of the paragraph in which this appears it might look as though I am saying that Julian represents 'quintessentially American values'. However, this is not the case. I place 'quintessentially American values' in inverted commas to indicate that it is not my phrase but someone else's, and therefore 'so-called'. Earlier in the same paragraph I hope that it is evident that the phrase comes from Sullivan (2000:115) and that I am in fact discussing wider claims about TESOL professionalism. It may however be difficult to catch this without connecting it with the discussion of Sullivan much earlier in the book (ibid.:20). I was not therefore associating Julian with American values, but with what other people were referring to as 'American values'.

Of course we are all busy people who can never hope to read all the huge amount of relevant material which is available; but there are significant dangers in what Spack (1997:771) refers to as 'selective scholarship', where we pick and choose from a range of sound bytes of reference to support what we say. This is the major weakness of academic writing – unlike literary fiction and fine art where referencing is evaluated within the deeper subtleties of the text. It would not surprise me at all if somewhere else I found myself mis-quoted as saying that Julian Edge employs American values.

The third issue is what I consider to be a fundamental ideological difference which I have with Julian's 1996[a] paper as a whole. In this respect my standpoint would be equally supported by the corrected citation of his work with the definite article removed and a further sentence added. The issue I have is with the broader notion of TESOL values which he describes. I have just read his paper again; and a lot of what he says I would certainly agree with – the conflict between positive and negative aspects of TESOL. I also look at this ambivalence nine years later (Holliday 2005:137) – and could perhaps have cited Julian more positively in this respect. Nevertheless, in my book I am critiquing the deeper professional discourses of TESOL; and I see Julian's statement that TESOL culture possesses the values of diversity, inquiry, cooperation and respect as being an artefact of these discourses, and that a belief that these values exist contributes to the hiding of a deeper chauvinism. I should of course be pleased that Julian cites me very favourably in his 1996[a] paper; but this is all old material, and my 2005 book also critiques my own arguments from that period in the same manner.

10

SO WHAT?

Introduction

I was having difficulty finding a way into this chapter, when I realized that Jennifer Wilson, a current MA participant, had given me one – as well as giving me a genuine laugh-out-loud moment – with a recent posting to our virtual learning environment. Jennifer sent in some wonderfully enthusiastic and (to me) empowering feedback on the experience she was having on the teacher education module that we are doing together. She then wrote:

> I can just imagine Julian saying, 'Thank you. So what?'

And I thought, Jennifer understands just what I mean by the, 'So what?' that I so often use. And that, in turn, made me realize how easy it would be to misinterpret it. As a spoken utterance, 'So what?' usually carries a sense of interpersonal aggression, and probably an implication that there is no significance worth attaching to what has gone before. That, of course, is not what I mean. I want to celebrate what has gone before, whether that is in terms of something read, or thought, or felt, or done, or all of these things, and then to encourage the next step, the view towards the future in which that which is to be celebrated will find its developmental significance. 'So what?' I have come to realize, is the link that my own trajectory as teacher educator has forged for me with what Dewey (1931/1970) (see p.120 above) described as the revolutionary aspect of American Pragmatism, the idea that one's positions are justified less with reference to the past than with reference to the future; less, even, with reference to a traditional sense of truth than to an expression of hope.

Here is Rorty (1999:xxv), in trenchant form, on one aspect of this form of pragmatism:

We cannot regard truth as a goal of inquiry. The purpose of inquiry is to achieve agreement among human beings about what to do, to bring about consensus on the ends to be achieved and the means to be used to achieve those ends. Inquiry that does not achieve coordination of behaviour is not inquiry but simply wordplay.

Contained within this meta-trajectory of linear purpose, however, are the cycles of thinking and doing that we shall want to keep in mind, cycles in which behaviour itself will need to be reflected upon, cognitively and affectively, and that reflection articulated in order for its significance to be shared and understood. We will want to remember, too, the internalizing and externalizing effects of reflexivity-in-action, as well as the cycles of prospective and retrospective reflexivity that shape the nature and direction of pragmatism's purposeful, but never predetermined flight. It is with all this in mind that we can revisit the dimension of becoming methodological and see our methodology/pedagogy as an emergent phenomenon – embodied in, and growing with, the teacher educator in a style that encourages teacher-learners to join in.

With specific regard to this chapter, I mean the *So what?* of its title to insist on a certain amount of responsibility on my part to pull together as many of the hanging threads of this book as possible into a weave coherent enough for me to feel sufficiently satisfied with it, and for readers to be able to evaluate it from their own perspectives.

The road running on

This is no time to hold back. One has roots and wings to some purpose. In general terms, the purpose is to allow learning to be a risky enterprise, rather than only the creation of an audit trail. Necessarily, according to everything that I have been arguing, specific *So what?* statements arise for me. Some help me encapsulate my current position, some point ahead into my future.

With regard to the former, I feel that I have now developed a better understanding of a working life that is reflexive, existential and pragmatic:

Reflexive, in the sense that I am more aware of shaping and being shaped in ways that I have tried to communicate throughout this book.

Existential, in the sense that I used the term at the end of my own contribution to Chapter 9 (p.156), and about which I want to say some more. In an overview of his '*existential psychotherapy*', Yalom (1991:4ff.) posits four '"*givens*" *of existence*' with which we must all learn to deal:

> The inevitability of death for each of us and for those we love; the freedom to make our own lives as we will; our ultimate aloneness; and, finally, the absence of any obvious meaning or sense to life.

In some small ways, I see the flight of Icarus (in action research) as a response to the first of these and the reflection of Narcissus (in reflective practice) as a response to the last, coupled with a determination to construct meaning through mutually respectful interaction (in Cooperative Development), which responds also to the third. Yalom's second existential 'given', our freedom to make our lives as we will, seems to me to be the most demanding – the challenge to respond to one's freedoms, no matter how great or small they may (seem to) be. This is where I find my exploration of reflexivity to be most helpful.

Pragmatic, in the sense that I insist on the freedom to search and re-search and research the methodological, the technical, the theoretical and the intellectual, while remaining equally aware of the need to make my findings count in my actions. Pragmatic, too, in the sense of a future-orientation as far as my evaluation of those actions, and my learning from them, are concerned.

Allow me one more example of such shaping, reaching out retrospectively from my methodological past to help me form my forward-looking position on becoming/being pragmatic. One paper that I regard as truly seminal with regard to the development of the contemporary TESOL scene, at least from a linguistic perspective, is Hymes' (1972) On Communicative Competence. Couched as a critique of the then dominant representation of language as a formal system, separate from its use, Hymes proposed for language (in my paraphrase) four dimensions of being and becoming: the possible, the feasible, the appropriate, and what actually happens. The possible relates to unconstrained systemic potential, the feasible relates to what the human brain can actually deal with in real time, the appropriate relates to social context, and what actually happens relates to, well, what actually happens as languages slowly change.

I have come to see these four dimensions as much more broadly useful, and certainly so in matters of teacher education and development, where they look like this:

- The *possible* relates to the ideas and procedures generally available to me from what I read and hear, from previous experience, and from my own creative thinking.
- The *feasible* relates to the subset of those ideas and procedures that I believe I could technically make use of in a particular context.
- The *appropriate* balances technical questions of feasibility with my (informed-by-others) view of the cultural and educational suitability of ideas and procedures for a particular context.
- *What actually happens* demands my sensitivity as I try to influence relationships between stability and change and evaluate the outcomes of those efforts, remembering (in the absence of a god's-eye view), that I need an appreciation of the way things look to others, as well as to myself.

My professional development engages my sensitive perception of what actually happens in interaction with my awareness of what might be possible in order to discern affordances that unite my concept of what is feasible and appropriate. I look for my development along all these dimensions.

My work as a teacher educator involves helping teachers engage their (increasingly sensitive) perception of what actually happens in interaction with their (growing) awareness of what might be possible in order to enable them to discern affordances that unite their (expanding) concept of what is feasible and appropriate. And then their work comes back to shape me. Most recently, Christopher Roland, a current MA participant, wrote in to the VLE of the Teacher Education module that we had just completed:

> This course has certainly left me in a certain place regarding some of the EFL reading I would like to do – a different place to the one I started in – and I'm very, very happy about that.

Not only does he capture in this feedback the (to me, very supportive) sense of *having undergone*, he also included in the report of his teacher education work that he submitted for assessment (that is, his statement of what he had been *trying*), a reference to Sandywell & Beer (2005) that is new to me, that helps me take my ideas forward, and that confirms our experience of *continuity* as I have used the term.

If one were to see this reflexive, existential pragmatism as a country, then awareness is its river, which runs the central length of it and sustains it entirely (cf. Maclean 1976).

Reflexive memo 10.1: In so saying, I acknowledge the dark-matter reflexivity that I have barely touched on: the shaping and being shaped of which one is not aware, the *trying* and the *undergoing* that seem simply to be the everyday business of getting on with life. To raise this issue now, fortunately, is only to repeat the point already made in praise of reflective practice (Chapter 2). One can argue that all teachers think about what they do and act accordingly and that therefore all teaching is reflective practice. What one means by *reflective practice* in such circumstances, however, is to be aware of the reflecting that one is doing and consciously to exercise a disciplined approach to it. Similarly with reflexive teacher education, what I mean by the term is consciously to explore the effects of reflexivity in one's praxis, to examine its roots and to glide, even sometimes to soar, on its wings.

Having reached out to shape this book, the strongest force of retrospective reflexivity that I am undergoing is the sensation of being shaped by a powerful motivation to read more of Richard Rorty. I said in Chapter 1 that I needed to read more of his work and I do not wish to go back and change that statement now. Writing a book, of course, takes a long time, and I have been reading Rorty as I have been writing this one. An ongoing temptation has been to go back and recast some of my earlier statements in the light of what I have since learned, but I have also felt the attraction of staying faithful to the chronology of the experience. My reference to '*transparent and true*' in Chapter 9 (p.156) is an example of the latter. In Rorty's (1999:48) terms, my contrast there between 'useful' and 'true' is meaningless, and, '. . . *we should try to replace it with something like the distinction between "less useful description of the world" and "more useful description of the world"* '. Rorty's position is that a search for 'truth' separate from statements that we can negotiate and justify among ourselves as most useful has proven to be unprofitable and should be abandoned.

On several fronts, I am finding that Rorty is helping me work towards a level of congruence that I had not expected to discover. My admiration for American Pragmatism has been explicitly on record for some time. I dedicated my (Edge 2001b) edited collection on action research to the memory of John Dewey, and used an extended quotation from Menand (2001) to introduce my (2006b) edited collection on TESOL in the new American empire. Indeed, the more I read in this tradition, the more surprised I am that it seems to feature so relatively little in our ongoing 'sociocultural turn'. In a lecture series in 1929, Dewey (1958:xiii) was saying:

> If . . . language, for example, is recognized as the instrument of social cooperation and mutual participation, continuity is established between natural events and the origin and development of meanings. Mind is seen to be a function of social interactions.

Rorty has helped me access this tradition and take my own thinking further. Briefly, let me recap some of the ways in which I find this to be true.

First, there is the line that I quoted in Chapter 3 that seems to me to chime so well with our needs in teacher education and does so at a more profound level than that of teacher education alone (Rorty 1998:19):

> Pragmatists think that if something makes no difference to practice, it should make no difference to philosophy.

Second, the theory/practice traumas that have plagued teacher education time out of mind are so well addressed by Rorty (1999:xxv):

> There is no deep split between theory and practice, because on a pragmatist view all so-called theory which is not wordplay is already practice.

Third, and purely incidentally, although still striking from the perspective of my own consistency, I find my commitment to *ablocutionary value* (see pp.70–71) validated in Malachowski's (2002:95) reporting of Rorty in the following terms:

> a 'good reading' of a text is *not* necessarily one that extracts its 'intrinsic meaning', its 'intended meaning' or any such thing, but one that puts the author's writing to the best extrinsic *practical* use . . . It is a *contextual* notion.

Fourth, I confess to a sense of real connection when I think of my (2008a) attempt to focus teacher education attention less on the necessarily interim products of teacher-learner theorizing, and more on the empowering process itself, and then read Rorty's (1999:120):

> This notion of a species of animals gradually taking control of its own evolution by changing its environmental conditions leads Dewey to say, in good Darwinian language, that '*growth itself is the moral end*' and that to '*protect, sustain and direct growth is the chief ideal of education*'.

Fifth, cementing the link to Dewey, Rorty (ibid.:49) makes explicit the unbroken continuum between the pragmatic perception of our socially negotiated reality and the concerns of ethics and politics, thus helping me with my theme of expansive reflexivity:

> Dewey was the philosopher who most clearly and explicitly set aside the goal common to the Greeks and the German Idealists (accurate representation of the intrinsic nature of reality) in favour of the political goal of increasingly free societies and increasingly diverse individuals within them. This is why he seems to me to be the most useful and most significant figure in twentieth century philosophy.

Sixth, and of particular significance to me in my own development, Rorty indicates a way to deal with a paradox to which I had previously had no convincing response other than an invocation of 'cultural bedrock', not when I identified it in Edge (1996a), and not when I invoked it on p.118 above. If I accept the right of others to develop their own sincerely-held positions, how do I draw the line when they sincerely insist on their duty to seek to impose their convictions on me?

This is where Rorty's concepts of 'final vocabulary' and 'irony' (Chapter 1, p.9) come into play in combination. He lays down three conditions that qualify a person as an ironist. Ironists (2000:45):

- have doubts about their final vocabulary;
- recognize that these doubts cannot be resolved in their final vocabulary;

• accept that their own final vocabulary is no closer to an external reality than another sincerely-held vocabulary.

He continues (ibid.:51):

> Since there is nothing beyond vocabularies which serves as a criterion of choice between them, criticism is a matter of looking on this picture and on that, not of comparing both pictures with the original.

At this point, Rorty's 'philosophical pluralism' faces the potentially difficult accusation of cultural relativism, of holding that any set of values and beliefs are as valid and valuable as any other. His response is straightforward (1999:276):

> Insofar as 'postmodern' philosophical thinking is identified with a mindless and stupid cultural relativism – with the idea that any fool thing that calls itself culture is worthy of respect – then I have no use for such thinking.

In the ironist terms of one's own final vocabulary, one must review what one can of human history and develop the description, or redescription, that is likely to be most useful in increasing humanity's ability to cope with ourselves and the rest of our environment and mutually to prosper in it. The greater the variety of descriptions available, the more likely we are to make useful discoveries, but none of this obviates the need to evaluate, in sub-philosophical, case-by-case terms, and to make judgments as to when and how to defend our own positions. He continues (ibid.):

> The reason to try persuasion rather than force, to do our best to come to terms with people whose convictions are archaic and ingenerate, is simply that using force, or mockery, or insult, is likely to decrease human happiness . . . The difference between pluralism and cultural relativism is the difference between pragmatically justified tolerance and mindless irresponsibility.

I find in reading Rorty something of what Rorty (1991:208) obviously found in reading Dewey, in the sense that, '*his vocabulary allows room for unjustifiable hope, and an ungroundable but vital sense of human solidarity*'.

It is perhaps asking a lot, without further adumbration, to ask my readers to consider the common relevance of this statement to contemporary discussion in TESOL about cultural politics, linguistic imperialism and the like, and to the state of war currently (summer 2010) raging in Afghanistan, but I have tried in this book not to back away from asking a lot of my readers, so I shall not start now.

Reflexive memo 10.2: I am aware that one does not end a book by introducing large-scale themes, the significance of which one has not fully argued, much less followed through. I pass on this advice to my graduate students on a regular basis. The reason that I am making exactly this mistake here and now is because this is where I am here and now, because reflexivity never stops, because I have undergone some change and am reaching out to identify where that change will take me, because to make that future-oriented point about reflexivity is more important to this book than to conform to the advice that I regularly give people about the construction of their texts. I have, therefore, achieved an inconsistency in my praxis and this, in itself, requires to be addressed. But not here.

Almost in conclusion

I want to try two more things. First, a very concise personal summary of what I have come to understand in the terms that I have developed to understand it with. Second, a more general (though inevitably equally individual) comment on the essential necessity of this work, work which I find satisfying, but difficult and demanding.

As I reflect on my time as a teacher educator in TESOL, I see that my employment trajectory in Action has taken me away from an emphasis on thoughtful Copying as I have accrued more time for the Reflection that has allowed me to develop my taste for Applying and for Theorizing. Along that trajectory, I have favoured the Revelatory in my attempts to encourage professional development and I have focused on individual, collegial, bottom-up processes rather than institutional, or larger-scale systemic concerns.

In the time that I have left, I shall be working to reintegrate more of an emphasis on thoughtful Copying, as it represents a kind of agreement, a dynamic kind of agreement, and a dynamic kind of agreement suggests an excellent basis for situated collaboration and development. I am less concerned about the possible under-emphasis on Emancipatory work, inasmuch as the Cooperative Development option that I introduce in Revelatory style does, itself, encourage Emancipatory development.

In all of this, I see an expression of the 'working-class intellectual' that I invoked in Chapter 3, making a path by walking it, enjoying new freedoms, making old mistakes, and frequently unsure of how to learn enough from individual experience to make larger-scale sense of it at the time. I acknowledge here the point made by Mauthner & Doucet (2003:425) that:

> It may be more useful to think of 'degrees of reflexivity', with some influences being easier to identify and articulate at the time of our work while others may take time, distance and detachment.

I see how I have reached out in terms of prospective reflexivity to shape, facilitate and constrain the affordances that I have made available via my work as a teacher educator. With regard to retrospective reflexivity, I see how my progress along this path has reached back to shape me in ways that I hope an awareness of its effects are enabling me to respond to.

With regard to expansive reflexivity, I see how working in this field has encouraged my development beyond boundaries that I was not even aware of when I set out. I remain, today, surrounded by colleagues in other departments who would shake their heads in amused disbelief if it were to be suggested that English language teaching has international political significance and needs to be studied in this light. I wonder how far back into my current final vocabulary I would need to go in order to begin to explain.

My stance in Chapter 3 was that I was nailing my colours to the mast of awareness in the conviction that awareness will see us through. I must return, therefore, as a working-class intellectual, to question who this 'us' might be, and how necessary this exploration of reflexivity is in terms of 'seeing a person through' as a teacher and a teacher educator.

First of all, I defend the right of those teachers who turn up to work reliably, who keep up with their subject, know their materials, respect their learners and help those learners achieve standards appropriate to their abilities, to draw a line and say, '*So far, this is what this society requires of me and what I am paid to do.*' I do not believe that there is any essential necessity for the kind of developmental work that has motivated most of my professional life, and which does make extra demands on time, effort and commitment. Not only is it not necessary, if one starts to include such efforts as a part of the definition of what it means to be a teacher, one provides those set above teachers in both public and private sectors with extra demands that can be made as of right. It can also, in broader social terms, exert moral and ethical pressure on teachers that I consider to be unreasonable. While I bow to no one in my admiration for the inspirational insights of Clarke (2007), therefore, I do not find myself in agreement with the following position as it might be seen as an expression of expansive reflexivity (ibid.:25):

> Being an effective teacher requires technical competence in planning and orchestrating lessons. But today we are forced to cope with a bewildering array of external demands, and if we are to do more than merely comply with someone else's mandates, we will have to become school leaders, community liaisons and political activists. Although the details vary depending on one's position and locale, it seems to me that this is a requirement of everyone in the profession.

No, such work is not necessary to be a good teacher. What *is* necessary is reflection on such issues in order to decide on their significance for oneself. And if one continues down that route (as a matter of choice), a part of that reflection needs to be reflexive as one engages with the issues that arise of prospective shaping and retrospectively being shaped.

The picture shifts, however, with regard to being a good teacher educator, because one does, I believe, have the responsibility to make an understanding of these options *available*. And if one has not, oneself, attempted to interrogate the bigger picture made available through reflexivity to ask or answer either the 'So what?' or the 'How come?' (see p.38), it is difficult to see how one can authentically make such an understanding available to others. As ever, there will be issues of extent and style, but while we might disagree about the necessity of extra-curricular engagement by teachers in the ways that Clarke indicates, I hope that there will be unanimity about the importance of awareness of their availability and significance. They need to be available for those who feel motivated to get involved, and an appreciation of their significance depends in part on an awareness of the interactive, linear and cyclical processes of reflexivity as they function in one's professional life. Interactive, because so much depends on how you get on with that (for example) first-year class; linear, because that class will run its course and come to an end; cyclical, because although time's arrow points only forward, and you are getting older, those first-year classes keep on coming round. Who understands that better than a teacher?

With regard to the necessity of engaging in this work, I read recently what I believe to be a perfect summing up of my position again in the work of Annie Dillard, whose encounter with a weasel you may remember from Chapter 3. In quite another context, she writes ([1982] 2008:43):

> You do not have to sit outside in the dark. If, however, you want to look at the stars, you will find that darkness is necessary. But the stars neither require nor demand it.

So it is, I believe, with reflexivity.

Over to you

I have attempted to achieve a number of goals in this book. Those attempts are scattered throughout the text, some of them emerging reflexively through my interaction with my own writing. I now intend to spell out, this time as a set of succinct statements, what I hope to have done. These positively expressed statements are not meant to sound boastful, nor is there any point in my suggesting that they are true. I have already done my best to justify them and they are true to the extent that you agree with them. I hope, at least, that you recognize them and that they provide a useful set of criteria against which the book as a whole can be judged. My only request in this regard is that, as you evaluate, you turn your thoughts to the future, to your own 'So what?'

1. The text has usefully separated out a concept of *reflexive* from *reflective*, thus obviating the need for confusion between the two terms and making possible further exploration of *reflective practice* and of *reflexivity*.

2. The text has communicated a cyclical sense of *reflexivity* in teacher education, according to which the teacher educator shapes the education on offer and is, in turn, shaped by the experience of offering it.
3. With regard to shaping and being shaped, it is sometimes useful to distinguish between *prospective* and *retrospective* reflexivity; sometimes between *externalizing* and *internalizing* reflexivity.
4. The terms, *vertical* and *horizontal* reflexivity can sometimes be useful to refer, respectively, to interaction between informing theory and professional praxis, and between different areas of professional praxis. Similarly, *expansive* reflexivity can be a useful term to capture experiences of horizon-expanding interaction between areas of knowledge and experience that one had previously thought unrelated.
5. The text has persuasively argued that an exploration of various forms of reflexivity might enhance the experience of being a teacher educator along lines of *coherence, consistency, continuity* and *congruence*.
6. The above concepts and terms have been embedded and embodied in an authentic autobiographical narrative of praxis.
7. The text has also used this autobiographical narrative to create a framework for teacher education, comprising interacting parameters of Copying, Applying, Theorizing, Reflecting and Acting.
8. The identification and exemplification of the elements of this CATRA framework have provided or provoked useful ideas, principles or procedures for teacher education praxis.
9. The connections between the narrative and the framework are at least idiosyncratically plausible and interesting; and/or the framework itself is worthy of consideration and critique; and/or the reader feels motivated to review his or her own autobiography in this reflexive manner.
10. Looking at the framework from a different perspective, the identification and exemplification of the interacting dimensions of *becoming methodological, becoming technical, becoming theoretical, becoming intellectual* and *becoming pragmatic* have provided or provoked useful ideas, principles or procedures for teacher education praxis.
11. The text has employed the mythological metaphors of Icarus and Narcissus in ways that are satisfying and/or likely to encourage further creative thinking about the praxis of TESOL teacher education.

As I look back at this list, it leads me to suggest that an exploration of reflexivity can be seen as central to all our personal and professional development. The attempt to understand and influence the cycle of retrospective and prospective reflexivity, the bi-directional interaction of internalizing and externalizing reflexivity, the vertically reflexive links to informing theories and the horizontal ones to other areas of praxis, the horizon-lifting effect of expansive reflexivity – this is, actually, what personal and professional development is all about. It is, in the most general terms imaginable, the organism's effort to discern itself in its context and, with regard to the human organism, the effort to influence that context and one's adaptive future in it.

What I am saying is that in this work might lie a difference between living in the monotone world of repetitive conformism, living in the discordant world of theory-and-practice, and living in a congruent praxis.

I am saying that the engagement with *reflexivity* is what Schön's (1983) *reflective practice* is all about, is what Prabhu's (1990) search for *plausibility* is all about, is what Kumaravadivelu's (2001, 2003a) interlocking parameters of *particularity*, *practicality* and *possibility* are all about.

While the effects of reflexivity will always exceed our ability to reflect on them, such reflection offers our best chance to influence those effects.

As you evaluate the book's success for yourself, perhaps with regard to those claims above, and/or in the light of the criteria I suggested at the end of Chapter 2 (p.25), it is my hope that you might find things to copy, things to apply, things to theorize, things on which to reflect and things to embody in action. Exactly how that will pan out for you and the teacher-learners with whom you work is impossible for me to say. What I can say, however, in hopes of being useful along these lines, is that I was taken aback by two questions put to me after I gave a talk on reflexivity in teacher education at the 2010 TESOL Convention in Boston.

The first question was, '*How can I introduce this approach for teachers in my situation, where the Ministry of Education lays down strict guidelines about what must be done and how it must be done?*'

What I *thought* was that the question, while clearly sincerely meant, expresses and reinforces the mindset of, '*Here is a theoretical statement by the speaker that we are supposed to apply.*' Any direct suggestions in response are likely to be met with an objection from the questioner based on specific information not previously available to the speaker. A response to this objection will elicit another one, and soon one is trapped in the '*Yes, but*' game of Transactional Analysis (Berne 1968), which most often ends with the speaker giving up in frustration and the questioner left with the feeling that this was yet another case of something that was '*alright in theory but no good in practice*'.

What I *said* was with reference to Kumaravadivelu's (2001, 2003a) afore-mentioned parameters of *particularity, practicality* and *possibility*. I said that I had been talking about a type of possibility that had arisen for me, but that how it might be practically meaningful for others in particular situations was not something that I could speak about in general, because that would be to deny the particular and the practical. I am happy to stand by that, but what I *wish* I had added is, '*Start with yourself. That is what I have been talking about. Not about introducing a model for teachers, but about being a teacher educator. Start with yourself and please report back to us.*'

The second question was, '*You have talked about the appropriate use of one's values in teacher education. Can you give guidelines for what is appropriate with regard to the use of one's values?*'

What I *thought* was that this was another (although different) misperception of the relationship between the general and the particular. Everything that I had been talking about was, in its most general terms, connected to the social negotiation of the individual-in-context. How could it be possible to give general guidelines for the individual-in-context?

What I *said* was, first of all, a reference to Johnston (2003) on values in ELT, along with an acknowledgement that I did not think that 'guidelines for what is appropriate' would be found there, either. I thought that guidelines did exist at the level of ways of raising one's awareness of what values were operating in one's praxis and then acting to bring them in line with the values that one wished to embody (issues with which Johnston (ibid.) does deal), but that beyond that, there were individual calls to be made. I gave a rather extreme example of one of my own from the late 1980s, when I said that I would not teach Iranian students sponsored by their government at a time when that government was also inciting the murder of the British author, Salman Rushdie (see Chapter 7), unless the students would disassociate themselves from that incitement. In the event, the students did not come and so the confrontation with my employers did not arise.

What I *wish* I had said, but had not at that point read, was the much more elegant way in which Rorty confronts the need to distinguish between philosophical principles and specific issues which have to be *'figured out sub-philosophically'* (Malachowski 2002:137) on a case-by-case basis, not looking back for permission, but looking forward for positive future potential. What I *wish* I had said was, *'Start with yourself and please report back to us.'*

Both these questions alerted me to fundamental issues of perception that I need to be able to address better than I did on that occasion.

★ ★ ★ ★ ★

Is that it?

That's it.

The last job?

The last one.

And you got away with it?

It's never as clean as you imagine it. There are always hits that you take, connections that don't hold up when you put your weight on them. But then, sometimes you see a new hand-hold, see a new connection. You know, sometimes 'our hero' gets unexpected support from someone who steps up out of the crowd. In fact, I think I learned more about why that last job almost always goes wrong.

Why is that?

It's not really so much that the last job has to go wrong, it's that by going wrong, it becomes the last job.

You mean, otherwise, our hero would have gone on?

I think so. Maybe so. It's like what I'm always telling course participants when they come to writing their assignments: prepare for disappointment. By the time you have finished writing about something, you are bound to have discovered so much more about it than you have managed to write. You may only feel ready to *start* writing. This is not failure; this is success, but it is a disappointing success, an unfulfilled success. A success that demands more effort, demands that you continue.

So, either this book was a failure, or it wasn't the last job?

Oh, that's hard. Did I say that?

I think you did. After all, you taught me how to listen and reflect back what a person said.

Hey, and you've turned out to be good at it! No, that doesn't feel right, then. That won't do. Let's try again. There has to be a way to acknowledge that you can't ever really finish, that you simply, at some point, have to stop. Our hero may ride off into the sunset, but the neatness of THE END is not on offer to the characters in the movie, only to the spectators in the audience. But we weren't only spectators. We were *in*, that was the deal.

So? So what?

So I need to know . . . No, I can't know. I need to *believe* that what I put out there, the hands I dealt, the chances I took with the cards that I got, that they had some kind of meaningful effect, that others will discern affordances for themselves. Oh, so that's why . . .

Why what?

Why it's so hard to stop when you can't finish. It does all fit together, you see? Well, most of it, anyway.

Tell me.

Oh, and I've just seen more, and that fits, too.

Do tell.

As a pragmatist, and to the extent that I have understood the Dewey and the Rorty that I have read, I am not looking to justify some version of 'the truth' dependent on past events or arguments. I am trying to articulate my best understanding against a criterion of what will be most useful in the future. The test of that will always lie ahead. To stop is to fail to test your articulation. But not to keep on attempting that future-oriented theorization would be an unacceptable failure of nerve. At some point, whether you are ahead of the game, or you've just been wiped out, you have to stop, even as you see the next possibility. That's why my original, naïve idea of a book to summarize, to round things off, was never really feasible, because that attempt to summarize, that so-called last job, always entails theorizing that looks to the future for the validation of its contribution. Who rides the pragmatist tiger can never dismount.

Clever line, but overdoing it a bit? Anyway, you are still left with the fact that you have to stop at some point – immortality not being an option. Also, you are left with the question as to whether this is indeed the last job.

Oh, no doubt. This was the last job. The point of spelling out that last 'tiger' paradox is to accept it. That is something else that I have learned by reading Rorty. It's a mistake to think that everything can be decided at the level of high abstract principle. Sometimes, pretty often, in fact, you have to work at a 'sub-philosophical' level in order to make good decisions on a case-by-case basis. The book, I think, like one of those course participant assignments, is a disappointing success. It was my best shot under the circumstances. It couldn't ever be anything more. I can live with that. There are a lot of things that I'm not going to get to say, but that would always be the case, because they arise from what I have just said and am in the process of saying – it's not as though there is simply a stock of already fabricated thoughts waiting to be said. And, for sure, I have had my fair share of chances to talk. Oh yes, this was the last job.

A disappointing success, contingent on circumstance, partly untested, by definition incomplete and anyway not necessary. That's it?

Yes, is that not enough?

Don't you worry that if you present the work in those terms, you undermine the reader's belief in how seriously you take it yourself, and therefore how much attention the reader should pay to it?

Yes, I do worry about that. And people have warned me about coming across like that before. But to me, you see, I am making big claims. This whole book has been the kind of reflexive experience that I see my working life as having been. I reached out to shape something and it reached around to shape me. Take one last example. In Edge (2008b), I wrote about being in a position to see some coherence in my professional life, though I wasn't sure whether that coherence was actually there in the episodes and events that I recounted, or was a *post hoc* imposition of my own. I now see the extent to which my thinking then was trapped inside a traditional Platonic, realism/idealism duality regarding where the truth lies – out there or in my head. I also see how my attempts to formulate a response to that question (ibid.:117) were my first steps in the direction of the Rortian pragmatism that this book has helped me discover. I now see that there is no 'coherence' other than what I can articulate and justify (and possibly get you to acknowledge). The coherence (or otherwise) is not a separate reality, either out there or in my head, that I am trying to represent; it is here in this communication, to the extent that I can justify it. This is still a bit of a conceptual struggle for me, but I find it exciting and energizing.

Furthermore, in saying this, I believe that I am making large claims about, for example, the relevance of philosophy to the life of a reflexive teacher educator. I am looking as deeply into myself as I can and I am soaring as high as I can. I feel my roots drawing in sustenance and I feel the sun on my wings. And if you warn me of immortality not being an option, don't think for a minute that I won't remind you of my (I hope at least partially) redeemed heroes, Narcissus and Icarus. A little piece of those myths might go a long way. I might also remind you that you started out by worrying not that this book might be too tentative or self-effacing, but that it would be too self-regarding and overambitious.

Mmmm. Fancy that.

So please don't doubt how seriously I take this work or this book. But in order to take them both as seriously as I do, I must avoid seeming to present them as more than they could be, even when successful: an incomplete, contingent articulation in my current final vocabulary, aiming not at demonstrable truth, but at negotiable hope. The best I can do under the circumstances. Necessary for me, available for others.

And is that what you call getting away with it, or not? How about a yes/no answer?

There is no reason to believe that what one person wants to say can be well expressed by a yes/no answer to someone else's question . . .

Oh, for goodness' sake!

. . . but, under the circumstances as I understand them, yes, I am hoping to have got away with it. I'm waiting to hear what you think.

★   ★   ★   ★   ★

It's late. So late that there is light in the sky. Even in an avowedly elegiac movie, anyone can tell that this scene is pretty close to the end of the story. The saloon has thinned out considerably. The girls have left with their clients. Joey has stopped pounding ragtime out of the piano, though Louise is now hunched over the keys, gently chording 'Visions of Johanna' (Dylan 1966) and humming the melody. The gunfighter brought in by the big rancher who commands most of the water rights remains, apparently half-asleep, in a chair to the side of the entrance. Around your table, a small crowd has gathered, slowly growing as the cards rise and fall and the money moves around and accumulates. The gambler deals once more. The tension rises.

You pick up a pair of fours, a seven, a ten and the Queen of Hearts. You change only two cards. (You never discard the Queen of Hearts. That's one reason why you'll never be a real player.) You draw an eight and the Queen of Spades. You can't help being lucky. Two pairs, queens over fours. The gambler changes just one card. Everyone else folds and there are only the two of you left in.

He looks up. For the first time all night, he looks you in the eyes. Smiles. Raises his eyebrows. Riffles the cards. Doesn't mind either way.

'I'm out,' you say.

A muttering runs through the crowd. The gunfighter unfolds himself from his chair, stands, stretches, flexes the fingers of his right hand and takes a step towards your table.

'That's not how it goes, my friend.'

'Says who?'

'Says me. And says my boss, who owns this place, who owns this town, who says who plays when, and who says how the story goes down.'

'I think you'll find that the point of this particular narrative has been much to do with not getting ourselves caught up in the schematic expectations of the past, even if we borrow their metaphors, but rather with discerning for ourselves the affordances that will allow us to move ahead, to cope better, to cooperate more, to flourish.'

The gunfighter's lips move silently as his right shoulder drops. The crowd scatters. His movements are almost balletic as his left arm swoops away from his body in order to maintain his balance, his knees bend into a half-crouch, and the Colt .45 clears its holster in a blur of hand, metal and leather. Simultaneously, however, the action shifts into extreme slow motion and, frame by frame, the gunfighter begins to become transparent. Just as the hammer of the revolver cocks into place, and the barrel achieves its horizontal, deadly stare, he disappears altogether. From various points around the room, there is a collective gasp.

The gambler, who has moved only to the extent of shifting his body sideways to the gunfighter's position, returns a small, silvered Derringer to its place beneath his coat.

'Saah,' he drawls, 'In terms of autonomous, conscious awareness, I believe you have just eliminated an unarmed man.'

You turn to face him.

'I also believe you had indicated a disinclination to continue with our entertainment here?'

You nod. He nods in return. You like to think that there was a kind of respect in that small gesture. You hope so.

Impassive, neither revealing the hand that he had held, nor showing any interest in looking at yours, he scoops together the cards and the winnings. You pick up your money. It looks about right. Maybe even a little more than you came in with. Anyway, now's not the time to count it. You head for the door. The piano has stopped. Behind you, you hear the scrape of a chair and someone says,

'Deal me in.'

You smile. No big last hand, then. No shoot-out. No riding off into the sunset. You step out onto the sidewalk and take a deep breath of chill morning air. Out at the edge of town there is a wind moving the trees; big birds soar overhead. Damn, it was good to have played for a while. You turn, one way or the other, and are soon lost in the early shadows.

Thoughts rage, of course, wanting to be heard.

'But it wasn't a *game*. I was never just "*playing*." That was a whole working *life*. The "game" was just a metaphor. Will they see that? Should I explain?'

Important not to lose your nerve now. You know full well that that's not how it works.

The camera pans back to the table, where the cards are moving again.

THE END . . .

REFERENCES

Akbari, R. (2007). Reflections on reflection: A critical appraisal of reflective practices in L2 teacher education. *System* 35 (2), 192–207.

Albert, E. (1972). Culture patterning of speech in Burundi. In J. Gumperz & D. Hymes (eds) *Directions in sociolinguistics* (pp.72–104). New York: Holt, Rinehart & Winston.

Alexander, H. (ed.) (1998). *The essential Dewey*. Bloomington, IN: Indiana University Press.

Allard, C., Goldblatt, P., Kemball, J., Kendrick, S., Millen, K. & Smith, D. (2007). Becoming a reflective community of practice. *Reflective Practice* 8 (3), 299–314.

Altrichter, H., Posch, P. & Somekh, B. (1993). *Teachers investigate their work*. London: Routledge.

Andrews, S. (2003). Teacher language awareness and the professional knowledge base of the L2 teacher. *Language Awareness* 12 (2), 81–95.

Argyris, C. & Schön, D. (1974). *Theory in practice: Increasing professional effectiveness*. San Francisco, CA: Jossey-Bass.

Aronowitz, S. & Giroux, H. (1985). *Education under siege: The conservative, liberal and radical debate over schooling*. South Hadley, MA: Bergin & Garvey Inc.

Atkinson, D. (2002). Comments on Ryuko Kubota's 'Discursive construction of the images of US classrooms' – A reader reacts. *TESOL Quarterly* 36 (1), 79–84.

Austin, J. (1962). *How to do things with words*. Cambridge: Cambridge University Press.

Bailey, K., Curtis, A. & Nunan, D. (2001). *Pursuing professional development: The self as source*. Boston: Heinle & Heinle.

Bakhtin, M. (1981). *The dialogic imagination: Four essays*. Austin: University of Texas Press.

Barber, K., Butorac, D. & Haak, S. (2005). Cooperative development: A discourse framework for individual professional development. Workshop at TAFEWA 7th Annual Best Practice Teaching Forum, Perth, December 2005.

Barber, K., Butorac, D. & Haak, S. (2006). Developing appropriate cultures of teacher learning. Paper presented at AMEP National Conference, Perth, July 2006.

Bartlett, F. (1932). *Remembering*. Cambridge: Cambridge University Press.

Bateson, G. (1999). *Steps to an ecology of mind*. Chicago: University of Chicago Press.

Bax, S. (2003a). The end of CLT: A context approach to language teaching. *ELT Journal* 57 (3), 278–287.

Bax, S. (2003b). Bringing context and methodology together. *ELT Journal* 57 (3), 295–296.

Bedny, G. Z. & Karwowski, W. (2004). Activity theory as a basis for the study of work. *Ergonomics*, 47 (2), 134–153.

Behar, R. (1996). The vulnerable observer. In R. Behar (ed.) *The vulnerable observer: Anthropology that breaks your heart* (pp.1–34). Boston: Beacon Press.

Berne, E. (1968). *Games people play*. Harmondsworth: Penguin.

Bernstein, B. (1971). *Class, codes and control* (Vol. 1). London: Paladin.

Bibila, S. (forthcoming) Teacher professional development in the era of Hermes. *TESOL Journal*.

Block, D. (2007). *Second language identities*. London/New York: Continuum.

Boon, A. (2003). On the road to teacher development: Awareness, discovery and action. *The Language Teacher* 27 (12), 3–7.

Boon, A. (2005). Is there anybody out there? *Essential Teacher* 2 (2), 1–9.

Boon, A. (2007). Building bridges – Instant messenger cooperative development. *The Language Teacher* 31 (12), 9–13.

Boon, A. (2009). I can see clearly now. *Modern English Teacher* 18 (1), 56–64.

Borg, S. (2006). *Teacher cognition in language education: Research and practice*. Chapter 7: Verbal commentaries. London: Continuum.

Boshell, M. (2002). What I learnt from giving quiet children space. In K. Johnson & P. Golombek (pp.180–194).

Bourdieu, P. (1977). *Outline of a theory of practice*. Cambridge: Cambridge University Press.

Bourdieu, P. (1992). *An invitation to reflexive sociology*. Chicago: University of Chicago Press.

Boxer, P. (1985). Judging the quality of development. In D. Boud, R. Keogh & D. Walker (eds) *Reflection: Turning experience into learning* (pp.117–127). London: Kogan Page.

Braine, G. (ed.) (1999). *Non-native educators in English language teaching*. Mahwah, NJ: Erlbaum.

Brogan, W. & Risser, J. (2000). Introduction. In W. Brogan & J. Risser (eds) *American Continental Philosophy* (pp.1–12). Bloomington: Indiana University Press.

Brown, J., Collins, A. & Duguid, P. (1989). Situated Cognition and the Culture of Learning. *Educational Researcher* 18 (1), 32–42.

Brown, K. (2000). Conclusion: Creative thinking about a new modern languages pedagogy. In S. Green (ed.) *New perspectives on teaching and learning modern languages* (pp.183–194). Clevedon: Multilingual Matters.

Browne, J. (1973). These days. On *For everyman*. Asylum Records. Open Windows Music.

Brumfit, C. (2006). What, then, must we do? Or, who gets hurt when we speak, write and teach? In J. Edge (ed.) (2006b) (pp.27–48).

Burns, A. (1999). *Collaborative action research for English language teachers*. Cambridge: Cambridge University Press.

Butorac, D. (2006). Inviting views of change: An effective framework for appropriate teacher development. Paper presented at TESOL-Italy National Conference, Napoli, November 2006.

Butorac, D. (2008). Managing Change in the Adult Migrant English Program. *Prospect* 23 (1), 4–15.

Butorac, D., Azzato, J., Bougie, M. & Purvis, D. (2005). Developing the community of practice in the AMEP. Paper presented at AMEP National Conference, Sydney, September 2005.

Campbell, J. (1973). *Myths to live by*. New York: Bantam Books.

Canagarajah, S. (2006a). TESOL at forty: What are the issues? *TESOL Quarterly* 40 (1), 9–34.

Canagarajah, S. (ed.) (2006b). *TESOL Quarterly* 40 (1). Special issue.

Capra, F. (1983). *The Tao of physics*. London: Flamingo.

Capra, F. (2001). *The hidden connections.* London: Flamingo.

Carr, W. & Kemmis, S. (1986). *Becoming critical.* London: The Falmer Press.

Carrell, P. (1983). Three components of background knowledge in reading comprehension. *Language Learning* 33 (2), 183–207.

Carroll, L. (1872). *Through the Looking Glass.* Ch. 6.

Casanave, C. & Sosa, M. (2007). *Respite for teachers: Reflection and renewal in the teaching life.* Ann Arbor: University of Michigan Press.

Charmaz, C. (2003). Grounded theory: Objectivist and constructivist methods. In N. Denzin & Y. Lincoln (eds) *Strategies of qualitative inquiry* (2nd edn) (pp.249–291). London: Sage.

Cheng, J-M. (2006). Awareness-raising through analyzing written discourse. Unpublished independent study paper, MA in Ed. Tech. and TESOL, University of Manchester, England.

Clandinin, J. (2008). Creating learning spaces for teachers and teacher educators. *Teachers and Teaching: Theory and Practice* 14 (5), 385–389.

Clarke, M. (1994). The dysfunctions of the theory/practice discourse. *TESOL Quarterly* 28 (1), 9–26.

Clarke, M. (2003). *A place to stand: Essays for educators in troubled times.* Ann Arbor, University of Michigan Press.

Clarke, M. (2007). *Common ground, contested territory: English language teaching in troubled times.* Ann Arbor, University of Michigan Press.

Clarke, M. & Edge, J. (2009). Building a communicative toolkit for leadership. In M. Christison & D. Murray (eds) *Leadership in English language education* (pp.186–199). London: Routledge.

Cobbett, W. (1817). *Political Register,* 6 December, col. 1094. Cited in Mengham (p.131).

Cobuild Concordancer (http://www.collins.co.uk/Corpus/CorpusSearch.aspx)

Cohen, L. (1992). Anthem. On *The future.* Leonard Cohen Stranger Music.

Cook, V. (1999). Going beyond the native speaker in language teaching. *TESOL Quarterly* 33 (2), 185–210.

Cook, V. (2000). Comments on Vivian Cook's 'Going beyond the native speaker in language teaching.' The author responds. *TESOL Quarterly* 34 (2), 329–332.

Coulthard, R. (1986). *An introduction to sociolinguistics.* Harlow: Longman.

Cummins, J. (1996). *Negotiating identities: Education for empowerment in a diverse society.* Ontario, CA: California Association for Bilingual Education.

Curtis, A. (2006). Dark matter: Teaching and learning between black and white. In A. Curtis & M. Romney (eds) *Color, race and English language teaching: Shades of meaning* (pp.11–22.). Mahway, NJ: Erlbaum.

Czikszentmihaly, M. (1990). *Flow: The psychology of optimal experience.* New York: Harper & Row.

D'Cruz, H., Gillingham, P. & Melendez, S. (2007). Reflexivity, its meanings and relevance for social work: A critical review of the literature. *British Journal of Social Work* 37, 73–90.

Dawkins, R. (1986). *The blind watchmaker.* London: Longman.

de Sonneville, J. (2007). 'Acknowledgement' as a key in teacher learning. *ELT Journal* 61 (1), 55–62.

Denzin, N. (2009). *Qualitative inquiry under fire.* Walnut Creek, CA: Left Coast Press.

Derrida, J. (1982). *Margins of philosophy.* Chicago: Chicago University Press.

Dewey, J. (1916). *Democracy and education.* New York: The Free Press.

Dewey, J. (1931/1970). The development of American Pragmatism. In H. Thayer (ed.) (pp.23–40).

Dewey, J. (1933). *How we think: A re-statement of the relation of reflective thinking to the education process.* Boston: DC Heath & Co.

Dewey, J. (1958). *Experience and nature.* New York: Dover Publications.

Dillard, A. (1982). (Reissued 2008). *Teaching a stone to talk.* New York: Harper Perennial.

Du Preez, J. (2008). Locating the researcher in the research: Personal narrative and reflective practice. *Reflective Practice* 9 (4), 509–519.

Dylan, B. (1966). Visions of Johanna. On *Blonde on Blonde.* Columbia Records. Sony Music Entertainment.

Edge, J. (1984). Feedback with face: peer microteaching in TEFL. *ELT Journal* 38 (3), 204–206.

Edge, J. (1985). Do TEFL articles solve problems? *ELT Journal* 39 (3), 153–7.

Edge, J. (1986a). Acquisition disappears in adultery: Interaction in the translation class. *ELT Journal* 40 (2), 121–124.

Edge, J. (1986b). Towards a professional reading strategy for EFL teacher trainees. Unpublished PhD thesis, Birmingham, UK: University of Birmingham.

Edge, J. (1987). Letter to *ELT Journal* 41 (4), 308–309.

Edge, J. (1988a). Applying linguistics in English language teacher training for speakers of other languages. *ELT Journal* 42 (1), 9–13.

Edge, J. (1988b). Natives, speakers and models. *JALT Journal* (Japan) 9 (2), 153–157.

Edge, J. (1989). Ablocutionary value: on the application of language teaching to linguistics. *Applied Linguistics* 10 (4), 407–417.

Edge, J. (1992). *Cooperative development.* Harlow: Longman.

Edge, J. (1994a). Empowerment: principles and procedures in teacher education. In R. Budd, D. Arnsdorf & P. Chaix (eds) *Triangle XII: The European dimension in pre- and in-service language teacher development – new directions* (pp.113–134). Paris: Didier Erudition.

Edge, J. (1994b). ELT culture and communication. *IATEFL Newsletter* 125, 18–19.

Edge, J. (1996a). Cross-cultural paradoxes in a profession of values. *TESOL Quarterly* 30 (1), 9–30.

Edge, J. (1996b). Keeping the faith. *TESOL Matters* 6 (4), 1, 23.

Edge, J. (1998). *The Foundation Module.* MSc in TESOL. Birmingham, UK: Aston University.

Edge, J. (2001a). Attitude and access: Building a new teaching community in TESOL. In J. Edge (ed.) (2001b) (pp.1–12).

Edge, J. (ed.) (2001b). *Case studies in TESOL: Action research.* Alexandria, VA: TESOL Inc.

Edge, J. (ed.) (2002a). *Continuing cooperative development: A discourse framework for individuals as colleagues.* Ann Arbor: University of Michigan Press.

Edge, J. (ed.) (2002b). *Continuing professional development: Some of our perspectives.* Whitstable, UK: IATEFL.

Edge, J. (2003a). Alternative discourses in teacher education. Interview in *ELT Journal* 57 (4), 386–394.

Edge, J. (2003b). Imperial troopers and servants of the lord: A vision of TESOL for the 21st century. *TESOL Quarterly* 37 (4), 701–709.

Edge, J. (2003c). *The Foundation Module.* MSc in TESOL. Birmingham, UK: Aston University.

Edge, J. (2004). Of displacive and augmentative discourse, old doubts and new enemies. *TESOL Quarterly* 38 (4), 717–721.

Edge, J. (2006a). Computer-mediated cooperative development: Non-judgmental discourse in online environments. *Language Teaching Research* 10 (2), 205–227.

Edge, J. (ed.) (2006b). *(Re-)Locating TESOL in an age of empire.* Basingstoke: Palgrave.

Edge, J. (2008a). Interested theory and theorizing as goal. *TESOL Quarterly* 42 (4), 653–654.

Edge, J. (2008b). Discourses in search of coherence: An autobiographical perspective. In S. Garton, & K. Richards (eds) (pp.232–247).

Edge, J. (2009). Making a difference in TESOL professional development. In H. Chen &

K. Cruickshank (eds) *Making a difference: Challenges for applied linguistics* (pp.171–187). Newcastle, UK: Cambridge Scholar Press.

Edge, J. (2010a). Elaborating the monolingual deficit. In D. Nunan & J. Choi (eds) (pp.89–96).

Edge, J. (2010b). Beyond approaches, methods and techniques. Course unit. MA TESOL. University of Manchester.

Edge, J. & Garton, S. (2009). *From experience to knowledge in ELT*. Oxford: Oxford University Press.

Edge, J. & Norton, B. (1999). Culture, power and possibility in teacher education. Paper presented at the annual TESOL Convention, New York, March 1999.

Edge, J. & Richards, K. (1998). May I see your warrant, please? Justifying outcomes in qualitative research. *Applied Linguistics* 19 (3), 334–356.

Edge, J. & Wharton, S. (2001). Patterns of text in teacher education. In M. Scott & G. Thompson (eds) *The patterns of text* (pp.255–286). Amsterdam: John Benjamins.

Edge, J. & Wharton, S. (2002). Genre teaching: The struggle for diversity in unity. In K. Miller & P. Thompson (eds) *Unity and diversity in language use* (pp.22–38). London: BAAL/Continuum.

Edge, J. & Wharton, S. (2003). Research in teacher education: reading it, doing it, writing it. In B. Beaven & S. Borg (eds) *The role of research in teacher education* (pp.49–53). Whitstable: IATEFL/Oyster Press.

Edge, J. & Richards, K. (eds) (1993). *Teachers develop teachers research*. Oxford: Heinemann.

Emerson, R. (1979). *Collected works of Ralph Waldo Emerson* (Vol. 2) (p. 190). Cambridge, MA: Harvard University Press.

Engestrøm, R. (1995). Voice as communicative action. *Mind, Culture and Activity* 2 (3), 192–215.

Engestrøm, Y. (2001). Expansive learning at work: Toward an activity theoretical reconceptualisation. *Education at Work*, 14 (1), 133–155.

Erlandson, P. & Beach, D. (2008). The ambivalence of reflection – Rereading Schön. *Reflective Practice* 9 (4), 409–421.

Farrell, T. (2007). *Reflective language teaching: From research to practice*. London: Continuum.

Fendler, L. (2003). Teacher reflection in a hall of mirrors: Historical influences and political reverberations. *Educational Researcher* 32, 16–25.

Finlay, L. (2002). 'Outing' the researcher: The provenance, principles and practice of reflexivity. *Qualitative Health Research* 12 (3), 531–545.

Finlay, L. (2003a). The reflexive journey: Mapping multiple routes. In Finlay & Gough (eds) (pp.3–19).

Finlay, L. (2003b). Through the looking glass: Intersubjectivity and hermeneutic reflection. In Finlay & Gough (eds) (pp.105–119).

Finlay, L. & Gough, B. (eds) (2003). *Reflexivity: A practical guide for researchers in health and social sciences*. Oxford: Blackwell.

Forbes, J. (2008). Reflexivity in professional doctoral research. *Reflective Practice* 9 (4), 449–460.

Francis, B. & Skelton, C. (2008). 'The self-made self': Analysing the potential contribution to the field of gender and education of theories that disembed selfhood. *Discourse: Studies in the Cultural Politics of Education* 29 (3), 311–323.

Freeman, D. (1998). *Doing teacher research: From inquiry to understanding*. Boston, MA: Heinle & Heinle.

Fullan, M. & Hargreaves, A. (1992). Teacher development and educational change. In M. Fullan & A. Hargreaves (eds) *Teacher development and educational change*. London: The Falmer Press.

Garton, S. & Richards, K. (eds) (2008). *Professional encounters in TESOL: Discourses of teachers in teaching.* Basingstoke: Palgrave.

Gass, S. & Mackey, A. (2002). *Stimulated recall methodology in second language research.* Mahwah, NJ: Lawrence Erlbaum Associates.

Gebhard, J. and Oprandy, R. (1999). *Language teaching awareness: A guide to exploring beliefs and practices.* Cambridge: Cambridge University Press.

Gibson, E. (1991). *An oddyssey in learning and perception.* Cambridge, MA: MIT Press.

Gibson, J. (1979). *The ecological approach to visual perception.* Boston: Houghton Mifflin.

Giddens, A. (1991). *Modernity and self-identity.* Cambridge: Polity.

Giroux, H. (1988). *Teachers as intellectuals: Toward a critical pedagogy of learning.* Brandy, MA: Bergin & Garvey Inc.

Giroux, H. & McLaren, P. (eds) 1989. Critical pedagogy: The state and cultural struggle. New York: State University of New York Press.

Goldberg, E. (2005). *The wisdom paradox.* New York: Gotham Books.

Gopnik, A. (2009). *Angels and ages: A short book about Darwin, Lincoln and modern life.* London: Quercus.

Gore, J. (1991). Practicing what we preach: Action research and the supervision of student teachers. In R. Tabchnick & K. Zeichner (eds) *Issues and practices in inquiry-oriented teacher education* (pp.253–273). London: The Falmer Press.

Graves, R. (1960). *The Greek myths* (Vol. 1). Harmondsworth: Penguin.

Gray, C. (2001). *Mentor development in the education of modern language teachers.* Clevedon: Multilingual Matters.

Griffith, T. (2004). Unless a grain of wheat . . . *TESOL Quarterly* 38(4), 714–716.

Grimmet, P. & Neufeld, J. (eds) (1994). *Teacher development and the struggle for authenticity.* New York: Teachers College Press.

Hales, T. (1997). Exploring data-driven language awareness. *ELT Journal* 51 (3), 217–223.

Harmer, J. (2003). Popular culture, methods, and context. *ELT Journal* 57 (3), 288–294.

Hawkins, M. & Norton, B. (2009). Critical language teacher education. In A. Burns & J. Richards (eds) *Cambridge guide to second language teacher education* (pp.30–39). Cambridge: Cambridge University Press.

Hedge, T. (2000). *Teaching and learning in the language classroom.* Oxford: Oxford University Press.

Hennissen, P., Crasborn, F., Brouwer, N., Korthagen, F. & Bergen, T. (2009). Uncovering contents of mentor teachers' interactive cognitions during mentoring dialogues. *Teaching and Teacher Education* 25, 1–8.

Herbert, F. (1965). *Dune.* London: Gollancz.

Hoey, M. (1983). *On the surface of discourse.* London: Allen & Unwin.

Hoey, M. (2001). *Textual interaction: An introduction to written discourse analysis.* London: Routledge.

Holliday, A. (1994). *Appropriate methodology and social context.* Cambridge: Cambridge University Press.

Holliday, A. (2005). *The struggle to teach English as an international language.* Oxford: Oxford University Press.

Holliday, A. (2007). Response to 'ELT and "the spirit of the times" '. *ELT Journal* 61 (4), 360–366.

Holliday, A. & Aboshiha, P. (2009). The denial of ideology in perceptions of 'nonnative speaker' teachers. *TESOL Quarterly* 43 (4), 669–689.

Hymes, D. (1972). On communicative competence. In J. Pride & J. Holmes (eds) *Sociolinguistics* (pp.269–293). Harmondsworth: Penguin.

Irwin, T. (1999). *Aristotle: Nicomachean ethics* (2nd edn). Indianapolis: Hackett Publishing Company.

Javier, E. (2010). The foreign-ness of native-speaking teachers of colour. In D. Nunan & J. Choi (eds) (pp.97–102).

Johnson, K. (1994). The emerging beliefs and instructional practices of pre-service English as a Second Language teachers. *Teaching and Teacher Education* 10 (4), 439–452.

Johnson, K. (2006). The sociocultural turn and its challenges for second language teacher education. *TESOL Quarterly* 40 (1), 235–257.

Johnson, K. (2009). *Second language teacher education: A sociocultural perspective*. New York: Routledge.

Johnson, K. & Golombek, P. (eds) (2002). *Teachers' narrative inquiry as professional development*. Cambridge: Cambridge University Press.

Johnston, B. (1997). Do ESOL teachers have careers? *TESOL Quarterly* 38 (4), 681–712.

Johnston, B. (2000). In search of the knowledge base of language teaching: Explanations by experienced teachers. *Canadian Modern Language Review* 56 (3), 437–468.

Johnston, B. (2003). *Values in English language teaching*. Mahwah, NJ: Erlbaum.

Johnston, B. & Peterson, S. (1994). The program matrix: A conceptual framework for language programs. *System* 22 (1), 63–80.

Kamhi-Stein, L. D. (ed.). (2004). Learning and teaching from experience: Perspectives on nonnative English-speaking professionals. Ann Arbor: University of Michigan Press.

Karmani, S. (2005). English, 'terror', and Islam. *Applied Linguistics* 26 (2), 262–267.

Kegan, R. (1994). *In over our heads: The mental demands of modern life*. Cambridge, MA: Harvard University Press.

Kegan, R. & Lahey, L. (2001). *How the way we talk can change the way we work*. San Francisco: Jossey Bass.

Kemmis, S. & McTaggart, R. (eds) (1988). *The action research planner* (3rd edn). Geelong: Deakin University Press.

Kirwan, C. (1995). Reflexivity. In T. Honderich (ed.) *The Oxford companion to philosophy* (p.753). Oxford: Oxford University Press.

Kolb, D. (1984). *Experiential Learning: Experience as the source of learning and development*. Englewood Cliffs, New Jersey: Prentice-Hall Inc.

Kubota, R. (2002). (Un)Raveling racism in a nice field like TESOL. *TESOL Quarterly* 36 (1), 84–92.

Kubota, R. (ed.) (2006). *Race and TESOL. TESOL Quarterly* 40 (3). Special issue.

Kubota, R. & Lin, A. (eds) (2009). *Race, culture, and identities in second language education: Exploring critically engaged practice*. New York: Routledge.

Kumaravadivelu, B. (2001). Toward a postmethod pedagogy. *TESOL Quarterly* 35 (4), 537–560.

Kumaravadivelu, B. (2003a). *Beyond methods: Macrostrategies for language teaching*. New Haven, CO: Yale University Press.

Kumaravadivelu, B. (2003b). Evangelical zeal not matched by humility, curiosity. San Jose, CA: *The Mercury News*, 15 September. http://www.christianaggression.org/search.php retrieved on 2 May 2010.

Kumaravadivelu, B. (2006a). Dangerous liaison: Globalization, empire and TESOL. In J. Edge (ed.) (2006b) (pp.1–26).

Kumaravadivelu, B. (2006b). Americans should be able to see Al-Jazeera English TV. San Jose, CA: *The Mercury News*, 30 November. http://www.globalpolicy.org/component/content/article/154-general/26645.html retrieved on 15 January 2010.

Kumaravadivelu, B. & Krishnaswamy, R. (2009). California school reform: 'It's the teaching, stupid.' San Jose, CA: *The Mercury News*, 21 December. http://mercurynews.com/opinion/ci14050303?source-email retrieved on 15 January 2010.

Lantolf, J. & Thorne, S. (2006). *Sociocultural theory and the genesis of second language development*. Oxford: Oxford University Press.

Lantolf, J. (ed.) (2000). *Sociocultural theory and second language learning*. Oxford: Oxford University Press.

Lantolf, J. & Appel, G. (eds) (1994). *Vygotskian approaches to second language research*. New Jersey: Ablex.

Lave, J. & Wenger, E. (1991). *Situated learning: Legitimate peripheral participation*. Cambridge: Cambridge University Press.

Lazaraton, A. (2003). Incidental displays of cultural knowledge in the nonnative English speaking teacher's classroom. *TESOL Quarterly* 37 (2), 213–245.

Lazaraton, A. & Ishihara, N. (2005). Understanding second language teacher practice using microanalysis and self-reflection: A collaborative case study. *The Modern Language Journal* 89 (4), 529–542.

Leont'ev, A. (1981). *Problems of the development of mind*. Moscow: Progress Press.

Leung, C., Harris, R., & Rampton, B. (1997). The idealised native speaker, reified ethnicities, and classroom realities. *TESOL Quarterly*, 31 (3), 543–558.

Levin, H. (1965). *Christopher Marlowe: the Overreacher*. London: Faber.

Liu, J. (1999). Nonnative-English-speaking-professionals. *TESOL Quarterly*, 33 (1), 85–102.

Llurda, E. (ed.) (2006). *Non-native language teachers: Perceptions, challenges and contributions to the profession*. New York: Springer.

Lortie, D. (1975). *Schoolteacher: A sociological study*. Chicago: University of Chicago Press.

Loughran, J. (1996). *Developing reflective practice: Learning about teaching and learning through modelling*. London: The Falmer Press.

Ludema, J., Cooperrider, D. & Barrett, F. (2001). Appreciative inquiry: The power of the unconditional positive question. In P. Reason & H. Bradbury (eds) (pp.189–199).

Lynch, M. (2000). Against reflexivity as an academic virtue and source of privileged knowledge. *Theory, Culture and Society* 17 (3), 26–54.

Maclean, N. (1976). *A river runs through it and other stories*. Chicago: University of Chicago Press.

Malachowski, A. (2002). *Richard Rorty*. Chesham, UK: Acumen Publishing Ltd.

Mann, S. (2002). Talking ourselves into understanding. In K. Johnson & P. Golombek (eds) (pp.195–209).

Marcus, G. (1994). What comes (just) after 'Post'?: The case of ethnography. In N. Denzin & Y. Lincoln (eds) *The Handbook of Qualitative Research* (pp.563–574). London: Sage.

Matsuda, P. (2003). Proud to be a nonnative English speaker. *TESOL Matters* 13 (4), 15.

Maturana, R. & Varela, F. (1987). *The tree of knowledge: The biological roots of human understanding*. Boston: Shambhala.

Mauthner, N. & Doucet, A. (2003). Reflexive accounts and accounts of reflexivity in qualitative analysis. *Sociology* 37, 413–431.

McIlveen, P. (2008). Autoethnography as a method for reflexive research and practice in vocational psychology. *Australian Journal of Career Development* 17 (2), 13–20.

McIntyre, D., Macleod, G. & Griffiths, R. (1977). *Investigations of microteaching*. London: Croom Helm.

McLeod, W. (1984). *Thesaurus*. London: Collins.

McNair, P., Hoover, A. & Neary, K. (1984). *The legacy: Tradition and innovation in Northwest Coast Indian art*. Seattle: University of Washington Press.

Mearns, D. & Cooper, M. (2005). *Working at relational depth in counselling and therapy*. London: Sage.

Medgyes, P. (1992). Native or nonnative: Who's worth more? *ELT Journal*, 46 (4), 340–349.

Medgyes, P. (1994). *The non-native teacher*. London: Macmillan Publishers.

Medina, J. (2005). *Language: Key concepts in philosophy*. London: Continuum.

Meijer, P., Zanting, A. & Verloop, N. (2002). How can students teachers elicit experienced teachers' practical knowledge? Tools, suggestions and significance. *Journal of Teacher Education* 53, 406–419.

Menand, L. (2001). *The metaphysical club: A story of ideas in America*. New York: Farrar Straus & Giroux.

Mengham, R. (1995). *Language*. London: Fontana Press.

Merleau-Ponty, M. (1968). *The visible and the invisible*. Evanston: Northwest University Press.

Milambiling, J. (2000). How non-native speakers as teachers fit into the equation. *TESOL Quarterly* 34 (2), 324–328.

Mitchell, J. (1977). Amelia. On *Hejira*. Warner Music. Crazy Crow Music.

Moorcock, M. (2001). *Elric of Melnibone: The tale of the eternal champion*. London: Gollancz.

Myers, M. & Clark, S. (2002). CPD, lifelong learning and going meta. In J. Edge (ed.) (2002b) (pp.50–62).

Nemtchinova, K. (2005). Host teachers' evaluations of non-native English speaking teacher trainees. *TESOL Quarterly* 39 (2), 235–261.

Norton, B. (2000). *Identity and language learning: Gender, ethnicity, and educational change*. Harlow, UK: Longman.

Norton Peirce, B. (1995). Social investment, identity and language learning. *TESOL Quarterly* 29 (1), 9–31.

Nunan, D. (1993). *Action research in language education*. In J. Edge & K. Richards (eds) (pp.39–50).

Nunan, D. & Choi, J. (eds) (2010). *Language and culture: Reflective narratives and the emergence of identity*. London: Routledge.

Olsen, D. (1977). The languages of instruction. In R. Anderson, R. Spiro & W. Montague (eds) *Schooling and the acquisition of knowledge* (pp.65–90). Hillsdale, NJ: Lawrence Erlbaum.

Paikeday, T. (1985). *The native speaker is dead*. Toronto: Paikeday Publishing Inc.

Palmer, A. & Christison, M. (2007). *Seeking the heart of teaching*. Ann Arbor: University of Michigan Press.

Park, Y. (2006). Will nonnative English speaking teachers ever get a fair chance? *Essential Teacher* 3 (1), 32–34.

Pavlenko, A, (2003). 'I never knew I was a bilingual': Reimagining teacher identities in TESOL. *Journal of Language, Identity and Education* 2, 251–268.

Pavlenko, A. & Blackledge, A. (eds) (2003). *Negotiation of identities in multilingual contexts*. Clevedon: Multilingual Matters.

Pennycook, A. (1989). The concept of method, interested knowledge, and the politics of language teaching. *TESOL Quarterly* 23 (4), 589–618.

Pennycook, A. (1994). *The cultural politics of English as an international language*. London: Longman.

Pennycook, A. (2001). *Critical applied linguistics: A critical introduction*. Mahwah, NJ: Erlbaum.

Pennycook, A. (2009). Is dialogue possible? Anti-intellectualism, relativism, politics and linguistic ideologies. In M. Wong & S. Canagarajah (eds) (pp.60–65).

Perkins, A. (2002). Continuing professional development: Sojourn or odyssey? In J. Edge (ed.) (2002b) (pp.97–103).

Phillipson, R. (1992). *Linguistic imperialism*. Oxford: Oxford University Press.

Phillipson, R. (2009a). *Linguistic imperialism continued*. London: Routledge.

Phillipson, R. (2009b). Review of Edge (2006b). *TESOL Quarterly* 43 (1), 163–166

Prabhu, N. (1990). There is no best method – why? *TESOL Quarterly* 24 (2), 161–176.

Prawat, R. (1991). Conversations with self and settings: A framework for thinking about teacher empowerment. *American Educational Research Journal* 28 (4), 737–757.

Prigogine, I. & Stengers, I. (1984). *Order out of chaos*. New York: Bantam Books.

Purgason, K. (2004). A clearer picture of the 'servants of the lord'. *TESOL Quarterly* 38 (4), 711–713.

Rajagopalan, K. (1999). Of EFL teachers, conscience and cowardice. *ELT Journal* 53 (3), 200–206.

Rampton, B. (1990). Displacing the native speaker. *ELT Journal* 44 (2), 97–101.

Randall, M. & Thornton, B. (2001). *Advising and supporting teachers*. Cambridge: Cambridge University Press.

Reason, P. & Bradbury, H. (2001). Introduction: Inquiry and participation in search of a world worthy of human aspiration. In P. Reason & H. Bradbury (eds) *Handbook of Action Research* (pp.1–14). London: Sage.

Reeves, A. (1994). Educational approaches for an international language. *Links and Letters* I, 51–70. Barcelona: Autonomous University of Barcelona Press.

Richards, J. & Nunan, D. (eds) (1990). *Second language teacher education*. Cambridge: Cambridge University Press.

Richards, K. (2003). *Qualitative inquiry in TESOL*. Basingstoke: Macmillan Palgrave.

Rickman, H. (1988). *Dilthey today: A critical appraisal of the contemporary relevance of his work*. New York: Greenwood Press.

Robison, R. (2009). Truth in teaching English. In M. Wong & S. Canagarajah (eds) (pp.255–264).

Rogers, C. (1980). *A Way of being*. Boston: Houghton-Mifflin.

Rogers, C. & Freiberg, H. (1994). *Freedom to learn* (3rd edn). New York: Macmillan College Publishing.

Rorty, R. (1991). *Consequences of pragmatism*. Hemel Hempstead: Harvester Wheatsheaf.

Rorty, R. (1998). *Truth and progress: Philosophical papers III*. Cambridge: Cambridge University Press.

Rorty, R. (1999). *Philosophy and social hope*. Harmondsworth: Penguin.

Rorty, R. (2000). Private irony and liberal hope. In W. Brogan & J. Risser (eds) *American Continental Philosophy* (pp.44–65). Bloomington: Indiana University Press.

Rose, S. (2006). *The 21st century brain: Explaining, mending and manipulating the mind*. London: Vintage Books.

Sallis, J. (2000). Imagination, metaphysics, wonder. In W. Brogan & J. Risser (eds) *American Continental Philosophy* (pp.15–43). Bloomington: Indiana University Press.

Sandywell, B. (1996). *Reflexivity and the crisis of western reason*. London: Routledge.

Sandywell, B. & Beer, D. (2005). Examining reflexivity: An interview with Barry Sandywell. *Kritikos* 2. http://intertheory.org/Beer-Sandywell.htm retrieved on 11 June 2010.

Schepens, A., Aelterman, A. & van Keer, H. (2007). Studying learning processes of student teachers with stimulated recall interviews through changes in interactive cognitions. *Teaching and Teacher Education* 23, 457–472.

Schön, D. (1983). *The reflective practitioner: How professionals think in action*. London: Temple Smith.

Schön, D. (1987). *Educating the reflective practitioner*. San Francisco, CA: Jossey-Bass.

Schön, D. (1992). The theory of inquiry: Dewey's legacy to education. *Curriculum Inquiry* 22 (2), 119–139.

Searle, J. (1969). *Speech Acts*. Cambridge: Cambridge University Press.

Segal, S. (1998). The role of contingency and tension in the relationship between theory and practice in the classroom. *Curriculum Studies* 30 (2), 199–206.

Shakespeare, W. (1591). Richard III. Act 5, Sc. 4.

Spack, R. (1997). The rhetorical construction of multilingual students. *TESOL Quarterly* 31 (4), 765–74.

Sprigge, T. (1995). The nature of relations. In T. Honderich (ed.) *The Oxford companion to philosophy* (pp.756–7). Oxford: Oxford University Press.

Spry, T. (2001). Performing autoethnography: An embodied methodological praxis. *Qualitative Inquiry* 7 (6), 706–732.

Stevick, E. (1982). *Teaching and learning languages*. Cambridge: Cambridge University Press.

Sullivan, P. (2000). Playfulness as mediation in communicative language teaching in a Vietnamese classroom. In Lantolf, J. (ed.) *Sociocultural theory and second language acquisition* (pp.115–132). Oxford: Oxford University Press.

Svalberg, A. (2007). State of the art: Language awareness and language learning. *Language Teaching* 40 (4), 287–308.

Swain, M. (1985). Communicative competence: Some roles of comprehensible input and comprehensible output in its development. In S. Gass & E. Varonis (eds) *Input in second language acquisition* (pp.235–256). Rowley, MA: Newbury House.

Swan, M. (1995). *Practical English usage* (2nd edn). Oxford: Oxford University Press.

Tannen, D. (1979). What's in a frame? Surface evidence for underlying expectations. In R. Freedle (ed.) *New directions in discourse processing vol 2: Advances in discourse process* (pp.137–182). New Jersey: Ablex.

Tedlock, B. (2003). Ethnography and ethnographic representation. In N. Denzin & Y. Lincoln (eds) *Strategies of Qualitative Inquiry* (2nd edn) (pp.165–214). Thousand Oaks, CA: Sage.

Thayer, H. (ed.) (1970). *Pragmatism: The classic writings*. New York: New American Library.

Thorne, S. (2005). Epistemology, politics and ethics in sociocultural theory. *Modern Language Journal* 89 (3), 393–409.

Toohey, K. (2000). *Learning English at school: Identity, social relations and classroom practice*. Cleveland, UK: Multilingual Matters.

Tsui, A. (2003). *Understanding expertise in teaching: Case studies of ESL teachers*. Cambridge: Cambridge University Press.

Tully, M. (1992). *No full stops in India*. Chapter 2: The new colonialism (pp.57–85). Chapter 9: The return of the artist (pp.268–296). Harmondsworth: Penguin.

van Lier, L. (1996). *Interaction in the language classroom*. Harlow, UK: Longman.

Vygotsky, L. (1978). *Mind in society: The development of higher psychological processes*. Cambridge, MA: Harvard University Press.

Vygotsky, L. (1986). *Thought and language*. Cambridge, MA: MIT Press.

Walker, A. & Cheng, Y-C. (1996). Professional development in Hong Kong primary schools: Beliefs, practices and change. *Journal of Education for Teaching* 22 (2), 197–212.

Wallace, M. (1991). *Training foreign language teachers: A reflective approach*. Cambridge: Cambridge University Press.

Wallace, M. (1998). *Action research for language teachers*. Cambridge: Cambridge University Press.

Waters, A. (2007a). ELT and 'the spirit of the times'. *ELT Journal* 61 (4), 353–359.

Waters, A. (2007b). Ideology, reality and false consciousness in ELT. *ELT Journal* 61 (4), 367–368.

Waters, A. (2008). Review of *(Re)Locating TESOL in a New Age of Empire*. *ELT Journal* 62 (1), 89–92.

Waters, A. (2009). Ideology in applied linguistics for language teaching. *Applied Linguistics* 30 (1), 138–143.

Wells, G. (1999). *Dialogic inquiry: Towards a sociocultural practice and theory of education.* Cambridge: Cambridge University Press.

Wells, G. (2002). The role of dialogue in activity theory. *Mind, Culture and Activity* 9 (1), 43–66.

Wells, G. (2007). The mediating role of discourse in activity. *Mind, Culture and Activity* 14 (3), 160–177.

Wenger, E. (1998). *Communities of practice: Learning, meaning and identity.* Cambridge: Cambridge University Press.

Wertsch, J. (1991). *Voices of the mind: A sociocultural approach to mediated action.* Cambridge, MA: Harvard University Press.

Wertsch, J. (1998). *Mind as action.* New York: Oxford University Press.

Wharton, S. (1999). From postgraduate student to published writer: Discourse variation and development in TESOL. Unpublished PhD thesis. Birmingham, UK: Aston University.

Wharton, S. (2008). Becoming a writer: Community membership and discursive literacy. In S. Garton & K. Richards (eds) (pp.218–231).

Wilde, O. (1892). *Lady Windemere's Fan.* Act 3.

Wilkins, D. (1976). *Notional Syllabuses.* Oxford: Oxford University Press.

Wilkinson, S. (1988). The role of reflexivity in feminist psychology. *Women's Studies International Forum* 11 (5), 493–502.

Williams, M. (2003). Rorty on knowledge and truth. In C. Guignon & D. Hiley (eds) *Richard Rorty* (pp.61–80). Cambridge: Cambridge University Press.

Wilson, E. (1998). *Consilience: The unity of knowledge.* London: Abacus.

Winterson, J. (1996). *Art objects: Essays on ecstasy and effrontery.* London: Vintage.

Wong, M. & Canagarajah, S. (eds) (2009). *Christian and critical English language educators in dialogue: Pedagogical and ethical dilemmas.* New York: Routledge.

Woods, P. (2006). The hedgehog and the fox: Two approaches to English for the military. In J. Edge (ed.) (2006b) (pp.208–226).

Wright, R. (2004). *A short history of progress.* Melbourne, Australia: Text Publishing.

Wright, T. & Bolitho, R. (1993). Language awareness: a missing link in language teacher education? *ELT Journal* 47 (4), 292–304.

Yalom, I. (1991). *Love's executioner and other tales of psychotherapy.* London: Penguin.

Yates, R. & Muchisky, D. (2003). On reconceptualising teacher education. *TESOL Quarterly* 37 (1), 135–147.

Yballe, L. & O'Connor, D. (2000). Appreciative pedagogy: Constructing positive models for learning. *Journal of Management Education* 24 (4), 474–483.

Yeoman, B. (2002). The stealth crusade. http://www.motherjones.com/magazine/MJ02/stealth.html retrieved 30 November 2007.

Zhang, X. & Head, K. (2010). Dealing with learner reticence in the speaking class. *ELT Journal* 64 (1), 1–9.

Zohar, D. (1991). *The Quantum Self.* London: Flamingo.

INDEX

ablocutionary value 71, 155, 167
academic 25,29, 74, 85–87, 153, 160–161
acting x, 11, 12, 45, 99, 119, 121–122
action research 2, 14, 17, 33, 37, 73, 84, 87, 97, 99, 119, 122, 124
action-in-context 95
action-in-discourse 95
activity theory 97
affordance 32, 41, 47, 60, 64–68, 73, 77–78, 81–82, 87, 91, 95–99, 100, 117–118, 125, 134–136, 165, 169, 175, 178
Afghanistan 109, 168
agency 46, 127
American Pragmatism x, 120–121, 162, 166
analysis 12, 22, 24, 35, 66, 68–76, 80, 120, 122, 130–136, 151–152
anticipatory reflection 17
application-in & reference-out 83–84
applied linguistics 56
applied science model 15, 48
applying x, 10, 12, 19, 45, 48, 63, 72, 74, 77, 82, 90, 96, 99, 122, 129–130, 133, 136, 164, 172
appreciative pedagogy 68
apprentice 15, 47, 50, 56
apprenticeship of observation 50, 52, 56, 98
Argyris, C. 17, 20
Aristotle 49
articulation 35, 48, 84, 91, 93, 95–96, 117, 176–177

as-if 12, 24, 47, 96, 122
aspiration-focused 68
assimilation/accommodation 35, 42, 50, 142
asynchronous/synchronous: communication 151
audit trails 36, 163
augmentative discourse 25, 42, 46
autobiography 78, 172
awareness ix, 7, 9, 17–18, 32, 37, 39–45, 59–63, 74–77, 80, 95, 103, 112, 115, 118, 121, 128, 134, 137, 139, 165, 170, 178

Bakhtin, M. 92
Bartlett, F. 142, 155
Bateson, G. 33, 39
Behar, R. 38
best method 69, 118
Boon, A. 90, 150, 152
boundaries 82, 96, 111, 116, 126, 128, 130, 136, 170
Boxer, P. 20–24, 77, 82
British Council 102, 140–141
Browne, J. 139
Brumfit, C. 107–108, 115

Campbell, J. 48
capitalism 106
case study 132
categorization 12, 20, 22, 24, 27, 35, 47, 74, 96, 122, 129
censorship 105

certainty 115, 119
Charmaz, C. 34
chauvinism 161
Christian 104, 114
Clarke, M. xi, 14, 16, 32, 39, 45, 142,
    170–171
classification 65, 74
Cobbett, W. 53, 68
coercive/collaborative relationships 158
Cohen, L. 117
coherence 40, 55, 74, 87–88, 96, 100,
    111, 118–119, 136, 144, 149, 155–158,
    172, 177
collegiality 15, 92
congruence x, 4, 40, 88, 96, 111, 117,
    119, 128, 136–137, 144, 149, 155–156,
    166, 172
consciousness 30, 45–46, 99, 160
consistency 23, 30, 40, 61, 63–64, 88, 91,
    96, 118–119, 136, 144, 149, 155–158,
    167, 169, 172
constraints 44, 64, 81, 91
constructivist-developmental: psychology
    30, 43
context 4, 19, 24, 32–35, 37, 46, 53,
    55–56, 60, 65, 67, 72–77, 81, 84–85,
    88–89, 91, 95, 100, 105–106, 108–110,
    117–118, 127–128, 132, 135–136, 141,
    143, 145, 148, 157, 164, 167, 171,
    173–174
context-in-mind 89
continuity x, 4, 11, 15, 38, 40, 61, 63–64,
    76, 88, 96, 111, 118–119, 128,
    136–137, 144, 149, 155, 157–158,
    165–166, 172
Cooperative Development 90–91,
    93–97, 122, 126–128, 136, 146,
    150–152, 155, 164, 169
copying ix, 10–12, 15, 17, 19, 48–50, 52,
    56, 58–61, 63, 67, 72, 99, 119,
    121–122, 127–128, 169, 172
craft and art 51, 60
craft model 15, 49
craft 17–19, 44, 48, 51, 60, 63, 119,
    121
criteria 25, 67, 73, 76, 79, 108, 127,
    132, 134, 153–154, 171, 173
critical pedagogy 18, 61, 135, 147, 157
Csikszentmihalyi, M. 43
cultural politics 100, 102, 105, 129,
    134–135, 168
cultural relativism 168
culture 6, 12, 15, 48–49, 55, 59, 68, 85,

100, 103, 109, 129, 143, 145, 147–148,
    157–158, 161, 168

dark matter 155, 165
Dewey, J. x, 18, 41–45, 47, 81–82, 99,
    120–121, 137, 139, 156, 162, 166–168,
    176
diagrams 13, 46, 159–160
Dillard, A. 43, 46, 171
Dilthey, W. 35, 45
dimensions of becoming 11, 172
discourse analysis 68, 71, 74, 80, 88, 97,
    133, 136
discourse of reflexivity 46
discourse pattern 65
displacive discourse 25, 79, 90, 99
distance education 83, 88
domination 88, 110
dyadic subject 93–95, 125, 127–129
Dylan, B. 178

ecology 31, 39, 104
educational colonialism 130
empathy 45, 147
empire 105, 107, 166
empiricism 120
empowerment 84, 116–117
Engeström, Y. 43, 92
espoused theory 17, 39, 82, 133
ethics 87, 99, 115, 121, 128, 167, 170
evangelical 114–115
existential 156, 153–165
experience 41–48
experiential learning 19, 41, 49, 55, 898,
    93, 103, 120, 137, 155
exploitative reading 69–71
exploration/articulation 83–84

failure 8, 36, 116, 139, 144, 154, 175–176
fair trade 106
fatwa 101–102, 115
feedback 15, 19, 24, 56, 58–59, 108–109,
    160, 162, 165
final vocabulary 9–12, 31, 35, 87,
    167–168, 170, 177
Finlay, L. 34, 36–38
first-person/third-person research 28, 154
fission/fusion 129
flow 43
free markets 106
future-orientation 120, 164

Garton, S. 105

globalization 12, 106, 114
grammatical signals 64
grand theory 93
Graves, R. 5–7, 100
grumpy old man syndrome 49
guilt 126, 152–153

hegemony 106
Heidegger, M. 31, 44
hermeneutics 35–37, 45, 47, 92, 95–96, 121, 150
Hoey, M. 64–74, 80, 97, 129–130, 133
Holliday, A. xi, 106, 113, 133, 147–149, 161
hybrid approaches 135
Hymes, D. 102, 164

Icarus xi, 5–7, 25, 95–97, 121, 137, 139, 141, 150–151, 156, 164, 172, 177
identity 18, 23, 38, 42, 48, 53, 56, 75, 153, 157–159
ideology 35, 102, 104, 108, 135, 147
illocution 66, 70–71, 100
imagination 14, 21, 44, 49, 53, 70, 89, 129, 162, 174
imperial troopers 106
in-service teacher education 58, 83, 122, 140
inside out/outside in 84, 92, 96
intellectual ix, 11–12, 15–17, 19, 26–29, 48–49, 60, 74, 85, 97–100, 104–105, 115–117, 121, 124–125, 127–128, 133, 136–137, 141, 156, 164, 169, 170, 172
intercultural 12, 68, 74, 106, 112, 141
intermental/intramental 94–95
internal/external relations 35, 40
internalizing/externalizing 43, 46–47, 92–93, 163, 172
interpretive reading 69–71
ironist 9, 167–168
Islamic 114–115

Johnson, K. 14, 17, 46, 50, 92–93, 96
Johnston, B. xi, 1, 14, 56, 140, 174
journeyman 49

Karmani, S. 115
Kegan, R. 30–31, 44–46, 99
Kemmis, S. 73, 118
Kolb, D. 7, 29, 41, 85
Kubota, R. 113
Kumaravadivelu, B. 109, 115–116, 173

Lave, J. & Wenger, E. 56, 72, 92,
lexical signals 64, 132
liberation 88, 110
Lin, J. 113
linguistic diversity 100–101
linguistics 11, 39, 52, 56, 79, 83, 129, 143, 160
local 16, 44, 50, 69, 81, 86, 88, 114, 126, 135, 141
locution 70,
Louise 178

making a fool of oneself 95
Mann, S. 90, 93
master 5, 15, 49, 51, 104, 110
Maturana, R. & Varela, F. 33, 39
mediation 92–93, 129
member checks 36
memorization 65
memos 34
Menand, L. 107, 118, 120, 166
metacognitive awareness 74
metalanguage 54, 58
methodological ix, 11–12, 34, 39, 48, 52–53, 55–56, 60–61, 68, 82, 98–99, 101–102, 117–118, 123–125, 128, 133, 135, 148, 156, 163–164, 172
methods review class 54
Mitchell, J. 6
modelling 5, 49, 61
morals 82, 120, 129, 167, 170
multiple realities 25
mutual shaping 31, 33, 35, 72, 116
myth x, 5–6, 29, 37, 48, 172, 177

Narcissus 5–7, 25, 95–97, 99–100, 121, 137, 139, 141–142, 150–151, 154, 156, 164, 172, 177
narrative x, 4, 14, 33, 98, 137, 143, 172, 178
native/non-native speakers 103–105, 111–113
negotiated syllabus 133
nominative/accusative 29–30, 45–46
non-defensive 91, 125, 127
non-judgemental 90–93
Norton, B. xi, 18, 145–146, 148, 157–158
Nunan, D. 14, 84, 96

order/chaos 45
organism/environment 33, 35, 39, 46, 53, 173

Overseas Development: Administration 101, 140–141

parameters of doing 10, 12, 19, 25, 90, 172
pedagogy 15, 18, 73, 83, 102, 163
peer micro-teaching 56, 58–59
peer review 36
peer-correction 21, 108
Pennycook, A. 18, 61, 72, 105, 109, 114
perceive/discern 32, 47, 65, 67, 73, 77, 91, 99, 117, 125, 134–135, 165, 173, 175, 178
peripheral participation 56, 72
perlocution 70–71
personal/professional 9, 116, 147
Phillipson, R. 105, 107–108, 111
philosophical pluralism 168
philosophy x, 8, 31, 39, 71, 120, 147, 166–167, 177
political correctness 107, 110, 130
politics 12, 34, 100, 104–105, 111, 115, 126, 167
postmodern 82, 114, 160, 168
power 5, 23, 40, 51, 84, 92, 99, 101, 106–107, 109–110, 115, 127, 129, 135, 140–141, 145–146, 157–159, 167
practitioner knowledge 95
pragmatic significance 66, 68, 70–71, 76, 115, 129, 131
pragmatic ix, 12, 18, 48, 98, 107, 117–122, 137, 156, 163–163, 167–168, 172
Prawat, R. 84
praxis 2, 17, 26, 39–40, 45, 51, 55, 63, 67–68, 70, 84, 87, 91, 94–97, 99, 100, 116–117, 119–121, 127–129, 133, 165, 169, 172–174
preferences (learning/teaching) 24, 54, 133, 134, 140
pre-service teacher education 23, 52, 63, 82
private/public 11, 153, 156, 176
Problem/Solution pattern 64, 76, 129–131, 133
problem-focused 68
proselytizing 104
public intellectual 116

qualitative research 33–36, 38–39
quantum self 117

racism 12, 103–105, 113–114

Randall, M. xi, 146–147, 149, 159
rational/reactive/reasonable 45, 137
Ray Charles Principle 47
Reason, P. & Bradbury, H. 84
recursive 45
reflection-in-action 16, 24, 34
reflection-on-action 16–17, 34
reflective approach 14–15, 18
reflective practice ix, 14, 16–18, 20, 25–26, 33, 88, 95, 99, 119, 136, 153, 164–165, 171, 173
reflective practitioner 11, 14, 18, 42
reflective rationality 79
reflexive practice 33, 37
reflexivity ix, 3–4, 7–8, 13, 18, 25–26, 61, 65, 69, 72, 75, 82, 95–98, 100, 108, 110, 112, 114–116, 118, 121, 128–129, 136–139, 152, 163–165, 169–173; expansive 75, 77, 97, 99, 117, 167, 170; horizontal 75, 77, 172; interactive 47; prospective 38, 47, 63, 77, 156, 172; retrospective 38, 47, 77, 156, 165, 170, 172; vertical 75, 77, 172
relational analysis 66–67, 69, 73, 75, 130–131
relationships 23, 31, 35, 42, 44–45, 59, 106, 123, 125, 128, 164
religion 12, 100, 104–105, 114–115
remedial language learners 53, 56
repertoire 29, 91, 129, 137
respect 15, 44, 51, 53–54, 60–61, 85, 106, 137, 146–148, 157, 161, 164, 168, 170, 179
responsibility 22–23, 38, 41, 44, 58, 60, 69, 70, 80–81, 84, 100, 118, 122, 129, 140, 146, 163, 168, 171
Richards, K. 28–29, 36, 84, 154
risks 22–23, 95, 119, 139
Rogers, C. 90
roots and wings 5, 138, 163
Rorty, R. x, 8–10, 39, 81, 87, 96, 117, 120, 137, 162, 166–168, 174, 176

Sallis, J. 31, 44
Sandywell, B. 37, 47, 165
schema 14, 31, 35, 42, 64, 68, 71, 113, 130–131, 142, 155, 178
Schön, D. 14, 16, 18, 20, 42, 46, 77, 79, 85, 173
scope for meaningful action 95, 127
selective scholarship 161
self-analysis 23
self-perception 23

semantic pattern 66, 76, 130
situated learning 84, 143
snobbery 26
sociocultural 11, 14, 43, 46, 92, 94–96, 119, 130, 166
Speaker/Understander 91–97, 122–128, 146, 150–152
status 36, 46, 61, 71, 75, 80–82, 113, 127
stepping back 31, 44–46, 65, 72, 99, 107, 156
stepping up 45–46
style of work 21–23, 63, 128
subject/object 30, 45
subjectivity 36–37, 45, 151,
supervision 122, 127

teaching practice 52, 56
technical rationality 63, 69, 72, 74, 77–79
technical ix, 10–12, 16, 23, 48, 76–79, 90, 98, 117–118, 164, 170, 172
theoretical ix, 2, 10–12, 15–16, 34, 48, 50, 55, 63, 68, 75, 78–80, 83, 85, 88, 90, 92, 95–96, 98–100, 111, 117–118, 121, 128, 156, 164, 172–173
theorizing x, 4, 10–12, 19, 45, 48, 72, 78–82, 88, 90, 92–93, 95–99, 117, 121–122, 127, 167, 169, 172, 176
theory 9–11, 16–17, 34, 39, 48, 62–63, 67, 69, 70–72, 74–75, 77–85, 87–88, 90, 92–97, 102, 119–121, 129, 133, 136, 145, 157, 166, 172–173
theory-in-action 82, 133
theory-in-practice 17
tradition 10, 15, 18, 34–35, 38, 49–50, 53, 60–61, 68–69, 71, 84, 99, 107, 110–111, 117, 120, 126, 135, 141, 152, 162, 166, 177

transformation of consciousness 30, 45–46, 99
transformative intellectual 99
translation 54, 56–58
transparency 36, 107, 152, 154, 156, 166
triangulation 36
trustworthiness 123
trying/undergoing 41–42, 47, 50, 52, 55, 60, 77, 81, 87, 95, 118, 139, 141, 156, 165

unitary concept/binary relation 31, 35, 45

values 5, 14, 20, 30–31, 40, 44, 101–102, 128, 135–136, 144, 147–149, 151, 158, 161, 168, 173–174
visible ethnic minority 113
Vygotsky, L. 43, 46, 92, 94

Wallace, M. 14–16, 18, 49, 63, 77, 79, 84
Waters, A. 59, 107, 110, 133
Wells, G. 43, 93–94, 127
Wenger, E. 56, 72, 92, 95
Wertsch, J. 92–93
Wharton, S. 72, 74
Wilde, O. 139
Winterson, J. 50
whole-people-who-teach 4, 39, 96, 107, 117, 144
wondering about/at 30, 44, 65
working class 26–27, 29, 60, 117, 141, 169–170

Yalom, I. 163–64

zone of proximal development 94